RADICAL RESILIENCE

RADICAL RESILIENCE

Athenian Topographies of Precarity and Possibility

Othon Alexandrakis

CORNELL UNIVERSITY PRESS   ITHACA AND LONDON

First published 2022 by Cornell University Press

Library of Congress Cataloging-in-Publication Data

Names: Alexandrakis, Othon, author.
Title: Radical resilience : Athenian topographies of precarity and
    possibility / Othon Alexandrakis.
Description: Ithaca [New York] : Cornell University Press, 2022. |
    Includes bibliographical references and index.
Identifiers: LCCN 2021015196 (print) | LCCN 2021015197 (ebook) |
    ISBN 9781501761430 (hardcover) | ISBN 9781501761447 (paperback) |
    ISBN 9781501761454 (ebook) | ISBN 9781501761461 (pdf)
Subjects: LCSH: Resilience (Personality trait)—Greece—Athens. |
    Marginality, Social—Greece—Athens. | Suffering—Social aspects—
    Greece—Athens. | Athens (Greece)—Social conditions—21st century.
Classification: LCC HN650.5.A97 A44 2022 (print) |
    LCC HN650.5.A97 (ebook) | DDC 305.509495/1—dc23
LC record available at https://lccn.loc.gov/2021015196
LC ebook record available at https://lccn.loc.gov/2021015197

For Jordana

Contents

Preface ix

Introduction: Disintegrations and Intensifications 1

1. Everyday, Illegible: How Being a Radical Became a Problem 30

2. Becoming Lost: Why Romani Boys Are Hanging
Out with Anarchists 64

3. Ordinary Ghosting: How to Yield Stability from Chaos 91

4. Common Matters: How Awkwardness May
Create Possibility 116

5. Radical Possibility: Why Some Solidarians Believe
Solidarity Doesn't Matter 146

Epilogue 171

Acknowledgments 173
Notes 175
References 179
Index 189

Preface

Every year the sirocco winds whip up the Sahara Desert. They carry particles of quartz, iron oxides, and carbonates from the ancient seabed, across the Middle East, over the Mediterranean Sea, and toward Southern Europe. The mountains that surround the Attica plain stall the winds, causing dust particles to accumulate into clouds, aggregate, become heavy, and settle in the form of fine grit or as muddy rain.

The precipitation of dust coats Athenian surfaces of all description: cars, balconies, sidewalks, drying racks, toys, plants, outdoor furniture, handles and latches, eyes and lungs. Athens looks, tastes, and smells a little different until the dust is absorbed. The Sahara is as much a part of the city as it is a part of those who live there—a very old aspect of the topological becoming of Athenian life.

RADICAL RESILIENCE

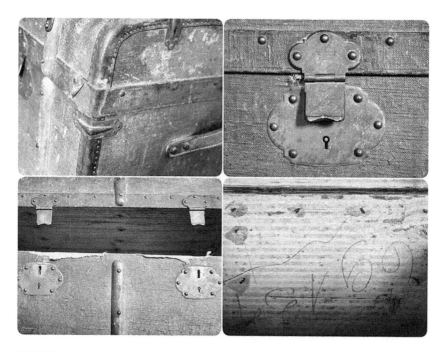

FIGURE 1. The trunk, in detail. Athens, 2019. Photo by the author.

DISINTEGRATIONS AND INTENSIFICATIONS

In the cellar at the back of my grandparents' home in Athens, an old trunk sat buried with two generations' worth of surplus furniture under paint-splattered drop cloths. The lid pushed heavily on my shoulder as I felt around inside. I don't remember what I was looking for, but I do remember it went out of my head the moment my fingers touched a stack of paper wrapped in the heavy fabric of an old coat. After a brief struggle, I held a collection of letters in envelopes, all tied together with a faded pink ribbon. There were thirty-two in total, postmarked between 1954 and 1956: messages sent, received, and saved together at a time of national recovery between the devastation of the Greek Civil War that followed World War II and the terror of the military dictatorship that would come several years later.

Sitting with my grandparents near an olive tree that grew in the garden at the back of the house, I undid the ribbon and handed the first letter to my grandfather and the second to my grandmother. I took the third one for myself. My grandfather used a large magnifying glass to inspect the address. My grandmother read something written on the back of the envelope she held—a quick note, jotted by someone decades ago. I looked over the first few pages of the letter I held but couldn't read the handwriting. The neatness of the script struck me, however, as did the care with which the letter had been folded: all edges aligned perfectly.

My grandmother took the letter from me and began to read aloud. The words were formal at first and then became increasingly tender—something about a room in a home and figs. . . . My grandmother was smiling when she stopped reading. She handed it to my grandfather, who looked it over quickly, folded it carefully, and tucked it back into its envelope. He took the stack from me, picked out the last envelope, skimmed the letter inside, and returned it to its place. He counted the envelopes, retied the ribbon, and put the stack on the table close to his coffee. He smiled and asked where I had found the letters. He had no idea they were in the cellar.

I asked about the letter writers. My grandparents had difficulty working out the kinship—they were members of the family, but not really. We settled on "great-aunt and -uncle," although I thought another "great" was warranted. They told me about the couple's difficult but happy life together, their struggles during the wars and occupation, about the end of their lives and that they had changed. My grandmother remembered a story my great-aunt used to tell about her childhood—something to do with being frightened of pigeons at the park and a tiny scar on her chin. My grandparents recalled how my great-uncle used to long for small luxuries during the difficult days of the Nazi occupation of Athens, like his newspapers and the smell of sweets with cinnamon and honey. The couple had lamented that they never had children.

My grandfather took the stack of envelopes with him when we went in. I followed him to the office, thinking I would look through the letters on my own. He sat at the desk, placed them in one of the drawers and locked it, leaving the key in the lock, as was his habit. I stood watching. "Don't open them," he instructed in a serious tone as he stepped by me. I followed him out to the hallway. "But—," I began.

He interrupted, "They were not written and saved all these years for us to read. They belong to the dead. We have a responsibility."

I thought I understood, so I nodded. This was not the time perhaps. The letters should not be inspected, alone, by someone who didn't know the couple. My grandfather continued down the hallway toward the kitchen. I went outside to find my grandmother watering the garden.

The letter writers grew up in Athens at a time of terrible violence and extreme uncertainty. The woman we were calling my great-aunt lost a parent during that period—the result of some violent episode that transpired in her home—and the man we were referring to as my great-uncle watched as injuries his father suffered during the war were compounded by hunger, permanently reducing his mobility. My grandmother tried to remember their wedding but couldn't. Maybe she wasn't there. "They always had flowers in their house," she said after a brief pause. I asked a few more questions, but the answers were unrelated. I wanted to keep probing but sensed I should stop. I had a feeling that these letters—safely tucked in an old trunk for decades, now locked in a drawer—were survivors of some kind of wreckage.

I was astonished when my grandfather told me later in the day that we would burn the letters that night.

"They were not written and saved for us to read," he repeated. "We must return them."

I quieted the growing panic in my heart and said, "We can't—they're important."

My grandfather nodded. "We will never understand the connection between those letters and the people who wrote them," he said quietly. "We must be respectful."

His words stayed with me all afternoon. Perhaps he was right, but I couldn't bear the thought of the letters on fire. It was as if we were throwing away the last opportunity to know these people through their own words—people who had no direct descendants, who I had no idea existed until that day. I felt that the letters belonged together, in that ribbon, in this world. They told a story.

That story remained in the near background of my thinking and fieldwork for this project. The letters and the lives of the letter writers—their struggles, experiences of near devastation, and change—became a point of returning for me. They inspired imagining, questioning, and nudged my engagements, at times, as I came to focus on matters of living through undoing. Indeed, the space of wondering that emerged for me around the elusive details of their incomplete biographies helped me to see and encouraged my attention to particular gaps and openings in the work I was doing. So, in the following pages I recall that story as I set up the main themes of this book, contextualize and situate the coming chapters, and outline the thinking that led to the concepts I use throughout. I also recall the story of the letters to sketch my positionality and state of mind, and the larger world of my fieldwork and writing, in an expanded and more personal way.

It was the summer of 2006: the verdict in the Enron trial had recently been reached, concluding a scandal that would be followed by a wave of corporate fraud investigations in the US and beyond and sowing uncertainty in the global economy. Saddam Hussein's trial, the killing of insurgent Al-Zarqawi in Iraq, and the thwarting of another major transatlantic terror plot marked accelerating change and instability across the Middle East. In Greece, politicians and commentators were concerned about government plans to change labor laws that guaranteed jobs for life in the public sector, moves to expand privatization, and the state of the "€700 generation": the growing legions of un- and underemployed youth facing uncertain futures (Chiotaki-Poulou and Sakellariou 2014). As the world edged toward the global financial meltdown of 2007–8, the Arab Spring, the rise of Daesh/ISIL (ISIS), and the war in Syria, Greece's economy was obviously tanking: small businesses were closing all across the country, and protests in Athens were becoming larger and more regular. Little did everyone know at the time how much worse things were going to get. I was in my second year of the doctoral program in anthropology at Rice University and about to begin a year of ethnographic fieldwork in central Athens. My interests had to do with political identity at the edges of the social mainstream. I had a loose plan to hang out with Roma, undocumented migrants, and anarchists. Many of the people I would meet in the ensuing year became long-term research participants, my interlocutors,[1] and some became my friends.

I returned from the field and began to write in the summer of 2007. I was still drafting dissertation chapters when, on December 6, 2008, fifteen-year-old student Alexis Grigoropoulos was killed by two special forces police officers in Exarchia—a neighborhood in Athens with a long history as a gathering place for antiestablishment actors (Economides and Monastiriotis 2009; Vradis and Dalakoglou 2011). This set off weeks and weeks of protest action that spread across the country and beyond. Most scholars talked about this as a kind of consolidation and tipping point (Kalyvas 2010; Panourgiá 2010; Sotiris 2010); although tipping into *what* was still uncertain. In the months and years that followed, further protest actions cataloged a growing list of devastating economic, political, and social problems, including increasing disenfranchisement and deepening disappointment among youth and young adults, mismanagement of public infrastructures, widespread corruption, government policy that actively discriminated against the most vulnerable members of society while benefiting the elite, and what was by then becoming an increasingly obvious impending national economic catastrophe.

By 2009, the effects of the global financial meltdown had weakened Greece's two largest economic sectors, tourism and shipping. The state declared a sovereign debt crisis the following year, in 2010, and began to take loans from the so-called troika—the European Union, the European Central Bank, and the International Monetary Fund—which came with a series of harsh neoliberal austerity measures (Featherstone 2015; Katsimi and Moutos 2010; Placas and Doxiadis 2018). In the years that followed, political dynasties fell, new parties arose, and matters related to sovereignty, democracy, and "national salvation" came to be on the minds of academics, political commentators, and ordinary Athenians alike. Then in 2015, Syrians fleeing war in their homeland, as well as others from elsewhere in the Middle East and various parts of Africa, began to arrive in Greece in massive numbers—thousands daily (Papataxiarchis

2016a, b). The Greek state was completely unprepared and financially unable to respond, local humanitarian efforts were quickly overwhelmed, and humanitarian aid groups from around the world began to arrive. The European Union stepped in with funding and a plan to regulate the migration through so-called hot spots (Fassin 2016). Subsequently, as tensions grew within the EU over migrant resettlement, and Greece's northern neighbors began to close their borders, migrants in the hundreds of thousands became trapped in the country. I would spend the rest of my graduate training, a postdoc in Hellenic studies at Princeton University, and the first five years of my current academic appointment thinking and writing about the unrest between 2007 through 2010, the utter devastation of the debt crisis and austerity measures that stretched from 2010 onward, and Greece's second crisis—the refugee crisis—that spiked in 2015 but dragged on and worsened to an outright humanitarian disaster as conditions in overcrowded refugee camps deteriorated, thousands of migrants found themselves on the streets, and human trafficking and labor and sexual exploitation proliferated.

Throughout this time, I continued to do fieldwork in Athens with the individuals and groups I met in 2006, and with others I came to know through them. As successive austerity measures were rolled out, every one of my interlocutors suffered compounding injuries of impoverishment, uncertainty, and demoralization. Gradually, I began to tune in to an aspect of their living through this situation that I found very concerning. As the years dragged on, and their lives became increasingly precarious and chaotic, most of the people I knew were becoming less interested or engaged in political processes and debates and—what was more alarming to me—were becoming socially distant. That is, they were becoming less involved with, and less responsive to, their friends, family, and broader established social networks—indeed, their familiar social worlds.

As a growing scholarship examined new modes of social collectivization, response, and resistance effervescing across the country (Rakopoulos 2015, 2016; Rozakou 2016; Dalakoglou and Poulimenakos 2018; Theodossopoulos 2014; Knight 2015b; Pautz and Kominou 2013), and a smaller body of writing explored the individual, day-to-day realities of subsisting under the crisis regime (Panourgiá 2016; Knight 2017), my focus on, and increasing concern with, political disengagement and fading away led me to wonder about the supple, sometimes fraying fabrics that hold a life together within and against the shifting tensions and other dynamics that animate the space between the individual and the social. In this, I was beginning to think not only about the conditions and possibilities that enable or activate expressions of the political, but also of the space beyond politics' edges: of those often compounding and accumulating minor moments and small locations where lives unravel and come to be separated out from others. I began to explore this theme further, and with a view toward thinking more systematically about what this life might look like among differentially positioned subjects, what it might lead to, and what it might reveal.

In a conversation I had with Athena Athanasiou for a book project on resistance and social justice, we discussed depoliticization as a normative aspect of the neoliberal regime in Greece, and indeed across Europe (2016). Athena was clear: Greeks had become subjected to a power configuration that repressed critical agonism and dissent. She observed that public discussions and debates around such things as cut services and pensions had become reduced to talk of economic management and national salvation, effectively limiting critique. She argued that exposure to austerity-driven exhaustion and the manifold violences of neoliberal governmentality discouraged many from participating in bodies-in-the-streets protests. She was also clear, however, that other diverse dissenting practices were nonetheless proliferating. Indeed, and as the growing resistance literature I have mentioned demonstrated, while traditional sites and forms of political participation were diminished, Athenians were politically mobilizing shared experiences of hardship in novel ways. Such undertakings as the establishment of work cooperatives, social solidarity movements, and the proliferation of more spontaneous and temporary acts of camaraderie, support, and care were expanding political imaginings and perhaps nurturing hope (Steinfort, Hendrikx, and Pijpers 2017; Douzina-Bakalaki 2017; Rakopoulos 2015; Spyridakis and Dima 2017).

This conversation, however, along with my ongoing reading on crisis response and related observations in Athens, did not reflect what I was seeing among my interlocutors. This conversation and scholarship sketched a field of practice that the vast majority of individuals I knew were *not* involved with—at least not intentionally, with any sense of investment, or in an ongoing way. To be sure, some occasionally benefited from solidarity activities, acts of care, camaraderie, and the like; but this was on-and-off and generally tapering away among them. This is not to say that my interlocutors did not need this kind of support. Indeed, they were among the new poor (*neóptohi*): victims of the politico-economic crisis, locatable among the valances of poverty produced, as Neni Panourgiá aptly put it, in the wake of the "neo-colonization of Greece by the global financial powers" (2018, 123). Nevertheless, they were not seeking support while they were suffering continued reductions on multiple fronts. Their suffering grew, but they became increasingly disengaged and isolated from their familiar social worlds. As the economic crisis dragged on and continued to drag them down, a dwindling of dissent, of appetite for agonism and willingness to reach out, distinguished those individuals I knew from others who, in one way or another, sought and otherwise actively preserved some relation to the diminishing conventional or the various proliferating novel forms of resistance practice. My interlocutors were increasingly alone.

Individuation driven and compounded by heightened competition and such diminishing austerity-driven feelings as shame, worry, and despair are well-documented aspects of neoliberal subjectivation. It was certainly possible to find evidence of this across Athens. However—and despite what one might assume, given the duration of the crisis and the relentlessness of impoverishment and uncertainty from continued and unrelieved austerity—as individuation was amplified and intensified, this was not accompanied by widespread isolation. That is, the economization of Athenians as subjects of a competitive struggle for survival was driving notions and practices of personal responsibility and self-advancement, among other forms of individuation, but was not necessarily leading to widespread isolation of the sort I had been seeing among my interlocutors. While the majority of Athenians were hustling while remaining engaged, involved, and otherwise socially invested, my interlocutors were not returning calls and were beginning to walk past friends blankly. Something else was triggering their pulling away from familiar social worlds. This was not happening all at once and not in a complete or total way, but at various times, at various sites, and with increasing frequency. The overall effect was that of a kind of ghosting from the familiar.

My mind went to the difficult possibility that perhaps I was tuning in to a subset of Athenians who were not only depoliticized and individuated but were also failing to continue on under the deteriorations they faced. Perhaps their deepening isolation evidenced a triggering of some kind of psychopathology. With suicide rates increasing 40 percent in 2010 over all previously recorded years, then, in 2011, another 40 percent above that of 2010, then increasing again in 2012, this was not an unfounded concern (Panourgiá 2016; Economou et al. 2011; Karanikolos et al. 2013). Perhaps some of my interlocutors were edging toward that terrible brink. Elizabeth Davis warned against this kind of thinking. In her article on the increase in suicide rates during the crisis, Davis demonstrated that although crisis explanations for the so-called suicide epidemic in the country seemed self-evident, we must be wary. This thinking, she explained, "obscures more than it reveals and produces as much as it represents" (Davis 2015, 1032). Attempts to understand suicide have always been confounded by indeterminacy arising from disjuncture between individual motives, acts, and social conditions. Accordingly, anticipating the possibility of suicide based on the presumed effects of social conditions on individual motives and acts would also be folly. Following her lead, I began to question my linear assumption that austerity-intensified individuation might result in isolation and possibly worse. The connection between deepening austerity and isolation remained in my mind; however, I began to think of isolation not as an effect of some unbearable accumulation of hardships or, indeed, as the other side of some tipping point beyond individuation. Likewise, I began to question whether one should think of isolation in absolute terms as a phenomenon of total disintegration. So, I began to consider isolation as a state of affairs triggered by crisis and austerity that entailed a related emptying; but I resisted the impulse to see those isolating individuals as having become so completely depoliticized and hyper-individuated that they should be edging toward some kind of "Durkheimian end" (Davis 2015, 1010; see also Economou et al. 2013). Seeking a more grounded, more nuanced understanding of the social isolation I was seeing, I began to tune in more closely to what my interlocutors were saying.

A common refrain among the individuals I came to associate with isolation, or ghosting or fading away, was, *auté den eínai zōé—this is not a life*. These words located the speaker along some edge. Insofar as the phrase would be uttered to me or others, it enacted a being-with in the social and expressed a critique of the existing situation; but it also marked a kind of liminality, a being apart. I would later come to understand the broader significances of this phrase—as I explain below—but from the beginning, it seemed to me to mark a reduced life in a space of duress between "with" and "apart": a form of barely living, reflecting a troubled sense of their relation to the social. Like many other victims of austerity, my interlocutors were struggling under crushing conditions of uncertainty, impoverishment, and various other forms of injury: they were being emptied financially, of symbolic and material resources, of energy and hope, and of their supports. Critically, however, and unlike others, they themselves appeared to be emptying some aspects of their lives. Some of this emptying could be explained as practical or strategic, as aimed at stanching the draining, slowing the diminishing, or otherwise reducing the harm, but other emptying could not. This other emptying created small voids and tensions that did not appear to me to be necessary or, indeed, logical. Their behavior evoked more an effort of self-activated reconfiguration than resolving crisis-driven reduction. It brought isolation, barely living, into view not as a total, general fading away, but as a site of potential refiguring one's being in the social.

Daniel Knight's exceptional ethnography *History, Time, and Economic Crisis in Central Greece* (2015a) became an invaluable resource for me as I thought further about, and sought to more clearly locate, ethnographically, this experience of isolation and this site of barely living. Using the idea of "cultural proximity," Knight explained how his interlocutors in Trikala, Central Greece, drew on memories of past prosperity and crisis to understand and ultimately respond to the social and economic turmoil they were facing in the present. He set out, in careful detail, how memories of historical events—as unsteady and imperfect as they sometimes were—became cultural resources assembled and shared in various intimate and more public social contexts and enacted, in part, through embodied practice. These resources not only imbued the crisis situation with content and direction but also informed the meaningful ongoing exchanges and actions of his interlocutors (see also Argenti 2019, 77–98). The Trikalinoi whom Knight knew had collectively "made sense" of their crisis experiences and were, by most measures, enduring accordingly. To be sure, I could read Knight's analysis in the lives of many of the people I knew in Athens, including at times those individuals who, at other junctures, would fade away. It was at the onset and for the duration of these episodes of fading away—some of which lasted as long as I knew the individuals—when Knight's work no longer seemed to accord in a comprehensive way. This, to my mind, again, marked an edge.

Those of my interlocutors who were pulling back from their familiar social worlds appeared to no longer belong there. They were struggling not only to make sense of the changes they faced, but, moreover, looking back, they struggled to make sense of their ruined lives. Expanding Knight's use of "proximity," I began to see that my interlocutors were experiencing increasingly greater distance from their familiar social worlds, distance that increased as the cultural resources that once rendered these worlds meaningful became progressively problematized. Again, aspects of their lives had been overturned, and their available resources to explain things were in one way or another coming up short—not because these resources lacked some kind of relevance, but because they had become contradictory, fragmented, or for some other reason no longer made sense. I kept hearing such urgent expressions as "this can't" or "this should not be this way." Unlike Knight, who could trace how Trikalinoi collectively drew on cultural references such as past episodes of hunger to render the crisis situation and individuals' struggles meaningful, I could not do the same among my interlocutors who were withdrawing from their familiar social worlds.

Among these individuals, failing normative explanatory frames—familiar narratives, life trajectories, shared values, promises and memories frayed or utterly emptied of significance, purpose, meaning—were undermining their ability to explain and otherwise make sense of things. Blow by blow, "trouble making sense" grew irresolvable contradictions, aporias, breaks or messy spaces that unsettled my interlocutors' familiar relations to various shared and collective matters. In other words, these aporias became sites of differential intensification, sites that drove disintegration or edging away from a social life where normative frames were maintained: not in the manner of turning one's back, but in the manner of looking elsewhere. The social effects of this form of austerity-driven psychic violence on memory and knowing were perhaps less abrupt or immediately legible, but arguably no less disruptive than the social effects of trauma, certainly over time (cf. Argenti and Schramm 2012). Ultimately, I came to locate my interlocutors along tumultuous fields that had shifted sharply, and in relation to social refiguring and deep questioning that was reverberating through and undoing even the more stable aspects of their lives.

How does one withstand not only the injuries of countless reductions, personal emergencies, and gaping uncertainties, but also disengagement, isolation, and spreading normative indeterminacy? As the situation worsened and my concern grew, I wondered what we might learn from my interlocutors' struggles. I also wondered what might come for these individuals. Refusing to mourn a future I couldn't know, to overwrite their lives with trajectories imagined from misery, absence, and an incomprehensible present, I cast my mind instead to possibility. Might we think of this state of affairs in terms of resilience? If so, I wondered what a *social topography of resilience*—an aggregate ground of coming through injury—might look like: how might it come about, what might this resilience entail, and what might it enable?

My grandfather held the letters as I prepared the wood for the fire. We were in the back garden again. I asked once more about the letter writers, about their lives during the years the letters were written. He said he didn't remember much. This cut me as I gathered the wood together. The silence that followed felt proleptic. I tried again. "Yes, but what was happening in Athens at the time?" My grandfather thought for a moment and answered, "That part of the story is the same for so many people." He avoided the question: another dead end. I lit the fire.

Silence descended again, and the fire grew quickly in the summer heat. My grandfather handed me the letters and said, "It is not sad, what we're doing. These are someone else's love letters. They wrote these for each other at a very difficult time in their lives. They wouldn't want us, or anyone else, to read them."

I looked at him. He knew more than he was telling me, of course. My grandmother joined us at that moment, sitting in the chair next to me. "Continue," I said, placing the letters on the ground. If I was going to be involved in this, I wanted to better understand the letters. My grandparents shared a look.

The letter writers had been married in the early 1950s. My grandfather made it a point to say they led unremarkable lives, like many other Athenians at the time. Wealth had not yet reached Greece, nor had tourists in large numbers; and although the violence of the preceding decades (the German occupation during World War II, and the street battles of the Civil War) had left deep marks on many city surfaces and on many individuals and their families, most were getting on with the work of building a life worth living. This was the case for the letter writers too. They had lost family members and economic resources and were struggling to live a peaceful lower-middle-class life.

"He saw sadness and violence everywhere in the city," my grandmother stated plainly. "He used to talk about it frequently." There would have been well-known places in Athens where large numbers of people had been rounded up and detained, or killed, or where the starving would have gathered—but this was not what my grandmother was referring to.

"No," my grandfather said softly, "the history is the backdrop. It happened to everyone. Personal things happened too, and this is what matters." I nodded.

My grandmother continued talking about my great-uncle. "It wasn't just those places, but other places too. Ordinary places. Places where people had been hurt accidentally or where he saw someone crying for whatever reason. And it wasn't just their sadness that bothered him—it was the idea that hurt experienced by people here and there had been forgotten. He felt it should somehow be recognized and remembered."

A million little ordinary violences, injuries, and losses forgotten. He couldn't stand the forgetting, and so he didn't. This man walked the streets of Athens with memorials in his head. Perhaps an echo of the cruelties he witnessed, either firsthand or though the accounts of family and friends; perhaps some trauma on which grief became stuck, slowly manifesting shadows—my grandparents couldn't say for sure. In any event, my grandfather pointed out, "These things didn't seem to hurt him. He never became obsessed with it, although he was harder to reach when money became tight. He felt worry very, very deeply."

I picked up the letters. It occurred me that they were written years after the two had been married. I mentioned this to my grandparents. My grandfather said, "Yes," adding, "Did you notice that they were all sent from and delivered to the same address?" The fire had now settled, and coals were beginning to gather. My grandmother told me that my great-aunt used to play the piano. Passersby would stop on the sidewalk to listen when she played. She remembered coming upon a small group of children trying to be quiet under her aunt's window. She recalled feeling very special when she walked up to ring the doorbell. She also recalled the piano falling silent, but my great-aunt not answering the door.

I loosened the ribbon and placed the first letter on the coals. It caught immediately—layers of old paper folded back as they burned away. My grandmother continued. She told me that my great-aunt had suffered several miscarriages. Some members of the family suspected this was somehow linked to her having suffered prolonged periods of hunger during the occupation. Others suspected she had been detained and beaten during this period. Whatever the cause, each time this had happened the letter writers would become increasingly distant from friends and family. My great-aunt would sit for longer and longer periods at the piano, and my great-uncle would take longer and longer walks when he wasn't working. This worried everyone, of course.

More letters went on the coals. I wondered if my great-uncle started to see shadows on his wife. I wondered about the circumstances that led to the wounds my great-aunt had suffered, and how she was coming to experience her body. I also wondered if the letters were not a response, of sorts, to the ongoing unfolding of personal crises. Perhaps these expressions of love helped push some point of traumatic gravity—the miscarriages—away from the present, from a shared life now haunted by converging crises, slowly coming apart. Perhaps the regular pace of these expressions, and the fact that they were sent away from the home only to be brought back again and again, nurtured a kind of healing. "People have always found ways," my grandfather agreed, although he did not like my suggestion that the letters were a response. He offered an interpretation that was much less deliberate:

> They understood that terrible things had happened to them, and were happening again and again. Very personal things. Perhaps the miscarriages caused her to turn inward and him to see her differently? How could they not. Maybe we should say that the letters brought them some relief from all this. . . . There is sadness in every life—there must be, because we are human. But there is also happiness—there must be, so we may *continue* to be human. People feel this. They understand it in a different way. It creates energies of different kinds.

The manifold violences of war structured the lives of the letter writers. Without question, the injuries they sustained during this period contributed to the difficult years that followed. Yet, as others struggled on within and against the ruins and debris of their postwar worlds, the letter writers faced the cascading immediacy of further darkening and emptying. This created a strange place within their lives not unrelated to war, but also—somehow, and in a deeply personal way—set apart. This was not a place they came to on their own, but to which they were pushed. Still, this was also a place that in many ways belonged to the individual and, considering how it affected them, to which the individual belonged. It was a place of deepening isolation, of coming to see differently; a place from where love letters were written and shared.

The letters and the ribbon that held them are now gone. It hurt me to burn them. I still think about them. They held a kind of intimacy not shared by books and other writings meant for distribution and circulation—an intimacy between writer and reader that encouraged healing and, years after they had died, called for its own removal from this world. Being the last people still alive who knew the couple, my grandparents had the final say as to what should be done with the letters that sat for decades hidden in an old coat in a trunk at the back of their cellar. They understood that the writers were unable to destroy the letters themselves, even if they never intended them to be read by others: in some way, the letters helped them withstand the compounding violences they had suffered so they could find their way back to each other, and to a meaning-ful life threatened by growing isolation and sadness. It was up to us to do what they could not: a last gesture of acknowledgment of their return, so long ago, to the shared world they had now departed. Some archives are meant to stay with those who create them.

After this episode, I began to think about the marks violence and injury leave on people, the everyday things people do to sustain themselves, both alone and with others, and the changes and futures these everyday things make possible but do not assume. I began to think about perspectives that become closed off and perspectives that may be rendered legible and meaningful by living with injury and uncertainty, sites that sustain, and what it may mean to find one's way back toward a life worth living. The love letters also lingered on my mind: love letters written at a time when two individuals were struggling with emptying of their lives; love letters that must have felt strange to write when the writers were suffering from persistent and sometimes overwhelming sadness; love letters that in their writing, content, movements, and being read, gathered fragments of good toward no certain end. The love letters, and the conversations, concerns, remembering, and other thoughts they provoked and inspired in their final day and in the days that followed, began to gather together my thinking on coming back from injury at the time when Greece's slow-motion economic catastrophe was gaining pace and my interlocutors began to fade. Although I was not think-ing that the plight of the letter writers was directly connected to the plight of my interlocutors—at least not in terms of lingering matters, related experiences, or in some other historical constructivist mode—puzzling through the question of the letter writers' coming to sustain themselves and return from injury in the remarkable, deeply personal way they did prompted me to remain attentive to unexpected signs of returning among my interlocutors as early as 2006.

This attentiveness intensified as successive implementations of austerity policy triggered successive episodes of sudden mass impoverishment sharply expanding the Athenian precariat and as more, granular, idiosyncratic expressions of uncertainty, sadness, fear, and shame became increasingly legible and increasingly present in the social milieu of the city. I was looking more urgently for signs that the Athenians I knew were making some kind of return, that they were coming back. Yet things only worsened, and most of the people I knew continued to voice a growing list of difficulties. Most suffered further salary or pension cuts and were not finding new sources of income; many who were struggling to get by because of cut services and programs now found themselves unable to rely on family and friends who were facing mounting problems of their own. A few moved out of their homes because they could no longer afford rent. One had taken to burning pieces of furniture in a makeshift woodstove for heat in the winter. Another had exhausted her social network and so resorted to asking at local bakeries if anyone had dropped off clothing that would fit her children. Their lives were being ruined, a little more at a time. What small gains they made were, in every case, wiped out again. As the years dragged on, I thought, surely, they would all somehow come through the slaughter of austerity; but again, I looked for signs and found nothing. They were continuing to struggle with uncertainty and, at times, becoming inwardly turned—not intentionally, it seemed to me, but in the way of one who carries a heavier and heavier load, who lies awake night after night trying to figure things out.

The unfolding situation in Athens resonated with what was at the time a growing body of writing on precarity and its various aspects, led, in my reading, by Elizabeth Povinelli, Judith Butler, and Lauren Berlant. This literature provided the framing through which I came to understand that Greece had become subjected to the most drawn-out, coercive exercise of neoliberal governmentality in modern European history. It also provided a vocabulary and critical theory for thinking through the situation my interlocutors were suffering. I came to see how the successive implementation of austerity measures structured conditions of becoming dispensable and disposable for these people, rendering their lives more and more deeply precarious (Butler 2004) as economized subjects of a competitive economic struggle for survival (Povinelli 2011). This literature made apparent that as this grinding precarity intensified, so too did the "ongoing work of living" (Berlant 2011); as neoliberal governmentality further consolidated, my interlocutors' lives grew increasingly fragile. The picture was bleak indeed.

Still looking for hope, I came to focus on the figures of *living on* developed in this literature, and again I found some resonance with what was unfolding around me. Many individuals were engaging in what could easily be identified as alternative social projects. Likewise, it was possible to find cases where individuals were variously mobilizing shared conditions of hardship with others and, more broadly, were pursuing caring practices as they came to terms with precarious life. Like other subjects of neoliberal regimes, at least in the developed regions of the world, many Athenians were adjusting to precarity and, beyond this, coming to (re)build—bit by bit—something that perhaps could be seen as gesturing toward alternatives to the present situation. Yet, despite these tentative glimmers of positivity, I was not feeling hopeful. Not only were my interlocutors not in any sustained or intentional way involved, invested, or otherwise touched by these undertakings, but, more broadly, it also struck me as disempowering that hope should somehow be located in and in some ways pinned to enduring a perpetually bad situation. I was not so naïve as to think possible some kind of radically sovereign response exceeding the relations of power within which enduring subjects were situated; I was wary of locating political possibility principally within the socialities of a disappointing life. Yet I felt compelled to remain open to the possibility that hope could be found elsewhere, in some other form. What's more, I felt this literature's figures of *hopeful living on* occluded the experiences of those people who slipped in and out of durative undertakings and situations, who were not (re)building things at any level. What of all those people growing more isolated, whose lives remained dangerously close to ruin? What of those who were, like the majority of my interlocutors, on the edge, or in a state of, barely living?

I took a closer look at the literature for figures of *barely living*. I was coming to think of *barely living* as those individuals who were living a reduced life between "with" and "apart," a life of urgent refigurings triggered by sudden crisis-driven ontological uncertainties. Among these individuals the expression *auté den eínai zōé, this is not a life*—for me, an establishing idiom that helped to ethnographically locate my interlocutors—had a special significance. While many Athenians uttered this phrase in frustration, protest, and lament despite steadily enduring often at the limits of what they could take, I was more interested in those individuals, indeed my interlocutors, who expressed this sentiment with alarm, again and again, as they were pushed *beyond their limits* by compounding injuries that reverberated through their lives. They were individuals whose worlds had become too far reduced, who were coming to leave fewer and fewer traces in and on their familiar social worlds while engaging in new relationalities that would at other times have seemed senseless, relationalities that transcended normative exclusions, that tested and tried things. These individuals could not in some absolute way be located within observable domains of *living on* or enduring. They were wavering and unsteady. They suffered injuries that triggered holding on or letting go, within and against the social and other durative formations of their lives, while trying unexpected, unconventional, seemingly irrational things in sudden, temporary, and other ways that distinguished them from those who were more steadily getting by despite the bad situation. In thinking about and looking for a different location of hope, I came to focus on the forces and tensions that animated these wavering dynamics and related undertakings. Insofar as these entailed recurring minor returnings, I began to connect this wavering and associated trans-normativities with resilience.

It is important to note that the literature, and specifically Povinelli's *Economies of Abandonment* (2011), made space for the *barely living* as I was coming to see them. I read my interlocutors' situation within her consideration of Agamben's distinction between potentiality (*dynamis*)—which he defined (borrowing from Aristotle) as the duality of *can be* or *not be* that might foster new forms of life and new politics—and actuality (*energeia*) itself (1999). In this work Povinelli made clear that the distinction between potentiality and actuality was a false one: that it is never a matter of one or the other. That is, individuals who were *barely living* were also *living on*; individuals who were beyond their limits, insofar as they continued to survive by whatever means, were nonetheless enduring. Indeed, those Athenians I knew did not fit within totalizing categories; my interlocutors experienced and expressed *barely living* in the worlds they continued to inhabit. However, although my interlocutors were not outside this literature's formulations, it was difficult to relate their experiences to the way this work figured response under pressure, framed possibility, and located hope. This gap widened as I thought more closely about the dynamics and other matters at various locations of *barely living* within broader domains of *living on*, and as I began to question and expand my understanding of the forces, conditions, and other intensities that form and inform the political terrain Povinelli delineated in her work.

Then the refugee crisis hit in 2015. With this, another domain of violence, injury, and uncertainty driven by the same neoliberal biopolitical logics, and logistics, of human disposability that informed government response to the sovereign debt crisis was opened (Athanasiou and Alexandrakis 2016; Fassin 2016). Whereas the injury that flowed from state attempts to structure and regulate conditions of "becoming migrant" touched only a few of my interlocutors directly, everyone I knew in Athens expressed deepening disappointment, sadness, and even embarrassment as new suffering and social injustice driven by some global situations and state action or inaction became present, variously, as an aspect of life in Greece. These newly invigorated affects were resonant with, and in some cases overlapped and fed, those affective expressions of crisis life with which I was already familiar. From bad to worse. As the Athenians I knew continued on in deteriorating situations, there was no hint that something better might

come for them: endurance's promise of meaningful change had not material-
ized and could not be spotted on the horizon—certainly not at the realm and
scale of political governance, or even within small spaces at the register of informal consensus. In 2015, as the situation deteriorated further and on new fronts,
none of my interlocutors were talking about better futures; but they were also not
idle. My thinking about hope moved decidedly to the animations of resilience,
and I began to look more directly at resilience's relations with political terrains.
I started to wonder about change. Specifically, I started to wonder if we might
think of resilience not as a form of some politics-facing endurance, but in terms
of its negative space.

Perhaps unlike other places in Europe where crisis regimes effected injurious
changes more quickly, the long duration coupled with the intensity of austerity
measures in Greece, compounded by the failures of the state response to the
refugee crisis, drew out and expanded *barely living*, rendering this legible as a
concomitant condition to endurance's forms. As I came to this line of thinking,
the archive of the letters returned to my mind more clearly as a durative form, as
the site where the shared work of care that would ultimately foster (although not
assume) the writers' social reintegration was cultivated; which led me to wonder
how the writers came to pick up their pens in the first place. I began to wonder
what it meant to come to the resilient action of writing love letters under conditions of persistent injury, devastation, and deepening withdrawal. How do we figure coming to resilience in microsocial spaces of ontological emergency, among
individuals who find themselves beyond their limits? How might this coming to
and then undertaking resilient action resonate with the realms and scales of the
social, and ultimately the political? I began to seek a more critical engagement
with this figure of coming to resilience, to connect with and perhaps rethink
established understandings of resilience, what it might teach us about relationality, possibility, and the political more broadly. So, I took a step back.

My approach was to collect and assess what people were saying and writing about resilience both in the field and within the discipline of anthropology.
I began with what I came to understand as general "resilience talk" among my
interlocutors, in the media, and in other spaces, as the crisis regime consolidated
through 2014. This talk either directly or indirectly juxtaposed some possible
achievement of well-being to some evocation of risk or experience of adversity. Both concepts were quite malleable; that is, they were easily adapted to the
speaker's experiences, interests, and positionality at the time (see Panter-Brick
2014, 432). Some individuals discussed resilience in terms of a morally charged
language of preparedness. This talk evoked ideas of competitive individualiza-
tion and commodity logic of accumulation at the heart of advanced capitalism.
For them, resilience meant using one's resources to cope with or even benefit

from crisis-driven risk. Others figured resilience in terms of perseverance. This talk evoked possessive individualism and self-management very much in line with neoliberal narratives. For them, resilience meant weathering the storm by whatever means necessary. Those able to persevere were those able to withstand adversity. Both preparedness and perseverance tended to reduce resilience to matters of fitness that played well with what struck me at the time as a thinly veiled social Darwinism at the heart of "national salvation" narratives of austerity emanating from the state and its international lenders. Later, I would also understand these takes on resilience as in line with the ideology of market economy and biopolitical logics of human disposability on which the state and its institutions had begun to operate.

Then I would also hear resilience discussed by those who were by all accounts weathering austerity through various formations of social solidarity. This talk typically pointed to expressions of solidarity located in everyday social relations, informal social economies of various kinds, and group actions as sources of resilience. Here, in general, resilience was tied up with collective responsiveness to heightened risk resulting from austerity measures. For these individuals, resilience meant participation in various expressions of collective agency that eased shared hardships. This resilience and solidarity talk was commonly heard in casual everyday conversations about crisis and, specifically, how various forms of collectivity—"the people," "the community," "we"—would get through it. The heuristic at the heart of all this talk, namely that resilience referred to a kind of problem solving, played well across all three iterations of resilience (cf. Ungar 2008). Like "well-being" and "risk," the idea of "problem solving" was extremely malleable: a reflection of one's subject position.

I also came across the unfixed-ness of the concept of "resilience" and its general association with notions of risk as I took a closer look at the literature in anthropology. Early work in the discipline did not engage with this concept directly, although research and writing on collective resistance usually flirted with ideas of resilience. James Scott's influential ethnography of poor peasants in Malaysia was perhaps the best example (1985). In this work, Scott showed that through jokes, stories, and gossip, his interlocutors—poor, hungry peasants—positioned themselves as superior to their exploiters, effectively advancing their dignity in the face of ongoing humiliation and oppression. Critically, they also employed hidden forms of action such as foot dragging, desertion, false compliance, feigned ignorance, arson, sabotage, and so on, to resist their exploiters in more practical ways (1985, xvi). These hidden actions, he explained, were the "weapons of the weak" (1985, xvii). Their goal was not to change or overthrow the system, but rather to continue on and survive within it (1985, 301). Although he did not use the term "resilience" in this work, Scott's description of his interlocutors' drawing on moral strength and group solidarity to retain self-esteem and endure suppression by undertaking grudging compliance with a system that harmed them and which they morally and symbolically rejected is generally acknowledged as early writing on resilience.

Indeed, Scott's idea that a collective sense of moral superiority and dignity may animate sustained resistant albeit not transformative action articulated an understanding that hidden internal strength—variously construed—was a fundamental or essential source of resilience against external forces. This basic idea would appear in the near background of work on resistance in political anthropology for years to come. Yet while the literature on resistance grew rapidly (Taussig 1980; Comaroff and Comaroff 1991; Comaroff 1985; Ong 1987), contemplative writing on resilience did not. Instead, resilience remained a very flexible conceptual resource, sometimes used interchangeably with "agency" to examine various matters of endurance, engagement, and response, but was rarely taken up directly. Instead, the concept was typically applied with a view to unpacking the sources and resources animating collective action, which tended to fall into one of two distinct categories: sustaining action not aimed at achieving change (as per Scott), and collective actions of disruption resembling open counterattacks aimed at achieving broader social and/or political transformations. Among both bodies of work, the political force of resilience was formulated in structuralist terms, along lengthy time horizons and at the microscale in terms of ordinary everyday matters.

Likewise, in a related branch of writing on suffering and violence, resilience was closely associated with matters of agency, albeit in relation to recovery, living with, or coping (Koonings and Kruijt 2015; Jarrett 1997; Lewis 2013; Zraly, Rubin, and Mukamana 2013). In this context, the term "resilience" brought into sharper focus the sustained effects of violence on subjects (Green 1999; Feldman 1994). It located weathering or finding resolutions that would either make livable or resolve drawn-out experiences of distress and marginality within collective actions, but at various scales. Many of the themes developed in this literature would resonate with later writing on precarity and precariatization. The ideas of living with or coping with suffering and violence related closely with how anthropologists would come to write about endurance under neoliberal regimes. Interestingly, like my concern with endurance's disempowering implications, the suffering-and-violence literature sometimes questioned if resilience is not also a disempowering formation, with terms such as "determination" or "courage" posited or used as alternatives (Reynolds 2000, 169n5).

More recently the idea of resilience has gained popularity in medical anthropology, in work on climate change, and on research examining how communities recover from, or resist, catastrophic events of various kinds. Among other things, this work has contributed an important acknowledgment and careful consideration of the role of external forces such as livelihood and social relations in building, preserving, and activating resilience (Nahar and van der Geest 2014, 382–83; see also Barrios 2016; Nelson and Finan 2009; Philogene Heron 2018; Cons 2018; Silver 2008; Papadaki and Kalogeraki 2017; Anthopoulou, Kaberis, and Petrou 2017). This more dynamic view acknowledges and takes into consideration the important role of relationality and context—including history—in thinking on resilience. However, it continues to advance two implicit assumptions carried over from earlier writing that I began to see as problematic.

The first had to do with the way writing on resilience formulated collectives—an effect, I suspect, of an enduring if not always upfront preoccupation with revealing or accounting for the "sources" of resilience. Reading over the early literature especially, I noted a tendency to locate the resources and impetus for resilient action in the collective experiences and cultural resources of groups, communities, commons, and such (Feldman and Masalha 2007; Panter-Brick 2014). In other words, the sources of resilience tended to be derived from some assessment of being-together and having-in-common, even in later studies that took more complex views of "internal strength" or which considered examples of cross-cultural coming together at times of hardship (Dressler, Balieiro, and Santos 1997). As I show in the following chapters, however, the presumptions of wholeness based on such things as common history, or shared ideology or culture, that were at the heart of this approach render unnoticeable certain modes of relationality that I observed were fundamental to an understanding of how my interlocutors came to resilience. I came to think of resilience not in terms of activated resources shared by some collectivity—an approach, incidentally, that would resonate well with the way Knight talked about cultural proximity and endurance—but in terms of nonessential aggregation: as a kaleidoscopic effect of intersecting individual impulses to live on.

The second persistent assumption relates to the implication that resilience does not change a people's external situation. Most commonly, scholars have defined the effects of resilience in terms of a collective's capacity to "bounce back" from external pressure or experience of adversity while maintaining some form of completeness, both individually and as a group (Almedom, Brensinger, and Adam 2010). Importantly, even works that take up resilience in terms of collective resistance aimed at bringing about change tend to locate resilience as a force that sustains action, rather than a force of change in and of itself. Where resilience is discussed as transformative, such work posits that sustaining actions taken by resilient collectives challenge political and institutional status quos such that they may achieve structural changes. Again, change is accounted for in terms of actions sustained by forces of resilience, allowing individuals and groups to remain whole. This is not the understanding I seek to develop in this work. Here I show that coming to resilience can be world making. Insofar as this entails a nonlinear dynamic of reengagement with the social, coming to resilience is fundamentally related to the content, form, and direction of coming political agencies, collectives, and action. In this, I argue, coming to resilience is a pre-political intensity charging resilient action with broader transformative potentials. Becoming resilient entails the possibility of a radical becoming of the political.

As my research came to focus more clearly on resilience, and my understanding of resilience became more complex, I found myself spending more and more time talking with my grandmother and thinking, once again, about the letters and the couple who wrote them. The injuries most of my interlocutors were suffering were about to be redoubled by a new round of austerity. I mentioned this to her, noting that I didn't know how people would cope. She said something in response that changed the way I approached my fieldwork. Here is the entry from my notebook:

> Every part of a person can be harmed. When harm happens, we try to mend ourselves. One of the dangers of living through difficult times is that this mending can take us over or, if mending is impossible, we work endlessly to make it possible. This makes us less human. It separates what we do from our sense of ourselves in the world. The letter writers could have become fixated on hurt: he could have kept nurturing the swells of pain he tended while walking, and she could have spent more and more time alone with her piano and the ghosts of her children. Their situation asked for this. But they didn't. They realized what was happening to them, and instead of continuing to live with it and tending to it, they did something else. They wrote a different story for themselves.

This idea—of dehumanizing violence triggering some undertaking that may then activate critique, allowing individuals to pursue and realize some inter/subjective change and path to something else—became a point of methodological concentration in my research. I began to seek sites that encouraged, activated, or enabled critique, and those that were informed by new critical perspectives. My attention turned to injury and violence and to aggregating bewilderment and bad feelings, reorientations of grit, untethering and tethering. I found myself following unfixed, uncertain, unsettling, and contingent matters in the everyday lives of the people I knew to moments of intersection when as yet unsure possibilities of coming situations that promised to be different from the current life evanesced and intensified, but sometimes backslid and evaporated altogether.

Put differently, I began to develop an understanding of the space just below the surface of resilience, where the work of coming to some iteration of resilience was being done, where individuals were still coming to some possibility of imagining a better life. This was the dynamics of *barely living*.

Eventually, these sites led me to question the linear teleological idea that resilience entails a moving *from* hardship *to* well-being and some desirable future. I also came to question the optimisms of returning or preserving or advancing that were bound up with resilience. I questioned the often opaque presumptions of self-determination and mobilized relationalities telegraphed by notions of resilience. This questioning, together with my earlier apprehensions about research with built-in assumptions regarding resilient collectives and futures, inspired me to seek an approach to thinking about coming to resilience that broke with traditional approaches and concerns. I was drawn to a thread within poststructuralist political theory that approaches matters of activation not in terms of particular histories, projects, or commitments, but as they come into formation around local critical events (Laclau and Mouffe 2001; Laclau 1990; for a more current critical account of agency and new modalities of social mobilization see Butler and Athanasiou 2013 and Puar 2007). To my reading, this work encouraged attention to intensities and interactions, the traces these leave and, generally, to the critical potential of heterogeneities at various realms and scales. Thinking with Roitman on the governance of crisis events (2014, 65–66) and Athanasiou's reflections on the uses of crisis events in bringing forth ways of interpellating subjects into crisis normalities (Athanasiou and Alexandrakis 2016), I began to connect this poststructuralist approach to activation with Foucault's (1997) writing on critique and Butler's (2002) thoughts on desubjugation.

What emerged for me was an approach to unpacking the complexities of coming to resilience—a methodological and analytical point of departure—that attended to matters of messy relationality, realizations of new perspectives, and activations of critical agency. I kept close Foucault's idea that the norms governing knowledge and desire may be transgressed by individuals whose lives have become disorganized or unintelligible, who are unable to produce meaningful explanations based on established truths. I reflected often on his suggestion that in uttering *Why can I not make sense of what is happening?* these individuals engage in critique beyond the epistemological field of their lives, that is, beyond the limits of normative "ways of knowing." Together with Butler's explanation that this critique encourages a transgressive desubjugation, or freeing from forces of interpellation (2002), this work came to inform my thinking about how subjects may form themselves in ways that yield critical agency from normative violences to which they are subjected. Accordingly, I began to approach sites of coming to resilience as sites of trans-normative formation activated and catalyzed by injury and undoing, as sites that intensify becoming outside of oneself under conditions of shared yet differential precariousness.

With time, the repeated questioning, new perspectives and undertakings individuals pursued in desubjugation brought order, if not necessarily relief, to the neoliberal-fed chaos in their lives. Thinking with Deleuze (2009, 1997), I came to understand the ongoing repetitions of trans-normative questioning, understanding and doing as emerging new ordering milieus, which in turn sometimes connected, intersected, and gestured toward each other, forming a territory of coming to resilience made of evanescent sites of coming through injury. Not unlike spectral fields formed as light cuts through the dust of newly formed rubble, this territory was unfixed, variable and dynamic. In places, assemblages of particles became dense and heavy, rendering the spectral field apparent. In others these assemblages became disaggregated, thin, and more isolated. This territory, this field of particles, provided space for and encouraged unfixed relationalities grounded in, on, and of trans-normative ordering questions, perspectives, and undertakings. Whereas violences often interrupted these territories at the level of milieus, they also produced new activations of critical agencies—mobilizations that contest injurious interpellations—and the further possibility of new aggregations. As these violences became regular and knowable, particles consolidated into more steady territories, became heavy, and settled onto and into the rubble, effecting not only a topographic, but also a topological transformation providing new ground for the emergence of new cultures of intelligibility.

Thus, a schematic of coming to resilience—the conceptual innovation of this book—would entail a nonlinear movement through various interrelated and sometimes concurrent steps. We might consider these steps discursively as follows:

1. Chaos and ruination: loss of one's sense of order in the world. The familiar becomes strange. Ready answers to explain what is happening to one's life and to imagine a path to some desirable future do not come easily.
2. Desubjugation and seeking of stability: awkward feelings begin to mark one's coming to see, if not yet understand and question, the limits of the normative. Looking for an end to further awkwardness is tantamount to seeking stability.
3. Ongoing stabilization and new resonances: one's growing sense of order is an echo of ongoing engagement with normative limits. This ordering renders other trans-normative milieus, and the ongoing efforts undertaken by others to find order within them, legible as both shared condition and positionality. This intensifies becoming outside of oneself, and activates critical agency.

4. Shared efforts and new imaginaries: individuals find ways to stabilize with others and begin thinking once again about futures. This finding ways is often awkward and uncertain, but encouraging of new imaginaries. These imaginaries bring the individual into relation with possibility under shared conditions of stabilization, envisioning, and desiring.

5. Aggregations and sedimentations: individuals come into relation with resilience. Imaginaries and possibilities emerged by finding ways with others encourage the consolidation of nonessentialist, not-totalizable, collective trans-normative undertakings as territories of coming endurance. Awkwardness dissipates as the resonant actions of critical agents become oriented to the possibilities emerged within consolidations of unsettled and unsettling territories. Continued engagement with and within these territories settles them onto and into the Athenian topography.

This book is not intended to give a complete picture or account of Greece's sovereign debt crisis or the so-called refugee crisis. Likewise, it is not about the various expressions of resistance and other forms of collective response to these crises. This is a book about people living through terrible, drawn-out times of upheaval. It is about loss, picking up and moving pieces around, and the worlds that fade and the ones that may begin to become visible in the process. This book is about refiguring. It is about the transformative intensities people experience as they fall out of and find their way back to the social. It seeks to expand how we talk about the effects of persistent, compounding injury by tuning in, not only to the various responses triggered by erosion or to strategies of living diminished lives, but to the subtle ways lives beyond their limits bend and then inflect into shared worlds.

I have organized the chapters of this book to reflect the states of undoing and seeking stability that followed injury, and the new perspectives and activations that came as my interlocutors felt their way along newly diminished and still-diminishing terrains. My intention was to give the book conceptual coherence; however, I was wary of portraying resilience as predictable or direct, or of producing a portrait of coming to resilience that might be seen as specific to a single community or collective within Athens. So, rather than following one interlocutor or one group, this book moves around to consider the very different lives of various interlocutors. My hope was to create the effect of a kind of collage as this form privileges encounter, engagement, and assemblage. Collage is also about unfixed dialogue as opposed to telling. It exists in an unfinished state within and against a frame, continually restarting and reorganizing. Accordingly, the chapters that follow are written in an *ethnography-forward* way to facilitate and encourage different readings, ways through, and imaginings within and of the conceptual space of this book. Each chapter develops a story that at first pass may appear to be quite unrelated to the others; but taken altogether, variously, the chapters will allow the reader to begin to see resonances that render visible an undulating, unfixed domain of coming to resilience animated by common human impulses from within injury and erosion.

This book does not have a typical concluding chapter, as coming to resilience is never a complete project. In the final chapter, I have opted instead to tack back to my interlocutor from chapter 1 to highlight the transformative, world-making potentials of coming to resilience not only subjectively, but in terms of expanding social fields that edge toward collective resilient action. This tacking back also performs an approach to thinking about the political at times of crisis through matters of resilience. The space between these chapters, both in terms of the content of this book and in terms of an untold narrative of my interlocutor's *barely living*, evokes the negative space of the political. So, the beginning of the book takes a familiar line into questions of response to hardship and depletion by considering the life of a resistance actor engaged in protests and other forms of collective action; but it then deviates to follow along as multiple simultaneous and multi-scalar undoings—of the political sphere, of his memory, understandings of history, and ultimately his normative self-identity—precipitate his becoming disintegrated from the social in a manner that would become further unsettling and destructive. The end of the book rejoins this interlocutor as he attempts to put things together, and follows as they fall apart, and he tries again, and again, and this trying begins to intersect with other trying, and ultimately comes to flirt with possibility. In this we leave the familiar ground of response, solidarity, and resistance to crisis intact as a form of politics-facing endurance, while leaving it behind for a closer look at the small everyday spaces where a social topography of resilience coalesces as a radical space of pre-political intensity: a form of negative space of the political.

Chapter 1, "Everyday, Illegible," develops an account of crisis-driven confusion and isolation touching on a number of key moments of disruption and periods of mass precariatization since 2008. We meet Niko, an anarchist organizer, as he struggles to reconcile what he thought he knew about resistance and activism with the politics that played out in Athens between 2008 and 2015—a time he came to describe as utterly bewildering, as making no sense; a time when he struggled with deepening agitation, growing anger and confusion that sent him into a state of near self-destruction. Bringing political memory and critical events (Roitman 2014) together with a consideration of dispossession (Butler and Athanasiou 2013), I examine my interlocutor's break from the anarchist scene and eventual descent into ever deepening self-isolation. I argue that, as Greece's neoliberal regime consolidated, the process of interpellation by which ordinary subjects were incorporated into the neoliberal economy (Povinelli 2011) produced everyday states of "not knowing." For Niko and others, this "not knowing" was unmooring as it unsettled established communities and social projects, shared identities and commitments.

Chapter 2, "Becoming Lost," explores the way crisis-driven experiences of messiness and confusion can spiderweb in unexpected ways within and through a life, how they may reconfigure relationalities and produce intense hardships and multiple uncertainties that may ossify crisis worlds. I show how for individuals caught in these situations, within these uncharted milieus, the immediate work of finding some stability can begin to stand in for a meaningful life. In this chapter, I follow the story of a Romani boy, George, as he navigated the slippage between traditional understandings of "Romani manhood" and an emerging moral geography of manhood grounded in the neoliberal fantasy of an individualistic, self-sufficient, and market-oriented sovereign subject. I show that his multiple failures, misfires, and recurring breakdowns marked transgressions of particular social and cultural normativities. I argue that the "awkwardness" he experienced as he found and exceeded these ingrained limits, along with his eventual distancing from his childhood home, the Romani compound where he grew up, and his friends and family more generally, marked an experience of desubjugation (Butler 2002; Foucault 1997). Struggling with this experience of desubjugation, my interlocutor began to look for some stable situation. From here, I explain, George came into relation with the possibility of looking at his world from a new perspective.

Chapter 3, "Ordinary Ghosting," continues to explore living with not knowing and increasing awkwardness, focusing specifically on how new perspectives formed in desubjugation can enable critical agency. I focus on the experiences of a young nurse, Amalia, who began to worry as job losses and pension cuts made life difficult for her and her family, while, at work, those in positions of privilege took advantage of changing policy to advance their careers even as my interlocutor's salary was cut, her hours increased, and the flow of sicker and sicker bodies at the clinic intensified. Building on the previous chapter's engagement with Foucault and Butler, I argue that an awkward encounter between my interlocutor and the father of an ill migrant child made the multiple violences she endured both visible and legible as a quality of a coming Athenian life of which she too was a subject. Thinking with Deleuze, I show that her response to this coming situation, with others, produced an alternative terrain of the present defined by compassion and inessential commonality (1997). Further, I suggest that this co-emerged terrain resettled the sense of continuity inherent in the way Amalia imagined and lived her life, producing an unsettled and unsettling stability.

Chapter 4, "Common Matters," explores the crucial moments when individuals living with the injuries of having been interpellated into the present of increasing precarity and inequality begin to pursue potentialization within the new social fields of alternative terrains. We join Samba and Taj, undocumented migrants who, after finding themselves stuck in a country that had increasingly fewer opportunities to offer, came to work together as scrap metal collectors for a third man. This was an awkward work partnership shaped and made possible by new critical perspectives cultivated at the edges of the normative violences that sought to form them as migrants within/of the sovereign debt crisis. They knew the work they were doing offered no future. Yet they continued on working at the bare edge of personal stability in part because this site provided space to reflect and imagine, and in part because my interlocutors came to associate the work with positive effects: understanding, trust, and the possibility of hope. Drawing on Berlant's "consensual rubrics" (2011) and Deleuze's writing on sense and series (1990), I show that the sharing of hardship inflicted by neoliberal policies establishes spaces of intelligibility that reconstitute individual experiences as shared matters. The chapter pushes against accounts of injury as inactivating and depleting of agency (Ralph 2014), arguing instead that the sharing of memories (albeit troubled and troubling) and aspirations (albeit uncertain and otherwise distressed) occurring along neoliberalism's contact zones of abandonment may enact a collective politics of relationality beyond and against the normative premises of competitive individuation. I suggest that these sites—in this case, an awkward site of care that was in some ways positive and others less so—evoke an anti-foundationalist becoming-in-common encouraging imaginative work that may open individuals to resilient actions.

In the final chapter, chapter 5, "Radical Possibility," I return to Niko. By 2017, my interlocutor had begun to see things differently, to make human connections again, and was volunteering at a shelter for undocumented migrants. However, things were not going well. Those living and volunteering at the shelter began to fear a violent attack by members of the neo-Nazi Golden Dawn, and as tensions were growing, so too were divisions between volunteers—so-called solidarians—and residents. In this chapter, I propose an understanding of the shelter as a co-cooperative site of concurrent solace and potentialization grounded largely on an ethic of "finding ways." I argue that sites like the shelter can be world making in a way that is not reductive, not totalizable or essentialist. Thinking with Berardi's writing on harmonization (2012, 120–23), I suggest that when multiple undertakings of solace and potentialization intersect as they did at the shelter, they encourage an understanding of the subject as having become involved in a co-emerged methodology of action that facilitates continuing on, despite hardships, obstacles, setbacks, and privations, toward a better life. These sites may come to form assemblages within which intersectionalities produce intensities. In this, sites of practical co-cooperation like the shelter can be taken as interwoven with and within other sustaining and potentializing acts, encounters, processes, and spaces insofar as these touch the daily lives of individuals struggling against erosion, depletion, and the crisis-driven sense of uncertainty. Working with Deleuze's writing on refrains (1995) and thinking with Kathleen Stewart's writing on the compositional present (2010), I show that the overall effect of these reverberations and interweaving is tantamount to a topological reformation of the social, effectively providing new terrain for a remapping of the political.

Coming to resilience is not about "bouncing back"; it describes a site of radical reconfiguration: a reworking of one's cultural resources, reassembling and finding again one's place in the social. It brings to focus matters that make us human where these matters are remade.

Among my interlocutors, neoliberal governmentality and oppressive, drawn-out, relentlessly redoubling austerity caused catastrophes and groping to find a practical but also deeper ontological stability. These sometimes momentary, sometimes drawn-out periods of stability provided critical ground from where the people whose stories I convey in the following chapters came to self-author, at, beyond, and relative to the limits of the normative, at first alone, then with others. This enabled unexpected intersections and encouraged new expressions that had the potential to intensify disruptive reverberations across Greek political topographies from within the very texture of everyday lives made messy.

My grandfather died just before the official onset of the economic crisis in 2010, and my grandmother died in 2018 just as commentators and other observers began to hint at signs of a national economic recovery.

As the years passed, my grandmother had grown less inclined to talk about the difficult situation in Athens but was happy to discuss the letter writers. She would sometimes recall conversations she had with my grandfather about them. Again, the letters—their weight, the few words read aloud, their burning away—and the mystery of the writers' lives were a source of inspiration for me throughout my fieldwork and the writing of this book. I was drawn to the contrasts of sadness and love, despair and doing in their story. I was drawn to figures of strained stillness: to holding the erosion of one's world and quieting overwhelmingly bad feelings by writing and reading love letters. I was drawn to the timelessness of it all, to the loosening of anchorings and the slipping of trajectories. I was drawn to the idea of remaining alive in remaking, to finding ways toward hope in small spaces. These themes are at the heart of the chapters that follow.

My great-aunt had died, unexpectedly, years before her husband. My grandparents only heard about her death months after she passed.

"Our relationship with them had changed," my grandmother explained. "We grew apart. They were somehow different at the end. It is hard to explain." She continued, "We made an effort to reconnect with him."

My great-uncle remained trapped in his memory of his wife for the rest of his life. He refused to try anything new or to go anywhere different. Life for him was sweetest the day before she passed, so he held on to her as tightly as he could.

"I don't think he was unhappy in those days," my grandmother told me, adding, "He continued to live with her in his own way."

They had developed new habits in their final years together, which he continued. They walked together—something the family had noted with concern, given his earlier wanderings—but she would choose the way. "He talked about how the city looked different along her route," my grandmother recalled. She had begun to give music lessons to neighborhood children. Some of those children and their families would occasionally visit him after her death.

"Your grandfather was right about the letters," my grandmother said. "Keeping them would have been more than an intrusion. We didn't really know them anymore. Even when we tried to spend time with him, it was difficult. We couldn't communicate easily; like we had nothing in common. They had gone a different way. They found a life we were not part of."

My grandmother was not sad about this, and neither was my grandfather, as she recalled. The letters and the trunk that contained them came to their door after my great-uncle passed. My grandmother could not remember who had brought it, or why. They had not inspected the contents of the trunk carefully when it arrived. Although they knew it would likely stay in their cellar forever, thinking back, she now recognized that they thought of it as being on its way to somewhere else. It wasn't *for* them. It was only *with* them. In this, the trunk was forgotten, and the letters remained hidden. I began to wonder about the parts of our lives comprising forgotten and hidden things, their people, and the lives they lived.

EVERYDAY, ILLEGIBLE

How Being a Radical Became a Problem

June 2007: Athens, somewhere near the Exarchia neighborhood.

The black door before me was worn from years of use and exposure to the elements, its paint blistering and peeling. I searched the building's façade but couldn't find a street number or mailbox; in fact, the only mark I could see were the letters "Φ Α" scratched into the stone that surrounded the door. I looked at the directions I had written on a small piece of paper, checked the time, and reached for the door's brass handle. I pulled it tentatively. Somewhere within the old wood a mechanism released, and the mass swung silently on large hinges. Entering the foyer, I looked over my shoulder instinctively and removed my sunglasses. My heart began to beat more quickly as I stood in the dusty space fumbling with the clasp on my bag, trying to retrieve my notebook. Behind me a spring caused the door to close with a decisive thud, and I was blinded by the sudden darkness: my breathing quickened and I became aware of the muffled sounds of the street I had just left and the strange shapes in the shadows that now surrounded me.

As my eyes adjusted I began to see details in the cramped, graffitied space: The floor was a mosaic of the old style where stones were set in cement, then sanded down and polished to reveal their intricate interiors; two doors, one broken, stood on either side of me; a light fixture hung by its wires from the ceiling; and a spiraling staircase made of wooden slats held in place by an ornate iron banister curled up into the darkness. An acrid smell I could not identify hung in the air. I steeled my nerves and began to climb the stairs, as per my instructions. Never had I been so aware of my footfalls as I was at this moment.

On the second floor of this old house located near Athens's activist and political dissident district Exarchia—mere blocks away from the site were Alexis Grigoropoulos would be murdered the following year—I found a poorly lit lounge. I entered and introduced myself to the man already sitting in one of two seats away from the windows. There was no one else in the room. He smiled and motioned for me to join him. Striking two matches simultaneously he lit a handrolled cigarette, then tossed the matches, still burning, into a crumbling fireplace nearby. One bounced off the mantel and began to scorch the wooden floor. Neither of us moved.

The air was sweetened with the fragrance of freshly boiled Greek coffee, some of which I accepted in a small cup with a chipped handle. As my senses adjusted to the new surroundings I began to notice random pieces of broken furniture near the walls, ornate yet crumbling plaster details in the ceiling, and three other doors blocking my view of adjoining rooms. I didn't feel safe. The man sitting across from me had a bad reputation. He was a public disturber, a self-professed "freedom fighter and educator of the public," one of Greece's most aggressive anarchists.

Consider a man: tall and slender with neatly coiffed black hair and brown, probing eyes. Niko[1] was in his late twenties, but the sheer forcefulness of his presence made him seem younger. My interlocutor didn't work, though he looked well-dressed and carefully put together: his leather jacket was fashionably distressed; leather boots scuffed but not worn; an Omega timepiece was clearly visible on his wrist; an expensive motorcycle helmet sat on the floor near a window.

I asked Niko to tell me about himself. He launched immediately into a brief family history. His father was a butcher, and his mother was a violin teacher. He took care to describe how each looked: his father was a heavy-set man with a mustache, a square face, and chipped fingernails; his mother was thin with delicate features and flat arches that made walking difficult for her as she aged. He grew up somewhere in Attica with two older brothers in a home that had been in his family for two generations. His father's recent decision to sell their property to a developer in exchange for two apartment units in the new build and some cash came as a disappointment to Niko, but not as a surprise. He explained: "The erasure of ordinary houses to make way for apartment blocks serving national and corporate interests is happening all the time now. This is just another example of the destruction of our city and the degradation of its citizens."

After a beat, Niko explained that his parents were now living in the larger of the two apartments, he was in the smaller, and his brothers had moved to other neighborhoods. He began to chuckle. "They're productive members of society." Shifting his chair closer, he added, "I'm productive too, although in a different way!"

It took a while to adjust to the way Niko spoke. His words came quickly and forcefully, and everything he said seemed rehearsed. Was his father *really* a butcher and his mother a violin teacher—a knife-wielding mustachioed man who processed meat to feed people, and a delicate disciplined woman who educated people—or in other words, a figure of "Hellenic traditionalism" and a figure of European "high culture" whose labor, taken together, portrayed a vaguely familiar vision of some Greek modern future? Or was this a bit of fiction? As my doubting grew, so too did Niko's control of the interview. He kept a very close eye on my notebook, pausing whenever my writing became illegible and offering to repeat himself or clarify whenever I made a notation in the margins. Adjusting to the way Niko spoke meant performing a kind of active but acquiescent listening.

Although I had many questions, I thought it best to keep the interview moving forward, so I asked Niko to tell me how he came to be interested in politics. He explained that he traveled to England in his early twenties to study government and international relations. During this time away he began to see Greece "from a different perspective" and grew increasingly restless. I circled the word "restless" in my notebook. In response to this, Niko explained that he was not involved with anarchism while he was in the UK, although he liked the idea of the "dissident in disguise." It struck him, my interlocutor recounted, that only "shadowy figures" could break what he perceived at the time to be the growing ideological and economic chokehold the state, the EU, and international corporations were having on Greeks. When he returned to Athens, Niko continued, he took to sharing his views on various social media platforms. He cultivated a large audience, which he soon discovered could be mobilized when called on for support. In time he became more involved with various far-left organizations, but mostly anarchist and punk collectives. "I have over a million subscribers and followers across various platforms. That's a far reach. I can get things done." Looking me in the eye, he then added, "The problem with Greeks is they are simultaneously dependent on the system and afraid of the system."

Now, there were large, obvious gaps in Niko's story, and although I had managed to ask a question a moment earlier, I suspected he would not be open to my probing his answers at any length. I focused my attention on his last statement, which it seemed to me was dangled like bait. I had come across the idea that Greeks were both dependent and afraid of the government several times in the past, especially in my conversations with older Athenians—people whose reliance on the welfare state was troubled by still-vivid memories of war, occupation, political unrest, and the uncertainty and terror of the 1967–1974 military junta (see, for example, Panourgiá 2009, 32). A similar refrain also circulated among young adults who expected the state would provide education, work, and comfortable pensions—essentially to take care of them from birth until death—but who were wary of the corruption and disorganization that plagued the public service. I mentioned this to Niko. He scoffed. "Yes, young and old, they talk about dependence and fear, especially when they feel uncertainty and anxiety in their lives. But they all refer to *this unfortunate history* or *that unfortunate state of affairs*. The truth is, this situation is deliberate." He sat up straighter. "Greeks are simultaneously dependent and fearful of the system because the state wants them to be. Successive governments cultivated this purposefully in order to centralize the mind of the citizen."

Confused, I looked up from my notes, and he stopped talking. I began my question, "What—" but he interrupted: "Centralization is the master political strategy of every [Greek] government since the junta."

He went on to say that large centers of administration created the illusion of power, but *poorly functioning* large administrative centers achieved the added bonus of forcing citizens to strategize whenever they wanted something done: rather than thinking about their rights, citizens thought about what they could achieve through connections and bribes. Governments kept the system big and broken to keep citizens worried and busy while corrupt officials lined their pockets.

This last thought hung in the air as Niko took a deep breath. After a few moments of silence, during which he lit another cigarette, he continued: "Uncertainty and anxiety are a normal aspect of Greek citizenship. This is a form of misdirection that allows the state and its agents and partners to act with impunity while producing complacency among the people. Normal citizenship here is a numbed, blinded citizenship of exploitation, routine, and worry—but some of us still see clearly." What he said next caught me off guard:

"The only hope for Greece is with migrants."

Niko must have known his statement would surprise me. He smiled and nodded slowly. He explained that abused newcomers had not been subjected to the forms of control locals grew up with. They saw through things and were finding their voices—he claimed they were beginning to ban together, informally, to fight for rights. Being, in his opinion, both the most abused people in Greece and a critical cog in the economy, migrants, including undocumented migrants, were in a unique position to bring about social change. Niko was especially hopeful that second-generation migrants would become a major source of future support for anarchism in Greece.

"They're growing up in Greece, but not like Greeks. You remember Paris?" he asked, alluding to the rioting that spread across France in October 2005 following the death of two migrant youth who were hiding from police in Clichy-sous-Bois. "Soon people will be talking about Athens."

Eventually, Niko slipped into a tirade over police corruption, and the interview began to feel like a bad lecture. He became very animated as he cataloged illegal police activities, including human and drug trafficking and facilitating the importing of illegal goods. These activities, he asserted, were carried out by networks of local and international criminals working in cooperation with members of the police. He went on to suggest that the government had orchestrated these connections between police and traffickers to bolster certain sectors of the economy and to repress others. All this served the corrupt and the powerful. "Greek capitalism!" he spat. He claimed to have proof of everything.

Checking his watch, Niko leaned back in his chair. What came next was . . . well:

> You see, it is very complicated. Anarchy is not like it used to be. Today only some people support us, and our messages have to be edited to reflect their needs and interests, which are often dictated by the needs and interests of the state, or the few who run it. The state is powerful and organized, despite its appearance. They know how to manipulate people, how to take away rights covertly, and how to silence detractors even before the voiceless victims *want* to be heard. We have migrants hitting them on the fundamentals of human existence. We have the youth fighting their more overt attempts to confuse and further their own destructive, corrupt agenda. We have traitors from within their own ranks joining ours, helping the state in the morning and fighting against it in the evening—like hellhounds feeding on sin.[2] And I'm in the middle, coordinating the effort, tearing down the disguises, questioning the lies and the deception to help people to see more clearly. Remember me in the near future. A time will come in Greece when the weak will understand anarchy as their path to freedom, and we will be there to help them rip at capitalism and consumerism . . . [and] overcome the violent police.

While few researchers would take my interlocutor's depiction of citizenship and the workings of the Greek government at face value, most would probably agree that an anarchist organizer makes an interesting thinking partner on matters of responsiveness and political terrains. Indeed, Niko had much to say, especially after 2010, merely three years after the above interview, when Athens became a hotbed of both conventional and unconventional actions in response to accelerating precarity—actions that troubled state attempts to depoliticize crisis and thereby manufacture consent for the troika-mandated program of neoliberal restructuring, but also troubled the high-scale moral narratives on which established political projects of all description were founded, including anarchism.

Initially, Niko attributed this rise in action to what he described as a widespread "doubting" among Athenians: a sense of suspicion that led to questioning the motives and logics that informed the state's attempts to govern though crisis management. He suggested, happily, that as Athenian livelihoods were depleted, new everyday hardships "mixed with anxieties the government bred in its citizens for generations—it's all coming back to bite them." For Niko, the people (meaning both recognized/legal and informal citizens—basically anyone living and invested in the *polis*) would always see through state attempts to effect harmful changes with minimal backlash because, regardless of individual political orientations, almost everyone viewed state structures as untrustworthy. In other words, in the early days of the crisis, my interlocutor remained convinced that conventional and other kinds of actions were evidence of the population *carrying on*, as they always had, albeit with a little less.

However, Niko began to change his tune in 2013. At this time, large street actions were becoming less frequent, and more and more Athenians were cooperating in various efforts to relieve hardship and mitigate uncertainty. Papataxiarchis has described this as a shift from protest to initiative (2018, 235). These efforts ranged from simple but assuring expressions of understanding and sympathy, to bolstering commitments and camaraderie, to the formation of groups working to relieve specific needs. Niko, like many of his comrades, participated in such activities; however, unlike his comrades, he quickly became suspicious. He insisted that such schemes indirectly benefited neoliberal governmentality: "The state is more likely to inflict harm when it knows ordinary people will pick up the pieces. This is the problem with relief efforts"—a position that was now just coming to him, that he would repeat again and again in the coming years, but later revise as I explain in chapter 5.[3] He began to insist the only way forward was through militant action. This drove a wedge between him and many of his comrades who saw "ordinary" cooperative efforts as a stand against neoliberal policies. Niko explained, "It's their prerogative. They can do whatever they want, but they should know they've been compromised. They are no longer radical actors. They have lost their ability to disrupt the system because their actions support the regime! . . . They've bought in without knowing it."

Informing this accusation of ignorance or compliance with the government was Niko's sense that his comrades and those individuals who were now benefiting from their labor—so, almost all political actors in his circle—had fallen victim to a strategic move of the state. He began to think that the state was using job losses, cutbacks to services, and expanding personal debt to grow fear, shame, and hardship among the "less valuable"[4] sectors of the population. The worsening of everyday life, he thought, pushed individuals to seek relief anywhere they could find it, which pulled activists and others with means and motivation to offer various forms of immediate aid. He feared that the consolidating nexus of "humanitarian" needs and responses was effecting a slow blurring of the boundaries of established political commitments, communities, and their projects—a sentiment that betrayed Niko's understanding of the political as tied to particular qualified or recognized undertakings. So, according to my interlocutor, the combination of intensifying hardship and the rise of informal relief efforts effaced traditional forms of resistance while enabling normative violences perpetrated by neoliberal governmentality, or, as he put it, "People are abandoning their *political lives* for a piece of bread."

Familiar political discourses, spaces, forms, and actions are aspects of the social. These familiar entry points to examining response to neoliberal-fed hardship and injury are part of the territory of coming to resilience that bleed in and out of everyday scenes, activities, and strategies. In this chapter I will examine Niko's attempts to understand gradual changes both in the way Athenians were responding to neoliberal governmentality and in the modes of action other members of his anarchist collective were pursuing. I follow him along from his early successes in spreading anarchist ideology to 2008 when my interlocutor noted that politics in Athens were beginning to look different, through 2010 when the government declared sovereign debt "crisis" and 2013 when he began to struggle with changes not only in the political scene but also within the anarchist collective. This was the time when what it meant to be a radical became a question and a problem for Niko. This was the time when he began to see that the political terrain had shifted, and the forms of disruptive radical action with which he was familiar, and invested in, targeted political fundamentals that did not appear to be fundamental any longer. Ultimately, this chapter ends in July 2015 when a critical event led Niko to think that he no longer understood politics. This event—a seemingly absurd political happening—caused him, like many other Athenians, to express bewilderment, disappointment, powerlessness, and anger, but it did not result in my interlocutor taking action. Niko became silent.

This silence indexes "not knowing," a state of resetting and returning that many Athenians came to experience and grapple with from 2010 onward as their worlds became messy and confusing, and countless people faced various degrees of impoverishment or outright ruin. As I will show here and over the next two chapters, with no conventional solution to the spread and intensification of everyday hardships and uncertainties seemingly possible, and with these hardships and uncertainties becoming *ordinary* for many Athenians, the immediate work of preserving a life worth living began to stand in for a meaningful life. For Niko, who defined every aspect of his life in terms of radical resistance, the changes brought about by neoliberal austerity produced "not knowing," which in turn sparked what became for him an existential crisis. As his followers and comrades took up various sustaining actions, Niko slipped into a destructive spiral of wondering if his life had any purpose or value at all. Niko began to experience a state of desubjugation.

Two days after my 2007 interview with Niko, I was walking near Omonia Square when a moped buzzed onto the sidewalk near me. I could hear it approaching quickly on my left, so I stepped to the right and stopped thinking it would simply cruise by. It didn't. The moped came to a sudden stop, and the rider reached out and grabbed my shoulder. I stiffened, and then recognized the motorcycle helmet.

"You're uptight!" Niko said as he raised his visor.

"You're frightening," I responded impulsively.

Niko smiled, "I've heard that before."

He locked up his moped, and we walked toward a nearby metro station. I knew a quiet spot in a park near there. We were meeting for a follow-up interview. I had texted him after our initial meeting to thank him, and because I wanted to ask a few additional questions. One question led to another—too many to ask over text. He agreed to another face-to-face meeting, but this time I picked the location.

As we walked, I noticed that Niko was dragging his heels on the ground, making a rhythmic scraping sound. This seemed strange to me. He didn't appear to have trouble walking, and his boots were relatively new—that is to say, the soles were not coming unglued so as to catch the pavement unintentionally. What's more, he would stop dragging his heels when we approached something he had to step over or around. After some uninteresting small talk, I asked why he was doing this. It was definitely noticeable, and a little distracting. I suspected he was doing it on purpose.

"It's how I walk," he said, smiling, then looked down at his boots. "I wear through a set of these every few months. It's a classic form of anti-police action." At first my mind went directly to James C. Scott's examination of foot dragging as a form of everyday resistance in the context of repressed peasant societies (1985), but this was clearly different. I asked him to elaborate. Niko learned to drag his heels from an activist who spent time at a squat he used to frequent. In the old days, he explained, gangsters would hang a long scarf from their back pockets. It was very long, usually down to the ground. To assert their territory, rival gang members would pull the scarf. This would start a fight. Other people would also cause these scarves to fall, almost always by accident. Regardless, a fight would ensue. Locals learned to keep their distance. The police, on the other hand, saw the scarves as an easy way to identify gangsters. They would walk behind them in plainclothes, and pull. When the gangsters turned to engage, they would arrest them.

"People aren't stupid though, especially criminals," Niko continued. "They switched tactics."

To avoid arrest, gangsters continued to dangle scarves but would roam around in larger groups. Whereas other gangs did not hesitate to start a street brawl, the police—who usually patrolled in small groups of two or three—stayed away altogether.

"Until they got smart," Niko explained. "Instead of pulling the scarves, which would alert the gangster to react, the police would come up behind them and cut the scarves with scissors!"

Niko stooped down comically and pretended to be following someone. With a snip of his fingers he straightened up again, laughing. He explained that gangsters gave up this tactic, but his friends had revived it—with a twist. Instead of a scarf, they dragged their heels. Most people looked at them momentarily, but would go about their business. Police, however, would stare.

"They're trained to," Niko explained. "They can't help it. They see something unusual, and they stare at it. . . . I mean, all Athenians stare, but members of the police don't stop staring. It's their way of intimidating people they think are abnormal." Niko exaggerated his heel-dragging walk by kicking his feet high into the air like a member of the presidential guard on rotation in front of the parliament buildings—or perhaps he was imitating the famous "Ministry of Silly Walks" sketch by Monty Python.[5] Either way, he looked ridiculous, and we both chuckled.

"We look to see who is staring at our feet. Police officers stand out—we see them watching us. This way we know who to keep an eye on. This comes in handy, especially at protests when you don't always know where the [plainclothes] police or their thugs are hiding in the crowd." I smiled again at the thought of an anarchist looking "abnormal" to a police officer by imitating the walk of a soldier or (satirical) ministry employee.

"Anthropologists stare a lot too, you know," I offered jokingly.

"I have my eye on you too," he replied. "I don't trust you."

I felt this was a more honest start. I told Niko that I was interested in his recruiting methods and in his social media presence more than in the street actions he coordinated. We hadn't talked about this at any length last time. Niko nodded and added that he also felt we left out many details.

"Let me start again," he said as he lit a cigarette, "but the right way this time."

Now, before continuing, it is important to say a few more words about my fieldwork with this interlocutor. During this second interview, Niko made very clear what he wanted from me in exchange for his ongoing participation in my research—terms he occasionally revisited and updated. Specifically, he requested that I include in my published work "a history of anarchism in Greece." I agreed and offered to help him develop this history, but he declined my help. So, I now emphasize that over the next few pages I will share Niko's take on the history of anarchism in Greece (rebutted and further contextualized by me only occasionally, and in consultation with Niko), as he recounted it during this second interview.

I should say, I explained to Niko that the history, as he presented it to me, was in many ways ambiguous and suggestive. At some point I sent him notes and edits, but he rejected them. He was quite happy with the account as he had presented it and I had recorded it. He insisted that readers should feel free to do the work of interpretation and filling in meaning as they saw fit. In the spirit of this suggestion, then, I encourage you to read his anarchist history as a negatively capable account that simultaneously deflects and invites particular interpretations. Indeed, it should be read as a rhetorically powerful and self-justifying personal narrative that opens a window to the political project in which Niko was involved, which he actively and skillfully advanced, and in which he was very deeply invested. In many ways, this history helps to further locate and position the Niko I knew in the early days of my fieldwork. As we will see toward the end of this chapter, it also maps a familiar terrain of knowledge and action that came to be problematized and was ultimately lost as the crisis dragged on. Now, back to the interview.

Niko considered himself a modern revolutionary: the "result," as he put it, of a long line of revolutionaries. He talked about some of his political heroes. He mentioned the editors of the first Greek anarchist publication, *Light* (*Phós*),[6] Emanouil Dadaoglou, who led a (failed) revolution against King Othon in 1862, and Alexandros Schinas, the educator who assassinated King George I in Thessaloniki on March 18, 1913.[7] Niko then paused the history lesson to say he respected anyone who followed the "core anarchist philosophies" as set out by Bakunin and Tolstoy. He suggested I look at how the philosophies of these thinkers continued to influence writers in well-known anarchist periodicals such as *Solidarity* and *Riot*. He also suggested that I could find these periodicals archived on Facebook. I looked up at Niko and lifted an eyebrow.

"Yes, I use Facebook. I use Facebook a lot. We'll get to that, but you need to know more about Greek anarchism first. I want you to hear this story because it is not well known," he explained.

Niko was not wrong about the history of anarchism not being well known. Anarchism is underexplored and underrepresented in the historiography of Greece, and not by accident. As Neni Panourgiá has explained, the history of the Left in general has only been written in fragments and intervals within a larger history that has not always included it (2009, 12–13). Until the mid-nineties,

Right and even Centrist-leaning politicians and others in positions of authority discouraged—and at some points in time even prohibited—the writing of the history of the Left as a conscious historiographic endeavor. Whenever the Left was represented, various groups ranging from labor unionists and communists to anarchists and others were lumped together—a politically expedient move that consolidated an immediately intelligible "enemy of the state." This idea of a singular Left, of course, was fiction: leftists claimed many different identities and identifications. Differences existed even within specific leftist political projects. According to Niko, "There are many different flavors of anarchism—something for everyone! . . . and we don't operate in isolation. We collaborate with punks, eco-warriors, students, communists—lots of people. I'd say my followers come from across the spectrum. Only an idiot would close his ears and shut his eyes to like-minded people. The leaders of other leftist groups might criticize us at times, but they know we pose a greater threat together. This is not new. We've always worked together to some extent."

So, the history Niko recounted began with a genealogy of anarchist founders, then moved through early practitioners and to the early and mid-twentieth-century anarchist thinkers who published pamphlets and periodicals at a time when action declined. We chatted for a moment about anarchism being excluded from the history books. Niko suggested that we should see this as a "crime against knowledge." He picked up at the point of the movement's resurgence, a time when leftist politics in general became stronger in Greece: the fall of the military junta in 1974. "I was too young when anarchists found their voice again— I have no memory from this period, but I know what happened from my older comrades."

Niko talked about anarchists supporting student protesters at the Polytechnic University the night when the junta attacked, which precipitated Greece's return to democracy. This involvement with students ended up being a long-term strategy for anarchist organizers. Niko talked at length about the student movements that proliferated in Athens between the 1980s and the early 1990s. This was a time, he explained, when anarchism became relevant once again, gaining a broad public. This was also a time when an older generation of anarchists left, making way for a younger, more violent generation with close ties to punks to take over. "Anarchists were on the streets!" he exclaimed. "We reset and dug in." Indeed, support expanded, resulting in a proliferation of anarchist collectives and activities. Niko rattled off some highlights of the period:

- Between 1982 and 1983 anarchists founded the Anarchist Federation party. This was mostly an exercise in political criticism led by a handful of activists.

- Students formed a number of anarchist-communist groups, with the Group of Anarchist-Communists of Nea Smyrni[8] (Omáda Anarkhoko-mounistón Néas Smírnis) being the most influential.
- The leaders of the Nea Smyrni group worked with the established publisher Free Press (Eléftheros Típos) in Athens to produce *Anarchist* (*Ánarkhos*), a leaflet dedicated to promoting their activities and spreading the political theory of Peter Kropotkin and Murray Bookchin[9] (a mix of classic anarchist philosophy and more modern anarchist perspectives on decentralization, anticapitalism, and ecological awareness).
- On November 17, 1985, the police murdered a fifteen-year-old youth, Michalis Kaltezas, sparking anarchist-backed riots in Athens and Thessaloniki.
- In November 1986, another group appeared, calling itself the Anarchist-Communist Cell of Ano Liosia[10] (Anarkhokomounistikós Pirínas Áno Lio-síon), which published the magazine *Autonomous Action* (*Aftónomi Drási*) in partnership with a small circle of anarchists (not anarchist-communists) from Piraeus. The magazine ran until 1991 and included articles that criticized local municipal activities, engaged with global current affairs, and encouraged the formation of a unified anarchist community.
- On January 8, 1991, a thirty-eight-year-old teacher, Nikos Tembonera, was murdered by thugs of the New Democracy government who were attempting to quell student protests. This sparked anarchist-backed riots, which in Patras, where the teacher was killed, culminated in the burning of the local police station and town hall. This prompted the minister of education to resign.

With a growing base and an active agenda, various anarchist organizers across Greece saw the mid-1990s to the early 2000s as a prime time for a second wave of recruitment to what they were now billing as a more inclusive "anti-authoritarian movement" (*antiexousiastikí kínisi*). The challenge, Niko explained, was to connect with an upcoming generation of young people who had no experience of the periods of political unrest of the seventies and eighties (see also Giovanopoulos and Dalakoglou 2011). My interlocutor had a solution:

"Listen now," he said smiling, "this is how I saved anarchism in Greece."

At the time, the most influential anarchist publications included *The Children of the Gallery* (*Ta Paidiá tis Galarías*); *Red Thread* (*Kókkino Níma*);[11] *New Topology* (*Néa Topoloyía*); *Anares*; and some others. Although these works tried to separate themselves from earlier anarchist publications by, for example, refraining from publishing "how-to" guides for carrying out street action or descriptions of ideal modes of organization, they nonetheless resembled the publications of the 1980s in that they were intended for internal audiences and others with specific interests in anarchism. To make these works more accessible, some publishing groups put their materials online. However, the publications did not reach a broad audience, nor did they appear to attract new followers. Niko offered his comrades a different strategy.

My interlocutor thought anarchists should communicate like the people they want to attract. He also distinguished between what he called "blind recruitment" and "social recruitment." During the early 2000s, one key blind recruitment technique Niko employed involved sitting at cafés popular with younger people and sending messages to mobile phones in the immediate vicinity via Bluetooth. These messages—including photos and videos—were often funny and communicated a sharp antiestablishment sentiment, usually at the expense of the police. They all contained links to websites where my interlocutor and others would upload and share similar antiestablishment digital content.

"For this style of communication to work, the kids' phones had to be set to receive incoming Bluetooth connections. Not a problem. Playing with their phone's settings before ordering became a habit for young people, because many cafés offered coupons to patrons over Bluetooth," Niko explained. "They'd find a place to sit, pull their phones out of their pockets, turn on Bluetooth, and place the phone on the table. Seeing phones on a table told me the kids sitting there were open to receiving messages. So I sent them."

"How did you know this strategy was working?" I asked, wondering if he was using a hit counter or some similar technology on his website to monitor traffic.

"I knew when I sat at a café one afternoon and my phone received one of my own messages!" Niko explained.

Niko also made use of text messaging for social recruiting. During the early 2000s he used group texting to distribute messages to his growing list of contacts. He thought to use group texting because student organizers employed this form of communication to keep in touch with other student leaders during coordinated school occupations—an adaptation of the way students communicated with their friends regularly.

"I was always in and out of schoolyards in the early days," he recalled. "They're prime recruiting ground—all you have to do is find the cool kid," Niko said, trying unsuccessfully to suppress a chuckle, "and offer them help. Done. They appreciate you, and as long as you're cool, they talk you up to their friends. Soon, you're getting messages from these kids too."

Niko made it a point to say he was not out there to "convert" people to anarchism. Rather, he claimed he was helping people find something they were already interested in.

"I told my comrades from the beginning that you can't *make* an anarchist. You can only reach people who are already interested—people who already have an anti-authority bent. Thankfully, in Athens, that's a lot of people!"

Niko then spoke emphatically against the idea that technology allowed him to reach groups and individuals of opposing political dispositions[12]—to convert anyone with a data connection, as some of his comrades hoped (cf. Rafael 2003).

"Supporters of the Right will always support the Right. They might see your message, but you can't convert a fascist!"

Niko went on to tell me that he used the latest communication technology to keep in touch with his supporters. We talked about Facebook, Myspace, Twitter, and various blogging platforms. We also discussed what he called "another level of communication": direct messages sent to other anarchist organizers and recruiters in Greece and beyond. He asserted that anarchism was, and remains, internationalist. Communication with these individuals usually had to do with resource sharing (such as contacts, experiences, expertise) and strategy (mostly to do with recruiting, avoiding monitoring, mobilization). This "other level" completed the picture, Niko concluded. He compared his work, again, to the work of anarchists of the 1980s and earlier—especially those who wrote and circulated pamphlets and periodicals. Although the digital content he distributed did not contribute to debates about anarchist political philosophy or communicate a rigorous critique of the ruling class, it depicted ideas and emotions that fostered awareness among his audience of a common, continuous struggle. He repeated that his story was part of a longer story, an ongoing political project that was steadfast in its commitment to anarchist values and ideals, persistent in its production of disruptive texts, responsive to changes in the political climate, and attentive to the lives of its supporters.

I had difficulty reconciling my initial interview with Niko and this follow-up. At our first meeting, my interlocutor talked about how he became involved with the anarchist struggle, about aspects of the current political terrain, and he discussed future political strategies. He told me "how it is." During our second meeting, Niko focused on positioning anarchism as a political force in Greece—one that had not been adequately registered despite anarchism's persistence in the country and, in his view, its broadly consequential contributions and interventions. Although we talked about his family in the first interview, it struck me as very performative, whereas our second interview was somehow more personal. We were a little more familiar with each other, to be sure; but that wasn't surprising. The second interview felt more personal in that Niko was being at once more contemplative, careful, and introspective. It felt as though I was being let in on something that mattered to him—something that was happening. Indeed, despite the history lesson—or perhaps because of the history lesson—the second interview was definitely forward looking in a way that involved me.

This, together with his insistence that I include his history lesson somewhere in my published work, led me to think that perhaps Niko saw a chance to shape our relationship such that it might generate some kind of political effect that was not possible through his comrades, established networks, or communication with the social mainstream. Perhaps I represented to him an opportunity to advance anarchism in a different way. This fit with the more personal feel of the second interview. Indeed, in asking me to record and incorporate in my work his "history of anarchism," I began to think that Niko was pursuing an opportunity to extend his political work—perhaps a soft form of the recruitment he pursued elsewhere—to new audiences, through me. Seen this way, the second interview could be understood as part of an established project for Niko in which he cultivated sustained relationships to spread and collect information, find supporters, and gain influence. Looking back, this also explains why Niko did not want my input on his history lesson: just my attention.

Yet, there was something personal beyond this, again to do with history. I began to think I was tuning in to *how* Niko imagined pathways and fashioned projects: in this case, one that involved me (and you). I was tuning in to Niko's taking stock of opportunities and to his forward-looking thinking. In this, the past did not figure as some ordered narrative, like the one he shared with me; rather, it figured as a flexible resource on which he drew to orient, inform, and backstop his various political initiatives insofar as past examples could justify these activities as needed, reasonable, and potentializing, and moreover imbue them with authority. In this, the past helped locate, structure, and activate future-oriented political projects. I was beginning to understand that Niko seemed to be pursuing an ongoing relationship with me (someone he saw as positioned well beyond his usual sphere of influence) because this strategy had worked for him in the past, as it had for others. He would later tell me that the mode of intervention he sought to achieve through our relationship—the insertion of his history into this text—was inspired by the use of malicious code by hacker comrades. "Don't take it personally; anarchists have always done this sort of thing."

Ultimately, I would come to realize that, in those days, Niko was constantly imagining directions and plotting projects that he pursued at every opportunity. As I started to focus on this further, I also came to see just how central, flexible, and in some ways capricious a resource the past can be. Past examples provided resources that oriented, informed, and justified; but these same resources would also become sites of differentiation and friction among individuals who participated in the same collective projects. This realization helped me to understand how and why my interlocutor later split from his comrades. As we will see, whereas his comrades and followers responded to the neoliberal regime by undertaking initiatives and actions in response to immediate needs produced by accelerating precarity, Niko remained dedicated to the kinds of actions he had been involved in for nearly a decade. This caused tension between him and his comrades, leading my interlocutor to become uncertain about the future of the anarchist political project and the people he thought he understood, and even about the basis of this understanding. This break within the collective was not the result of a simple disagreement over something practical that festered into something bigger but, I will argue, a result of a differentiating revision in the way members of the collective interpreted and valued certain aspects of the movement's history, which in turn resulted in an inability to agree on projects. In this, neoliberal governmentality troubled the normalizing premises of shared sense that both grounded the collective and formed the heart of Niko's "fiction of the self."

Close to six months after Niko recounted to me his history of anarchism and shared with me his online recruiting strategies, I received an email from a Hotmail address I didn't recognize. I would have deleted it, but my name was in the subject line, and the first line of the message preview on my screen read, before fading, "It's Niko. You might be interested in a meeting I'm holding next Friday with Mustafa from . . ." I clicked. The message did indeed appear to be from Niko and contained details of a meeting he had organized with a man he claimed represented a large group of migrant workers. This piqued my interest, but I wasn't in Athens at the time and couldn't join him at the meeting. I replied, telling him I'd have to miss it, but that I was very interested in his work with migrants. He wrote back almost immediately, "The revolution is coming. You should join us."

I was becoming used to Niko's flair for the dramatic. This message certainly excited me, but I tried to put it into context. Niko was expanding his network to include migrants, as he indicated he would at our first meeting. The way he was going about doing so was in line with the way he recruited students: connect with the leader, and let them recruit for you. Reaching out to working migrants specifically was also a logical next step for Niko. Historically, and especially in Italy and Spain, anarchists were very successful in finding support among dissatisfied labor groups—again, this is something he mentioned during our first meeting. A recent explosion of undocumented migration to Greece had both grown the migrant labor force and sparked a flurry of racist responses, ranging from hate speech to physical attacks on the streets—a phenomenon repeated across Europe. Anarchists were among an increasing number of self-fashioned informal activist groups attempting to help this population (see for example Rozakou 2012). However, whereas other groups sought to support migrants by attending to "rights and resources," as Niko put it, his group took a different approach.

I reconnected with Niko via Skype after his meeting with Mustafa. It had gone very well, he said. He explained that Mustafa was also an organizer, but of a different sort. He connected newly arrived migrants with jobs. To date he had placed between forty and fifty individuals in a variety of jobs, including day laboring, cleaning, and scrap metal collection. I interrupted:

"Mustafa sounds like a criminal, Niko." I minimized the Skype window and began to search through my field notes for an interview I had done with a migrant from Nigeria.

"I know," he replied, "but he's not," Niko added quickly. "The people you're thinking about are those guys who trap workers in terrible conditions and take their money. They really are evil. Mustafa is more like a translator."

Niko went on to explain that his new contact did not take payments from the people he helped. He was a well-established second-generation migrant who was eager to help people from his father's homeland, which he had visited often as a child. Migrants would connect with him after arriving and settling. He kept a list of people and skills, then connected them with opportunities when these came up. With time, Mustafa's reputation grew, and migrants of various backgrounds began to contact him for help.

"Now listen to why all this works," Niko continued. "Mustafa asks migrants he helped place in jobs to contact him before they move on. This way he can make sure he has someone to fill a job before it becomes available." Niko was beaming. I was still suspicious.

"And what's in it for him?"

"You'd be surprised how useful it is to have lots of people around you," Niko responded wryly. "Anyway, he's a good person." I couldn't get Niko to elaborate further on his new contact's motivations.

Mustafa, it turns out, was in a difficult position. Several of the people he placed in jobs were experiencing violence where they worked. These people—a woman from Nigeria and two men from Bangladesh—had been in Athens for only a few months. They were in positions Mustafa had filled in the past, leading him to wonder if others had been victimized as well. Especially worrying was the fact that the job the Bangladeshi men were doing was for one of the local municipalities. Specifically, they were working on contract in garbage collection. This contract was not with the men directly, but with someone else who had been injured and, not wanting to lose his right to the work, arranged with Mustafa to have the position filled for a percentage of the wages. This had been a lucrative arrangement for everyone, Niko reported eagerly.

"The Bangladeshi guys had work, and the Greek guy was happy knowing he had a job waiting for him. Think of it like job sharing. And," he added, "Mustafa's guys also had the chance to pick up random work through the people they met on the job. One of the guys just painted the house of one of the other truck drivers."

Niko's plan was to talk to the victims, gather information, and then return to the collective to make a plan of action. He explained that he preferred a targeted intervention in these cases, rather than a broad "declarative move" (to use his words). By making it clear to the perpetrators of racially motivated violence that their actions were wrong and would not be tolerated, Niko expected to solidify his relationship with Mustafa, who could help spread a positive message about the collective to others within the migrant community. After gathering further support they would be able to mount larger street actions of various kinds.

This was the first time I heard Niko refer to a strategic move intended to benefit not "anarchism" in general, but the "collective" specifically. This exchange provided a small opening into a space to which I had no access. Again, Niko was involved with a small group of particularly active anarchists in Athens—a group that was, if not closed, at least very suspicious of outsiders. This is to say they were not open to people they did not already know. Niko once described the prospect of my interviewing the collective as "vanishingly difficult." One had to have several contacts within the collective and already be part of their conversations (if indirectly) to gain permission to join them. "It's about trust," Niko said, "built on compatibility." Asked to clarify what he meant by "compatibility," Niko explained he was referring not only to personal political beliefs, but also to sense (*aísthisi*) and predispositions that were in line with the motivations and modes of action undertaken by the collective.

Anyone familiar with the anarchist scene in Athens would recognize these sentiments. It was not at all unusual to have outsiders vetted before they could participate fully in an anarchist collective—a practice that persists today. This process usually entailed individuals presenting themselves or being presented to the group, followed by a conversation among members of the collective, and a verdict—however reached—as to whether or not and to what degree the individual would be welcomed into the collective. Squats and other anti-authority projects supported, created, and/or maintained by anarchists and others with similar ideological leanings employed comparable vetting processes, if not consistently, then when called for by some internal group or individual (see, for example, Adib 2018).

In subsequent conversations Niko would tell me that he felt he belonged with the collective, while rejecting my tentative suggestion that his comrades were like family.

"It's different," he interrupted. "I don't feel close to them, but we go together . . . you know? We share a sense for how things are and how they should be. That's all, really. We're not brothers and sisters . . . there's no father! We're people who see things similarly and rely on the support we provide to each other in the struggle.'"

Niko's words suggested that his interpersonal relationships with other members of the collective mattered insofar as they reinforced the collective, through big and little expressions that communicated a shared ideology, willingness to act, and *sense of things*. The idea of belonging to a collective as being predicated on shared ideology and action has been explored at length in anthropology. The same cannot be said, however, about shared sense. What exactly is a shared sense, and how do individuals come to understand their sense is shared? Is a shared sense the same as shared understanding, or does it refer to something different?

Anthropologists have discussed *sense* and *sensing* in terms of making encounters meaningful (Stewart 2007), wayfaring or movement in general (Hage 2005; Massumi 2002), and affective geographies (Thrift 2004; Navaro-Yashin 2012) but not in terms of belonging and collectives—at least not without tying sense to shared histories and abstract conceptions of cultural affiliation (Raffaetà and Duff 2013). Research on shared material attachments and shared practice is also unhelpful here, as this work tends to refer to the accrual of "sense of belonging" in a way that effectively reduces sense to a feeling intensified or attenuated by what we might refer to as social mechanics. The way Niko talked about shared sense, not only during this exchange but also later when I asked him about this directly, was more in tune with how we might talk about entanglement and simultaneity as emergent knowledge making.

To help me think through the way Niko used the word, I turned to Gilles Deleuze, who envisioned the sense individuals apply to evaluating the phenomena they encounter in the world as a kind of surface along which events are evaluated, understood, and assigned significance (Deleuze 1997, 2009; see also Das 2000). A shared sense can thus be understood as a shared surface—a common ground in the world (cf. Ahmed 2004, 198). Shared sense, this surface, also constitutes a norm along which belonging is construed. In this, the collective is always becoming in relation to itself and according to the norms that demarcate inclusion. Collective actions or projects must thus resonate with the collective norms. Insofar as projects appeared to be understandable and otherwise in line with what was possible under the sign of their collective practice, the shared sense among the group would most likely be positive and supportive, in turn opening the possibility of that project coming to be taken up and incorporated, variously, into the common ground.

The way Niko talked about compatibility evoked this shared sense as being at the heart of his relation to the group. For my interlocutor, the collective was more than just a group of like-minded individuals willing to act together in pursuit of their ideals. The collective was composed of individuals who could be trusted to support actions—almost impulsively—that were consistent with a particular view of the world, one that was in line with Niko's own view. So it was no surprise that Niko sensed the collective would support his initiative to reach out to migrant workers because exploitation, violence, and increasing desperation would drive this population to take action against the police, the state, and corporations in general. In fact, support for reaching out to this population was unanimous and enthusiastic.

I reconnected with Niko some months after his conversation with Mustafa. We met at a café for a drink. He told me that he followed up on Mustafa's complaints by talking to the migrants involved and then reported back to the collective. As he expected, the other members of the collective jumped on the opportunity to help a migrant organizer. They dispatched comrades to visit the workplaces of the Bangladeshi men and the Nigerian woman. Niko explained that, unfortunately, they had mixed results. Whereas the Bangladeshis reported a positive change in the attitudes of their coworkers, the Nigerian woman lost her job as a result of the visit.

"I'll spare you the details, but we found the guys giving the Bangladeshis a rough time and helped them to see the other side," Niko said, smiling. "Let's just say things got a little out of hand when we went to help the girl. Her employer was a pig."

Feeling bad that they caused her to lose her job, the collective helped Mustafa to find her a new job.

"It's the least we could have done," Niko said, looking at his phone.

Niko saw this initial action on behalf of Mustafa as an overall success. His new contact seemed satisfied, and Niko was making plans to reach out to other groups of migrants and to informal advocates who worked with them. The members of the collective also began to visit the areas where migrants lived. Their contacts grew steadily. This led Niko to host a community meeting in Kypseli, an area of high migrant concentration. "I wanted them to see me, and to understand that we were there to help," Niko explained. I, however, began to think Niko and his comrades were playing a dangerous game. It seemed to me that they were selling protection like a gang might: your attention and loyalty for our muscle and resources. Suggesting this to Niko sparked an angry response. He insisted that politics was about relationships and that they were simply building relationships with a group of people who needed their help. He repeated several times that the collective did not punish people for turning their backs on them—and that this happened often. They were there to connect, to support and help people (in his words) to "become free."

As I will discuss in chapter 5, the conversations we would have some years later would reconsider the meaning and, importantly, the various limits of "helping others." What's more, Niko would begin to understand the relationship between anarchists and their supporters and audiences differently: less in terms of cooperative endeavors, and more in terms of what I came to think of as *co-cooperation*—alignment and resonance of distinct albeit compatible projects. Although it was not obvious to him in the final days of 2007, Niko would later point to this time as the beginning of a new project.

As 2007 ended and 2008 wore on, critical commentators and scores of protest actions in Athens cataloged a growing list of compounding social, economic, and political troubles. It seemed to me that Greece was on the verge of a transformative political moment, for better or worse. I would eventually come to understand the broad intensive questioning I was seeing in Athens as part of a larger global trend of questioning the parameters, modes, and ethics of neoliberal governmentality and which was casting doubt, as Povinelli would later point out, on the legitimacy of this mode of governance (2011). Niko agreed with this assessment. Throughout 2008 he had been involved in numerous protests and other actions targeting particular state agencies, the government in general, and large corporations such as banks. Mobilizing supporters to participate in these actions was easy, as most people in his network were struggling in low-paying jobs—or jobs that did not pay at all, such as once-lucrative but now effectively dead-end government internships—and few people saw any possibility of positive change. Many also resented what they saw as a broken education system, the daily challenges of living with neglected and often crumbling public infrastructures of all kinds, and growing social inequality, among many other frustrations and deepening concerns. Motivation to participate in action was high, even if life was becoming more difficult. Most Athenians I talked to joked that protesting had become a "national pastime." Niko suggested this sentiment was myopic: "Greeks have always taken action against those who try to harm them. It's just that the world has become a much more violent place. The increase in action on the streets is an effect of global pathogens."

For his part, Niko was splitting his time working to bolster the protest scene and organizing the still-growing population of working migrants. He had become especially interested in connecting migrants with students—something he hoped to achieve by leveraging the connections second-generation migrants already had within schools. Niko saw his two projects as complementary, as developing two fronts of resistance against the same problem: impoverishment (understood very broadly) caused by global elites. Then, in December 2008, he would see his various efforts come together.

On the evening of December 6, 2008, Alexis Grigoropoulos arrived at the Exarchia neighborhood of Athens with a small group to celebrate a friend's name day.[13]

As the evening progressed, the group decided to walk from this friend's home to a nearby café on Messologiou Street. As they approached the café they heard shouting and the distinct sounds of people running away from some nearby happening. Curious, Alexis broke off from the group and stood in the middle of a nearby intersection to see what was going on. At that moment a police officer spotted him, raised his gun, and shot Alexis dead (Vradis and Dalakoglou 2011).[14]

The gunfire could be heard along the street where Alexis's friends were standing, and echoed across Exarchia Square, which was packed at the time with young people. The last moments of Alexis's life were witnessed by twenty to fifty individuals who ran to the scene in response to his friends' cries for help. Niko was in Kypseli at the time. He received word of the shooting from four different contacts, almost simultaneously. He arrived just after the boy's body had been removed, to find scores of young people milling about.

"I was stunned, like everyone else," Niko began. "The Greek police are violent and ignorant, but they don't usually commit cold-blooded murder—and in our neighborhood, no less. The collective used to meet a stone's throw from the murder scene!"

The next day Niko passed by the site of the murder with a few other members of the collective and some supporters. By then the site had become adorned with candles and flowers. They were on their way to the campus of the nearby Polytechnic University, where hundreds if not thousands (according to Niko) of young people had already begun to gather. At some point, Niko explained, the mass split into two groups: the first headed to the Central Police Headquarters, and the other went to the Parliament building at Syntagma Square. Niko went to Syntagma Square, where he found a garrison of riot police waiting. At some point protesters, including Niko, started throwing stones and Molotov cocktails at police, banks, and other nearby businesses (Panourgiá 2010). The growing intensity of this barrage caused the police to fall back to their secondary positions, dig in, and respond with water cannons, tear gas, and stun grenades. The uprising lasted nearly a month, spread to several cities across Greece, and inspired sympathy protests in other parts of Europe and beyond. It also drew to the streets a wide variety of actors: anarchists, unionists, pensioners, university students, soccer (and other kinds of) hooligans, mainstream political party supporters, and documented and undocumented migrants.

"This was all spontaneous, Othona," Niko said. "I mean, I relayed messages as they came to me and tried to coordinate people who said they were coming, but I didn't arrange anything. My contacts just joined the action on their own. It was beautiful."

Pundits and observers were surprised by the persistence of the action, the absence of a clearly articulated demand or complaint beyond a general expression of anger,[15] and by the diversity of actors who were taking to the streets—actors who, in other spaces, expressed competing and in some cases completely incompatible political views (Vradis 2009; Economides and Monastiriotis 2009). Common frames of analysis failed to explain the politics we were witnessing. Indeed, familiar categories like "solidarity" and "civil action" appeared to function better as descriptive tools than as analytical prisms. Even meta-analytical frames didn't work. As I've discussed elsewhere (Alexandrakis 2016b), the December events (as they came to be known locally) did not resemble proceduralist politics— that is, politics grounded in the actions of autonomous individuals pursuing their own self-interests. The actions also exceeded the terms of communitarian politics—that is, politics grounded in the actions of self-identified groups engaged in resistance and advocacy in order to acquire public recognition and empowerment. Some observers wondered whether Greece was undergoing some kind of fundamental "political realignment" (Kalyvas 2010, 351; see also Gourgouris 2012). Niko was less uncertain.

"It's simple. All these people are fucking suffering. The architects of this mess have pushed everyone too far. They've broken politics. No more Left! No more Right! No more thinking in small boxes. The people are waking up."

The December events made Niko ecstatic. The political ramifications of the changing world he described in 2007 were unfolding before his eyes. His optimism was unbridled. His network—from anarchists to students and migrants— was mobilized and cooperating with others. The establishment was in shock. Niko began to circulate materials online trumpeting the "seeding" of a new direct global street politics. His supporters remained energized and active through the rest of 2008 and into 2009 when Niko and his comrades began to sense that a new opportunity to further intensify the fight was around the corner.

On April 23, 2010, the Greek state formally declared a sovereign debt crisis and requested an international bailout. On May 2, the government began to implement an aggressive austerity program in exchange for economic aid from the European Union, the European Central Bank, and the International Monetary Fund—the "troika." During the coming years, successive governments dismantled public services and oversaw a series of salary and pension reductions, increased taxes, and layoffs that resulted in sudden mass impoverishment. The Greek middle class was devastated, and the lower class came to struggle further, while the so-called reforms protected financial institutions.

Niko helped coordinate efforts at the first general anti-austerity occupations and protests. He also helped organize street actions as austerity measures were rolled out over the following years: cuts to pensions, public-sector firings, moves to privatize, and so on. These actions were largely peaceful. Then, in the summer of 2013, things began to change. Following the practice of pushing through major legislation by decree, the government—without debate, without consulting its coalition partners, and without due public warning—closed the public broadcaster, ERT, in an attempt to meet a troika deadline pertaining to the reduction of the public workforce and spending. The spontaneous shuttering of ERT and the replacement of regular television programming with prerecorded classical music performances evoked memories of the classical music piped over the public airwaves just before the onset of the military junta in 1967 (see Panourgiá 2009, 125). Niko saw the closing of ERT—an event that brought the current crisis situation into direct conversation with earlier periods of terror, violence, and restricted civil rights that remained part of the public consciousness—as an opportunity to "step up" action beyond typical street protests and occupations.

"We wanted to support ERT journalists who were resisting the government by continuing to broadcast. We thought the revolution should be televised,"[16] he said, furrowing his brow, then smiling. "We knew some people who could do things with electronics, who could keep these journalists on the air."

Niko was telling me this several months after the ERT protests died down. "Instead of protesting on the streets, I was trying to make contact with ERT technicians. I was also thinking about how to gain access to the building once the protests were over. I bought a bulletproof vest."

It seemed to me that resistance action in Athens was becoming more dangerous since 2008. Before this time larger organizations, including labor unions and party organizations, planned big marches and protests at the city center, while autonomous groups and NGOs usually planned low-grade disruptive actions such as blockades, and smaller autonomous groups (including anarchists) focused on property destruction against government and corporate businesses. Large-scale violence was unusual within large protest bodies, although fights did break out at night and along the edges of protest spaces where operatives of opposing groups would target protest organizers and participants—something activists of the 1980s and 1990s warned me about early on during my fieldwork. Surprisingly, violence against smaller groups causing disruptions and those targeting state and corporate properties was less common. Sustained interventions, like occupations of schools and other buildings—which happened with surprising regularity in Greece—were relatively nonviolent.

However, things were changing. Anarchists, hooligans, and criminals were burning buildings, smashing cars, and otherwise causing havoc during public actions more frequently now, both within the main spaces of protest action and along various edges. The police and groups of thugs were also acting more aggressively toward protesters. Yet perhaps most alarmingly, the neo-Nazi Golden Dawn Party was acting boldly against migrants, refugees, and others it deemed social abnormalities and national enemies, not only during protests but also in social, economic, and private spaces including squats, workplaces, and in their neighborhoods and homes. Niko's talk of wearing a ballistic vest to break into a government building so he could steal equipment with which to spread antigovernment messaging was not only consistent with his personal trajectory but seemed to me to reflect the zeitgeist of the post-2008 protest scene in Athens.

Yet, there was another side to all this. Athenians of all description were pursuing forms of nonconfrontational, nonviolent collective action in response to growing hardships afflicted by neoliberal policies. These actions included the setting up of local free clinics like the Metropolitan Clinic at Elliniko, food-sharing schemes, social supermarkets, collective education spaces, time banks, alternative bazaars, urban gardens, urban eco-initiatives, barter networks, and other, "ordinary" expressions of commitment and camaraderie, which seemed to be steadily on the rise. Athena Athanasiou has called these "alternative engagements with the political" (Athanasiou and Alexandrakis 2016, 258; see also Rakopoulos 2014), that is, actions and/or projects that insofar as they were a collective response to shared hardship also provided a space in which democratic agonism could thrive. Niko overlooked these undertakings. Instead, he was becoming more intently focused on carrying out militant action.

It was a cool February morning in 2014. I was waiting on a street corner near the Exarchia neighborhood to meet a local resident, Alex, and several migrants. Alex had organized the meeting so I could get to know his friends, and so the group could walk me over to Platia Victoria where an undocumented migrant had recently been attacked by Golden Dawn thugs. Alex and I had known each other for years. He had recently moved to Exarchia to be closer to the university and began to hang out with a diverse group, including other students, activists, artists, and a number of Bangladeshi men who played cards in the square near his home. I would drop in to see him occasionally when I was in the area. Alex was very concerned about the plight of his neighbors—all his neighbors. The violence in nearby Victoria had not made the news, but word reached him over Facebook. A conversation with his Bangladeshi friends confirmed the happening. Alex saw the attack as part of a pattern of neo-Nazi violence in Greece. He felt compelled to do something—even something as small as calling his anthropologist friend with an interest in the plight of migrants.

The street corner was crowded with people, so I backed against the wall of a building, trying to stay out of the way. Alex arrived first, and we were soon joined by his friend Anik. A third man, Sabbir, texted Anik to say he couldn't join us, so I stepped away from the wall, thinking we were ready to walk to Victoria. Alex asked me to wait, saying that he had invited someone else to join us—for "our protection." I told Alex that I thought he was being silly, but Anik said he felt uneasy around Victoria after the events of the previous week. Our conversation was interrupted a few minutes later by Niko, who brushed by me to stand next to Alex. Alex didn't seem to know him and tensed up. Things remained uncomfortable for a moment until Niko explained that Alex's contact was a member of his collective. This man told Niko about our excursion to Victoria, and, wanting to "make new friends," Niko volunteered to come instead. Alex relaxed.

"It's nice to see you, Othona," Niko said, eyes down as he lit a cigarette. "A coincidence of the highest order!"

I looked at him skeptically, "Really?"

Niko inhaled deeply. "You're an academic. Perhaps you don't believe in coincidences?"

We talked as we walked to Victoria. I noticed that Niko was not doing his usual heel-drag. I also noticed that his left hand was bandaged. It came out that Alex had posted something about bringing me to Victoria and linked to my university page on Facebook. When Alex reached out to Niko's comrade to arrange protection for Anik and Sabbir, this man began to keep tabs on Alex's Facebook page. He contacted Niko when he saw a "Canadian anthropologist" would be joining them. Niko decided to surprise me. Alex and Anik thought this was all rather funny, but I became uncomfortable. I noticed Niko was using his relationship with me to gain the trust of my friend and Anik. In fact, Anik began to talk openly about the work he was doing at a restaurant, his living arrangements, the loan he secured from a friend of a friend, and more. I began to feel that I had somehow compromised this man's safety.

When we arrived at Victoria, Anik walked us to the area where he thought the attack occurred. Niko had broken away from our group as soon as we entered the square—he was standing close to a kiosk a short distance to our right. My attention became split between the conversation Alex and Anik were having about the growing sense of fear they shared regarding the spreading violence in Athens, and Niko who was now speaking loudly to a large man in a black T-shirt and jacket holding an open bottle of Amstel beer. A few moments later, Niko took a step closer to the large man and, looking him in the eye, cocked his head to the right. The man poked Niko in the chest and growled, "Don't speak to me like that." A heartbeat later Niko swatted the beer bottle to the ground with his bandaged left hand and struck the man's face with the open palm of his right. The man staggered back and fell over a park bench. He lay there stunned. Niko stood over top of him, called him a fascist, then walked away.

Anik was breathing heavily as we walked away from the square.

Niko caught up with us two streets over. He assured us that everything was OK. "I can smell them in a crowd."

"Who?" I asked, not wanting to make assumptions.

"Golden Dawn. That guy was one of theirs. We saw each other right away."

"He saw you? What do you mean?"

"Yeah. I didn't get into a fight. I *continued* a fight. You understand that anarchists are the natural enemy of fascists. We're in active conflict now. They're trying to spread to new areas, but we're pushing them back. His cell will think twice before trying something in Victoria again." Turning to Anik he said, "You should go back there with friends. We'll support you."

Niko walked with us for a few more minutes. After answering his phone, he broke off in another direction. The encounter seemed surreal to me, and Anik still looked uneasy, but Alex was energized. He was going to go back the next day, he said. "Niko could use another set of eyes."

Niko was still recruiting—this much was clear. The recruiting strategy, however, had evolved. It seemed that Niko and the collective were using Facebook and other social media not only to aggregate followers who could be provided with curated political messaging and perhaps mobilized when action was needed; they were also creating content about their collective intended to position them as an alternative "social service provider" to the broader community. Alex told me he had contacted Niko's friend before our walk to Victoria after reading a Facebook repost about how this man confronted a group of fascists who were picking on a migrant on his way home from work. The same man was also mentioned in a story about food sharing in Exarchia. Critically, these stories did not appear to be written by the anarchists themselves, but by members of the community who seemingly benefited from their activities.

Alex posted about Niko's actions at Victoria, and his story was shared over a hundred times within an hour. It seemed a new narrative of the anarchist defender was forming. I emailed Niko to ask about this. He didn't want to meet me, explaining he was too busy. He said simply that one of his contacts had been threatened by Golden Dawn, so he recruited some friends to protect the man on his way to and from work. A fight ensued. Niko then organized regular patrols of the neighborhood. He had since been more involved in "protection" than organizing action. Trying to get a sense of how great the threat of Golden Dawn was to Exarchia and the surrounding area, I wrote back to ask if the entire collective had become involved in this kind of protective work. Two weeks passed before I received the following response: "Some of us are. We've split."

By 2014, neoliberal-fed chaos had ruined untold Athenian lives. The anarchist collective was struggling too. In later conversations Niko would tell me that the majority of his comrades were beginning to question the ethics and, frankly, the practicality of focusing their efforts on street action at a time when most of their supporters were worrying about paying their bills and putting food on the table.

For his part, Niko thought it was unethical to give up on street action, especially at this time of increased hardship. He was adamant that this is when the people had to push back the hardest, although he did admit there appeared to be dwindling appetite for street politics. His calls were bringing fewer and fewer people. This certainly concerned him. "It should not have been that way," he insisted.

Instead, the collective talked about sowing dissent through the work of helping the people around them survive the slaughter of austerity. Niko rejected this tactic, arguing, as I mentioned above, that there would be no end to austerity if people found ways to live with it. The state, he insisted, would continue to impoverish people and communities it deemed without value unless those communities pushed back. To support his position, he pointed to the gains students made during the nineties. He said that had anarchists simply helped students live with conditions imposed by the state, their worsening situations would have become normalized. For Niko, resistance—and fierce resistance at that—was the only way forward. His sense was that the collective would come around to his thinking. It didn't.

Although I was not able to interview the other members of the collective, it struck me that the gradual shift to alternative engagements over taking action in the street was more complex than it seemed at first. Specifically, the collective members didn't support just any alternative engagement; instead, they preferred projects that communicated, either in form or content, a direct critique of the state. For example, many of Niko's comrades were involved in barter networks portrayed by participants as a "counter-economics" that was fairer and more humane than the mainstream economy; others participated in collective education spaces organized in direct response to corruption within academic administrations and poor learning experiences, supports, and outcomes at public schools at all levels now exacerbated by funding cuts. The food delivery scheme I mentioned earlier also communicated a critique of the state. Participants collected food donations at an occupied site, then redistributed the food to people in need. Some people received only ingredients, while others were given cooked meals—requests were made via text message, email, or through the organization's website. Participants talked about the work they did as a necessity now that social services were being cut. They contrasted the innovation, initiative, and community spirit of their group to the state, which they saw as creating empty spaces and depleting livelihoods.

Niko instead maintained that (to borrow his words) a "non-humanitarian" response to suffering was more a challenge to authority than "quelling the anger of the suffering masses." Although he participated in the food scheme to show solidarity with his comrades, he quit in a huff after his request to see the organization's contact list was rebuffed by the organizers. This incident produced a sustained conversation within the group—initiated by Niko—over the question of whether alternative engagements were in line with anarchist politics. The difference of opinion widened as they debated if alternative engagements were contributing to what they all agreed was a dropping-off of participation in street action.

It struck me at first that the issue at the root of this disagreement stemmed from a small difference in the way members of the collective understood the anarchist project in Greece. Both Niko and his comrades agreed that Athenians had to be "woken up"—that is, they had to be brought to see oppression. They also agreed that this awakening could lead to political action. However, whereas Niko drew a direct line between the distribution of disruptive materials and action, his comrades seemed to believe that action could *also* result from undirected conversations within critical social spaces: under the right conditions, people would come to see oppression on their own. These differing perspectives appeared to me to be in tune with the different roles Niko and his comrades played in the collective. While they all worked together to organize action—an undertaking that involved evaluation of the situation and available resources, debate and coordination—Niko was also a recruiter. In this role, my interlocutor's primary strategy was to disseminate "knowledge" that would resonate with receptive individuals (in his view, individuals not heavily affected by state efforts to craft governable subjects) who could later be mobilized. This line of thinking was consistent with Niko's descriptions of earlier successful periods of anarchist expansion through recruitment, and action.

With time, however, I would come to understand this small difference as indicative of a deeper divide between Niko and his comrades, a divide that—with the social, economic, and political changes brought about by austerity measures—would threaten his inclusion in the collective. I am referring specifically to the difference between how my interlocutor and his comrades understood activations of political responsiveness. Niko talked about political action in terms of knowledge, networks, and street action. Individuals would come together when called on to resist some happening or situation that threatened equality and freedom. He was very clear about this. Having plotted and worked tirelessly to move the anarchist cause forward through the painstaking establishment and broadening of various channels by which he spread information, mobilized supporters, and coordinated street action, Niko not only backed his view with experience but insisted that his efforts had ensured the collective's most notable successes. His comrades, however, experienced collective resistance first within the social spaces where actions were discussed and debated, often with allies, and so were more likely open to the possibility of another kind and quality of resistant force—one in which political responsiveness was cultivated and informed by the social form of struggle. Niko's sense that activated political responsiveness meant street action was out of step with his comrades' sense that political activation could also take other forms—alternative forms—emerged from critical socialities. Although Niko did not contest the way his comrades talked about responsiveness, he nonetheless struggled to relate resistance talk that was newly oriented to the potentials of defiant social spaces with his experience, ongoing projects, and plans for the future. For Niko, the people had to be brought to see how the state curtailed freedoms, coerced people, and exposed them to violence. He was deeply invested in the spreading of knowledge from person to person, and he knew that the network could be activated to bring action to the street directly against the state. His comrades did not disagree that the people had to be brought to understand their subjugation and encouraged to resist, but suggested that the people, under the right conditions, would come to this themselves and may resist in other ways.

Questioning the motives, commitments, and experiences of individuals and groups responding to precariatization in unconventional or unexpected ways was not uncommon in post-2010 Athens—certainly not among long-time activists, be they anarchists or not. These were not simply expressions of uncertainty or concern about the effectiveness, appropriateness, or legitimacy of the actions of others—expressions probing the normative limits of the political—but also revealed a broad defamiliarization of the sociopolitical landscape. Indeed, established political projects and communities founded on high-scale moral narratives were being disrupted. In other words, and to borrow again from Deleuze (1995; see also Biehl and Locke 2010), these expressions marked a subtle deterritorialization such that one's own becoming was rendered less certain. Niko and his comrades—like other activists of various political stripes—were finding themselves on shifting terrain. The work of figuring out this new ground and locating oneself on it was urgent and, critically, beginning to produce subtle fault lines that troubled the shared sense that was so foundational to the collective form.

As Niko explained, the members of the collective were no longer confident that everyone would support the actions other comrades undertook. Interpersonal conflicts also grew between him and a number of others who became passionate about alternative engagements. On a personal level, Niko was struggling, he explained, with a growing fear that the state's project was succeeding: the willingness to engage in confrontational street action among Athenians had waned, and his collective—one of the most active anarchist groups in Athens—was beginning to split. How could his comrades have taken the wrong path? As he put it, "How could handing out fucking cookies bring down the state!" Yet, rather than leave the collective—something my interlocutor admits he considered—he threw himself into the fight he thought was correct, and allowed those who held different visions to work in the spaces and in the ways they felt were appropriate.

"We were still connected, you see. They were in touch with the people, building relationships. This was good," Niko recounted in 2016. "I was still fighting the *real* fight, though. I was taking it to the fascists. I was hoping the people my misguided comrades were helping would take to the streets again as soon as they felt safe."

It's arguable that the Niko whom Alex met in 2014 was more dangerous than the Niko I met in 2007. Again, Niko became involved in street battles against supporters of Golden Dawn after one of his contacts was attacked. As time went on and participation in protest actions in the street dropped off, patrolling and fighting became a daily activity for my interlocutor. Niko saw an opportunity to solidify his following, attract new people, and promote a sense that street action was possible again by encouraging the circulation of stories over social media about their efforts against Golden Dawn. This strategy had some success, but it required Niko and his comrades to keep fighting. What's more, Niko's comrades were beginning to participate in projects my interlocutor thought were a waste of time. Feeling the rift growing between him and the collective, Niko threw himself completely into protecting his most vulnerable contacts—migrants—while looking for opportunities to disrupt Golden Dawn. By 2014 he wore his bulletproof vest every day and always carried a weapon. Niko was angry, struggling with a feeling that he was being abandoned by the collective, increasingly uncertain about the future, and always ready to fight.

In the spring of 2015, Niko was once again preparing for a fight, but not against Golden Dawn. He was beginning to prime his contacts for street action. The Syriza government led by Alexis Tsipras—a left-wing politician who began his political career as a member of the Communist Youth of Greece organization in 1980—was talking boldly about rejecting the troika's latest bailout tranche unless they changed the conditions tied to its payout. Talk of debt relief and halting or even reversing some austerity measures had Athenians buzzing. Niko's contacts were more than buzzing—they were flooding his social media feeds with expressions of anger at the troika and Germany, which they saw as the driving forces behind the austerity measures imposed on Greeks, and with links to stories about Tsipras's roughish finance minister Yanis Varoufakis, a figure of clever defiance. Niko, along with the rest of the collective, sensed this was an opportunity to regroup, recommit to the anarchist project, and return to the streets. The government had to know that they would accept no less than complete freedom from debt, be it personal or downloaded state debt; a total stop to monitoring through licensing, regulating, auditing, taxing, and other mechanisms ramped up under the cover of economic reform; a reversal of the trend toward privatization of public assets; and the cessation of intimidation and censoring of independent journalists[17] and news outlets like Indymedia, which authorities had tried to shut down; among other things.

Then, on June 27, Tsipras announced a referendum on whether Greece would accept the bailout conditions proposed by the troika. The announcement came as a shock to Greece's lenders and as a source of elation to Niko and the other members of the collective, who saw it as a step toward returning power to the people. The referendum was going to take place on July 5. Niko wouldn't vote, of course, but he knew which side he supported. Ensuring a strong "no" to the bailout conditions was crucial. An overwhelming vote against the bailout was seen as possibly leading to Greece falling into bankruptcy, being cut off from global markets, ejected from the EU, and might have resulted in complete political disarray—or as Niko put it, "an anarchist paradise!"

Niko was involved in organizing various actions leading up to the vote. These were mostly low-intensity affairs involving smaller numbers, banners, chanting, and occasional disruptions of traffic and scuffles with police. Niko had no trouble getting people out to the street. He later told me that as the referendum question was rather ambiguous,[18] that everyone and every group was able to interpret the stakes as they liked. Some people saw a "no" vote as a rejection of austerity and neoliberal governmentality in general. For others, a "no" vote was a rejection of Europe. These differences were not a problem for my interlocutor. He crafted a message that he believed played to all sides: a "no" vote was a rejection of "annihilation."

The rally on the night of the vote reminded my interlocutor of the December events of 2008 and the early anti-austerity protests of 2010. It seemed to him that everyone was on the streets again. "I just walked around all night. You saw me! I didn't do anything. There was no need."

I did see Niko that night. He looked as if he hadn't slept in days, but he was ecstatic—floating on air. I left the scene after midnight and could hear the roar of the crowd over two kilometers away at my apartment in the Mets neighborhood. The sounds of honking and chanting woke my young daughter at some point later that night. She found me following the news on my phone in the next room and asked what was happening outside. I immediately thought, "The revolution!" Perhaps Niko was rubbing off on me.

In the end over six million Greeks turned out to vote—62.5 percent of those eligible to participate in the referendum. Over three and a half million people voted "no." In other words, 61.3 percent of voters rejected the bailout conditions imposed by the troika. This was the result Tsipras wanted. He vowed to use the mandate given to him by the people in the next round of negotiations. This was also the result Niko wanted. He told me that in the days after the referendum his social media feeds were exploding, and he felt the collective coming together again. The group made plans to get together to talk strategy. It was time to harness the momentum, Niko had told them. The people had seen and felt the violence of the state, and rejected it. He wanted to have a clear path forward as events unfolded, unlike December 2008 when everyone was caught off guard.

Yet, everyone *was* caught off guard. Three days following the vote, the government formally asked for a three-year bailout worth 53.5 billion euros and pledged to start implementing economic policy overhauls by mid-July. Many people thought Tsipras was simply restarting negotiations. Things began to look grim, however, when on July 13 the government accepted a bailout package that contained larger pension cuts and tax increases than the ones rejected by Greek voters in the referendum. Not only had the "no" vote *not* resulted in an easing of uncertainty and suffering for Greeks, or in Greece leaving the Eurozone, or indeed the European Union, but Greeks would now have to bear the weight of austerity measures that were harsher than those proposed by the troika before the referendum was held. A rebellion by Syriza MPs led to Tsipras's resignation on August 20, prompting a snap election. However, Syriza won the ensuing election, and Tsipras was returned as prime minister.

Although his accounts were still visible, Niko stopped posting or reposting on social media after July 2015. We talked over Skype a few times during the latter part of that year, and we met in Athens during the summer of 2016. Between July 2015 and the time we met, Niko slowly split from the collective and gave up the fight against Golden Dawn. He became isolated, disillusioned, angry, but also deeply confused. It seemed to him that everything went wrong.

"That shit should have sparked a revolt," Niko said when we met again in 2016. He was referring to the bailout agreement of the previous summer. Looking at a large stain on the sidewalk, he added, "Their heads should have been on pikes before sunrise the following day."

The conversation went on like this for a while. Niko expressed disbelief that people could live with what he perceived to be a complete failure of representative politics, a breakdown of democracy, and ultimately the "*fuck you* spat in the face of a population daring to hope for something better by an elitist masquerading as the working everyman."

I asked if he was thinking about starting a new group, a new collective. Niko shook his head. He said he knew he was heading somewhere dangerous before the referendum, that by offering protection he was becoming a thug too. What's more, he still rejected the projects his old comrades were involved with, for having "achieved nothing." Beyond this, he said he couldn't stop thinking about July 2015 and the revolt that should have come but never happened. It had become an obsession in his life.

"All the pieces were in place, weren't they? Still, this was the first time egregious state repression did not result in action. Maybe they've won," Niko added. "Maybe I should say it was a good fight." He looked down at his scarred hands, clenched them, then opened them again. "I don't know. I don't trust anyone, anything. Not even myself. I'm so unsure, anxious. . . ." He looked at me with bloodshot eyes, then focused on something in the distance.

Political memory and political events feed back, resonate, and reverberate into other aspects of life, producing meaning, while reinforcing each other. They can ground collective projects, cast futures, orient, and reassure. This connection became messy for Niko as Athenians were interpellated into "crisis normality" as economized and racialized (not to mention gendered and sexed) subjects of competitive economic struggle. With his social and political self-formation tied to an understanding that repression can be known and that response to repression should directly engage political actants and structures, Niko interpreted the more malleable, nuanced, and even "ordinary" responses to successive injuries perpetrated by the neoliberal regime at first as a misfire of political will, and eventually as an outright abandonment of political life. Unable to make sense of the world unfolding before him, unable to connect what he knew and what he was witnessing, my interlocutor found himself in a position where the past, the future, the social and the political, became disorganized. Niko fell quiet.

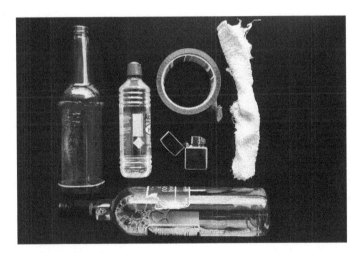

FIGURE 2. Elements of a Molotov cocktail: empty bottle, fuel (mix of gasoline, motor oil, and soap), rubbing alcohol, tape (either packing or electrical tape), a rag, and a lighter. Athens, 2019. Photo by the author.

BECOMING LOST

Why Romani Boys Are Hanging
Out with Anarchists

"Can you explain what the devil is happening in this world? Come today—but tell me something I won't mind forgetting."

I hung up the phone and left right away.

Vasilo lived at the Roma compound in Halandri, a suburb north of Athens. She had seven children and a number of grandchildren. Her two oldest children—daughters—were both married, and both had several children of their own. Her middle three—two sons and a daughter—were living with family and friends at other Roma compounds. Her two young sons—both thalassemia sufferers—lived with her at the Halandri compound.[1]

Vasilo's life was comfortable if not easy. She collected government benefits for her five youngest children—extra medical allowances for her youngest sons—plus benefits for a set of twins she gave to a friend in the early 2000s. Her husband's death a month after the twins were born (which prompted the informal adoption) meant she also collected a survivor pension, an old age pension, and a modest disability benefit. Money was rarely a problem for Vasilo, but the circumstances that led to this financial security kept producing other kinds of worries.

"I could change things, you know," Vasilo once told me. "I could make my life easier, but the problem is I've become used to it. I know how to manage."

I met Vasilo shortly after her younger son had been diagnosed in 2002. She was one of my key interlocutors during both my MA (2003) and PhD (2010) fieldwork. The day we were introduced, Vasilo had just returned from the hospital where her son had begun regular blood transfusions. An orange binder stuffed with medical records was tossed casually on a nearby bed. One boy was sleeping on the cement floor near a lamp; the other was sitting listlessly in an old plastic lawn chair. Vasilo offered me a cigarette and a glass of lemonade. She was gruff but kind and very perceptive—she struck me as the sort of person you'd want in your corner should a difficult situation arise.

I took a bus to a stop near the compound, then continued on foot. I arrived at the outskirts of the compound half an hour after Vasilo's phone call, at about two thirty in the afternoon. The easiest route into the tangle of the forty to fifty houses that made up the compound was along a hilly street that divided the site in half and connected it to parallel thoroughfares. Behind me, as I approached the compound, was a typical Athenian suburb consisting mostly of low-rise apartment buildings. Beyond the compound to the left stood a large fenced-off office tower and its parking lot. Beyond the compound to the right was a small field overgrown with thorn bushes. Straight ahead beyond the end of the compound was a busy road lined with shops of various kinds. Overhead, wires hacked into power lines dipped into several Romani homes. These homes fed power to the rest of the compound via buried extension cords. While the compound homes had fully equipped kitchens and bathrooms, they were not connected to plumbing. Individuals would bring water from the outdoor taps of neighboring apartment buildings, and waste was dumped into ditches along the street and into holes outside homes. The homes varied in shape and size, but were all single level and made of cement blocks, pieces of wood, corrugated metal, and tarpaulins. They were very close together.

About halfway up the street, I turned left at a familiar point along the dirt path between two smaller homes. I made my way over deep ruts, around discarded building materials and broken playthings. The smell of rats wafted up from the hot ground. Most residents were milling about, bleary-eyed, unable to take their afternoon naps because of the intense heat. Nearly four years of unusually extreme late-summer temperatures made this delirious meandering-about a common sight at the compound. I found Vasilo sitting with her eyes half closed in an old office chair in front of her home.

In 2004 Vasilo expanded the home she had been living in since 2002, dividing the structure in two by erecting a plywood-and-cardboard wall in the middle of the main room and adding two rooms to each of the new sections. She gave one side to a family friend and the other to her pregnant daughter, Evi. This "architectural mitosis" was a regular occurrence at the compound: the result of growing families (cf. Karathanasi 2000). Vasilo built a home for herself—the home she was sitting in front of—on the opposite end of the compound, on top of a small hill away from other houses. She fitted it with a powerful woodstove and a large television. Being on a hill, Vasilo's home was the only place in the compound that received MTV Europe, making it very popular among adolescents. To accommodate the often-rowdy group, Vasilo knocked down the wall between the main room and her bedroom. "They were going to break it anyway, so I did it myself," she explained. Small piles of teenagers on her bed and on the floor would grow, shrink, and reconfigure all day long.

By 2010 the MTV crowd came to be joined by a much younger cohort. The deepening recession meant construction and maintenance jobs were becoming scarce, while licenses for selling in the street markets were becoming more expensive. Perhaps unexpectedly (at least for me), this closing off of the two primary employment sectors for local Romani adults produced a bump in demand for child care. I mentioned this in a conversation I had with Vasilo and a few of her neighbors in October 2011. By this time pockets were emptying, and, they explained, most adults in the compound were spending more time and going farther distances looking for work. They were very grateful for Vasilo: parents simply left in the mornings, trusting that she would care for their kids. According to one father, "People get nothing for doing nothing—so we go out and do something. We have no choice."

Vasilo nodded, "It's our way—it's the good way."

By the summer of 2015, Vasilo's house had become a second home for most of her young neighbors. Soon after sunrise the compound would empty of able, working-age people. Babies were dropped off with whoever had agreed to watch them, while older kids—toddlers and up—were simply allowed to make their way to Vasilo's home on their own. The daily movement of adult bodies out of the compound mirrored a daily movement of little bodies into Vasilo's sitting room. What was quickly becoming the new normal—deep economic uncertainty and intensive daily competitive struggle—drove these regular movements, these "good" movements, to borrow from Vasilo. They had worn pathways onto the compound—deepening traces of a Romani response to austerity (Napolitano 2015).

"I have no idea what is happening in this world," I said as I walked up to her. "How's George doing?"

She looked straight at me and chuckled but didn't smile. I knew she wanted to talk about him, but maybe I asked too soon. She smoothed her long dress.

"Can you believe I miss him? What an asshole. He's not a bad kid. He's just lost, maybe."

George—who was somewhere between fourteen and eighteen years old—was the latest boy to leave the compound.[2]

"All the young men are nearly gone now," she said. "Nobody else here worries about it, but I do. Where the fuck are they?"

"You know where they are," I replied, gesturing beyond the neighborhood. "Maybe they think they look good in black."

"Yeah, they're lost, but if we keep pushing them out, then so are we."

In the pages to come, I will explore how, as economic pressure was building and the compound was becoming increasingly empty, many young Romani boys began to spend their time at anarchist squats, where they found a sense of camaraderie with non-Romani, or *balamé* (to use their word), youth. Residents of the compound associated squats with the local drug trade and assumed that Romani boys who spent time there, and especially those who self-identified as anarchists, were becoming agents of "social decay." This impression led to a dangerously delimited logic: Romani boys unable to succeed in the changing economic landscape were becoming corrupted and posed a threat to the community. Romani elders, and the established and well-connected families who acted as gatekeepers of community inclusion, were the ones who took this idealistic view. They presumed that boys who turned to nearby anarchist squats had adopted values and had become involved in conflicts that would harm the compound and those living in it. These boys were discouraged from returning to the compound and from interacting with other Romani youth. For their part, the excluded Romani boys understood the hostility to which they were subjected as a social cost of their involvement with balamé; however, they also understood that this involvement was forced on them by the same individuals who were now keeping them out. They likened their situation to being stuck in a trap set by an older generation struggling to maintain authority as daily life became more difficult.

As I worked to understand the broad picture of everyday "life in crisis" in the compound without dissolving the fine articulations of daily struggle, as I accounted for the material effect of governmental reform and structural forces, and as I attempted to shed light on the ways that my Romani interlocutors sought means of making a life worth living, I began to understand the movement of boys away from the compound in terms of crisis-driven changes in the way my interlocutors were relating to each other. The Halandri Roma imagined and claimed identity in ways that were interwoven in the normative violence inherent in the various bordering practices—both self-imposed and those imposed on them—that regulate their interactions with balamé (see also Stewart 1997; Sutherland 1975; Williams 2003). One of the effects of the neoliberal reform agenda was to change the terms and the stakes of the established points of interaction between Roma and balamé within economic spaces, precipitating changes in the way my interlocutors negotiated differential belonging relative to labor practices.

As Halandri Roma began to reconsider and rearticulate the exclusionary demarcations that informed being together, the normative frameworks conditioning community inclusion also began to change.[3] From about 2010 onward, individual working-age Romani boys were faced with having to navigate gradual changes in these frameworks as they prepared for and made public performances intended to signal their desire and ability to take on new social roles and economic responsibilities.[4] This led to recurring breakdowns, failures, and misfires. Those individuals whose performances were unsuccessful were labeled "awkward" and faced social isolation within the compound. This awkwardness and the resulting isolation became a generative force that, for many, enabled new perspectives and propelled new trajectories.

I must note that although I focus on the experience of boys—and cis-gendered boys specifically—I observed that all young people living in the compound found themselves on uncertain terrain and in awkward positions at times when they attempted to take on new social roles and responsibilities, or when they tried to increase their social status within the compound. I focus on George and his friends because I spent most of my time with this group; however, the same unsettling forces and conditions that troubled my close interlocutors affected others as well.

Vasilo's word choice was apt: George was lost. In Greek, as in other languages, to say someone is "lost" (khaménos) can mean they have lost their bearings, their sense of location and direction on the ground. It can also mean they have lost their moral bearings—that the individual has become a "bad person." Generally, it evokes a state of being uncertain, or being on the wrong path. George was definitely on the wrong path. Everyone hated him. Deeply.

This all started in 2013 when he turned fifteen and, like other boys his age, became interested in making a change in his life, which meant he needed a job to show he was prepared and able to take on new roles and responsibilities. However, George knew finding a job would be difficult, not only because the economy was terrible, but also because he was Romani. Like most Romani children, George grew up hearing about the violence and discrimination his family and friends endured beyond the edges of the compound. However, it was at the local elementary school where George gained firsthand education in living with violence and discrimination. This was the same education his parents gained when they went to school. In the 1980s, the Greek state sought to cultivate national cohesion and national consciousness through schools by actively structuring student identity formation as part of the country's nation-building effort. Despite more recent attempts to modernize and to adapt the educational system to the changing international environment, schools remained ethnocentric and continued to be tolerant of stereotyping and prejudice (see Dimakos and Tasiopoulou 2003; Paleologou 2004; Gropas and Triandafyllidou 2007). Romani youth, along with students of non-Greek backgrounds, have been disadvantaged in Greek schools for over three decades.

As a young boy, George was bullied relentlessly by balamé children and, perhaps unexpectedly, by their parents. He dared not use the bathroom at school, walk the halls alone, speak in class, ask teachers or staff for help, or linger outside the school fence, where parents would sometimes spit at him or chase him away. George used to stay close to other Romani kids whenever they were near, and he tried to blend in with the crowd whenever he was on his own. The fact that he used to wet his pants regularly added to his troubles. From the age of five onward he was in fights and scuffles nearly every day, and certainly when he was wet. An incident at the end of second grade, in which a group of boys beat him and tried to urinate on him, prompted George's mother to keep her son home for a month. When George began school again the following year he was placed in a special "Roma classroom." The separation of Roma from other students was supposed to be part of a "culturally sensitive" education strategy devised by the principal; however, funding for the program was never found, and a teacher was never assigned to the class. After a few weeks, George's mother decided to keep her son home for good.

"Romani kids don't need to go to school for more than a few years. How long does it take to learn that balamé are in charge?" George explained. "Only stupid kids stay in school for more than a few years."

Having made the decision to keep him home from school, George's mother—like other Romani mothers who kept their school-age children home—began to take her son everywhere with her, showing him how to stay safe in the city. Put simply, he was now gaining a Romani education in how to find and respond safely and cleverly to the boundaries that separated him from balamé (Lydaki 1998, 1997). As I spent more time with my Romani interlocutors, both within and outside the compound, I began to see these boundaries more clearly. It seemed they would materialize whenever a Rom was present, but were otherwise invisible. I made descriptions of these ephemeral boundaries in a separate section of my field notebook, something a few of the local boys thought was very funny. They offered to help me write a manual on "How to Fuck Roma" (their title, not mine); here are a few entries rewritten by my interlocutors as directives:

- Keep compounds physically separated from balamé neighborhoods. The best way to do this is by mounding garbage around them. Garbage is free and repulsive so works well to keep Roma in and balamé out. Bonus: surrounding Roma with garbage reminds balamé that they are superior.

- All people must stare suspiciously at any Romani person entering a bus, a store, a restaurant, a movie theater, a public toilet, a park, a school. . . .
- Do not let Roma gather in large groups. This is especially important in hospital settings, where gatherings of Romani family members might cause a disruption or spread disease.
- City officials are not permitted to speak directly to Romani constituents. If local Roma want anything done, they must find a balamé advocate. This advocate will then be ignored, abused, and discouraged by city officials as a matter of standard procedure. The advocate must persist until city officials become irritated and make false promises to get rid of the advocate. In this way Roma receive the same level of service as other constituents.
- Officers running military registration centers must discharge boys arriving for their mandatory service as soon as it is discovered they are Romani. Do not give them guns, do not allow them to wear an official military uniform. This will only encourage them.

The above list hints at some of the physical, social, and even political limits Roma experience every day. The boys, including George, were also very aware of the boundaries that ran through the economy. Most of George's family and friends worked in what were known at the compound as "Romani jobs." During the 1990s and 2000s, various state-level strategies designed to head off what most politicians and economists at the time recognized to be the impending financial downturn caused a proliferation in work opportunities along the less monitored or regulated edges of the economy. This proliferation was due in part to Greece's failure to fully implement its own reforms, coupled with its failure to update labor policy (see for example Featherstone 2008; Pelagidis 2010). The informal or gray economy, as it was referred to by some economists, expanded under these conditions, became regular, and provided work for thousands of people, particularly subalterns, including Roma. When talking about "Romani jobs," my interlocutors referred to work in the gray economy, especially under-the-table labor or anything related to street selling.

During the early days of the financial crisis, Romani jobs were still very much available. Under-the-table work proliferated as companies sought to save money, and both licensed and unlicensed street selling became a greater possibility as police turned their attention to undocumented migrant sellers and became less interested in stopping people with "familiar faces." In fact, up until 2011, the Halandri Roma talked glowingly about Romani jobs as being recession-proof. They scoffed whenever anyone talked of the various early protests against austerity measures and other public expressions of anger and anxiety over reform and privatization: the clever, hardworking Roma were different from the lazy, entitled Greeks—a narrative inspired by the language at play in public debates at the time over the "Greek character."[5]

Between 2010 and 2013, however, auditors working for various state and supra-state agencies (the EU and ECB in particular) began monitoring and ultimately regulating the economy more closely, in part through new requirements for business tax reporting that made workers without official identification undesirable; random audits and inspections that shut down semi-legal businesses with expired, missing, or incomplete papers; the tracking of social security numbers; and new stricter and more expensive licenses for market selling. This brought about major transformations. In broad terms, many individuals who worked at the edges of the formal economy for semi-legal businesses, and especially individuals and semi-legal or illegal businesses serving legal businesses, wound down their operations or began to deal almost exclusively with clients and suppliers who preferred to operate entirely below the radar. Whereas the Greek state's pre-crisis inefficiencies and deficiencies permitted the thriving of economic gray areas, troika-mandated neoliberal austerity policy, and the heightened monitoring and increased regulation that followed, dialed up the contrast between formal and informal, legal and illegal, while shrinking the economy overall.

During this period Halandri Roma began to notice work opportunities beginning to dry up, especially in the construction and transportation sectors where many people worked. Unlicensed street market selling was also becoming risky again. Job losses hit Romani households hard. It seemed to me that the first austerity shock wave that destabilized so many balamé lives was beginning to reverberate into Romani lives—the first round of mass impoverishment of many to come—but my Romani interlocutors didn't see it that way. Talk within the compound of the worsening economic situation was decidedly focused on the moment. Rather than looking back at state actions and the ruinous trends that hit both their community and balamé, Halandri Roma discussed the crisis in present and future tenses only. "The government is fucking us," was the usual response when I asked about the mounting job losses hitting compound residents. My attempts to ask how the government was harming them, like my attempts to discuss particular policy changes—both, essentially, attempts to place the Romani experience in terms of a "Greek" experience—were usually met with, "They're racists."

As life became more difficult, and jobs became harder to find, my interlocutors began to draw a new contrast: they talked about how Roma were working to create employment opportunities while persevering at whatever jobs came their way, versus balamé who depleted their savings while living off the support of family as they waited foolishly for the economy to improve. Market reforms and a contracting economy may have faded the established borders in labor activity on the ground, but these borders were preserved in talk of (proper) Romani responses to crisis-driven job losses and hardship. Claiming a market-oriented ethic of endurance distinguished my interlocutors from balamé and came to be a marker of one's being a member of the Halandri Roma community.

By 2013 George had picked up on this. He complained loudly about having no money and told his friends he was willing to travel as far as necessary to find work. He would stop at nothing to make money. He talked endlessly about how, if given the chance, he would look for "hidden jobs," and if he couldn't find any, how he would create work opportunities for himself. Here, unfortunately, is where things began to go wrong for George. Like other boys who found themselves at personal crossroads—living like kids, but yearning for independence, responsibility, and social status—my interlocutor planned a daring expedition based on the example set by his older brother, Thanos, some years back.

It took Thanos two days to recover from what both he and George regarded as the best party ever thrown at the compound. It was 2008 and Thanos was (approximately) sixteen years old. George was (approximately) ten. Thanos threw the party to celebrate his return from two weeks of working as a driver for a company near Volos in central Greece. He spoke with bravado about finding high-paying mainstream work. This was a "found" job, an opportunity that came to his attention by way of his broader social network (a testament to the breadth and quality of his network). The compound was buzzing about the money Thanos made, the new connections he gained, and about Thanos's work not being typical Romani work—it was balamé work. Thanos had transgressed an important boundary.

George was very proud of his brother. In his eyes, Thanos had become a well-connected, mobile, and above all clever individual able to thrive in both Romani and balamé spaces. He represented an ideal George aspired to, an ideal that was also celebrated by others at the compound. Indeed, the party Thanos threw, like parties thrown by other boys who had gone away to find balamé work and returned with pockets full of money, was an established ritual. Returning involved the announcement of one's imminent arrival, the distribution of extravagant gifts to close family members the day before the event, and putting on of public displays of frivolous spending during the party that approximated those public displays demanded of older, established men acting as patrons and godfathers. It was not unusual to see fourteen- and fifteen-year-old boys returning from a few weeks of work throwing large parties at the Halandri compound, giving jewelry to their mothers and sisters, and giving away alcohol to friends, neighbors, and even strangers (on the social significance of alcohol among the Roma see Alexandrakis 2003, 70–88; see also M. Stewart 1989).

However, by 2010 these parties became few and far between as the economy collapsed and "balamé work" became more difficult to find. As noted above, Romani jobs were still available, but Halandri Roma began to notice that things were changing. Most people talked about agents of the state becoming problematic: several people involved in transportation had been stopped and searched by police; others were turned away from job sites because auditors were conducting inspections; still others found themselves unable to buy wholesale goods because they couldn't produce the correct paperwork to access warehouses and ports. This activated a variety of protective responses. Most people began to work as much as possible to secure the jobs they had and to build their savings. Even those individuals who did not work appeared to be preparing for some kind of downturn: groups of older Romani men would roam the nearby neighborhoods to collect useful things from the garbage; homes with obvious damage were being repaired, while others were upgraded with better insulation; travel for leisure stopped almost completely.

Older Romani boys were perhaps one of the first groups to sense the changes in the economy. While everyone was preparing for something on the way, they were already dealing with the disappearance of fast-money balamé work opportunities. The neoliberal reform agenda coupled with the economic downturn took from Romani boys an important means of self-determination. We might think of this in terms of social abandonment through dispossession, and we might draw connections between the experiences of Romani boys and the experiences of other Greek youth who, because of spreading hardship, demoralization, and social and economic suffering, were being denied promised futures or the means to access them (Athanasiou 2011). Nobody at the compound, however, spoke in terms of experiences shared with a broader "Greek" or "Athenian" population; but older boys—including those who would gather daily at Vasilo's—did express anger at being stuck or being left behind "like kids," owing to the worsening job market.

In the lead-up to the summer of 2013, George had become very unpleasant: he was acting aggressively toward younger children; he drank heavily; he stole items from friends and neighbors; and he fought with anyone who could stand to spend any time with him at all. It was clear to most people that George was frustrated, but his behavior made it very difficult to feel badly for him. To be clear, the aggression, drunkenness, stealing, and fighting were not new. George had always gone out of his way to irritate the people around him. When he was younger he did things like shout over others randomly when they were speaking, spy on private conversations and intimate moments, deliberately break objects in other people's houses, call people by nicknames they didn't like, and on and on. Over the last year, however, his behavior had become even worse. His mother was worried he might begin to experiment with criminal activities, so she decided to send him out of the compound for a few weeks. She initially planned to send him to visit her sister near Loutsa, where he could "swim and calm down."[6] However, George, sensing this was his opportunity to make a change, convinced her to send him to Crete to visit his cousins.

Vasilo asked me to talk with George when he returned from Crete—she thought he was acting strangely, and maybe I could find out what was wrong. I was doubtful. Up until then I had spent only a little time with George. To me he was just another kid at the compound. I interacted with him mostly when I was playing with Vasilo's sons, but we rarely spoke one-on-one. I pointed this out to Vasilo, but she thought I should talk to him anyway. She told me I would probably find him near an old car on the south side of the compound. Sure enough, he was there. He loved that car. It was a rusty, sky blue, 1983 BMW 320i—and it was his. He slept in the BMW. The non-functioning vehicle, given to him by an uncle, had been parked there for the last two years. When George looked at his car, reruns of his favorite show, MTV's *Pimp My Ride*, ran through his head.[7] I gestured to the car as I approached, and smiled.

"It has so much potential," he said as he stood up. "The tires in the back are fatter than the tires in the front—did you notice? They did that on purpose. It's fast."

I nodded. "It's nice, but all the tires are flat," I said with a smile. George laughed for a little too long. We sat down.

George had been drinking that afternoon, but he was still lucid. He wanted to talk about the two weeks he spent on the island. He told me he found work as a security guard at a warehouse, or more accurately a large shed (judging from the pictures on his phone) that was operated as a warehouse by two men George met on the island. He had met the men at a gas station—they struck up a conversation with him and his cousins, which eventually led to job offers. Now, most people would have thought twice about accepting a job offer made by two men they just met at a random gas station in the midst of a recession—but not George. His cousins walked away, but my interlocutor went with the two men.

Sitting by his BMW he told me how lucky he was. "I was at the right place at the right time. I made lots of money." There was more to this story, I suspected, but George didn't want to talk about it. He said it was "private," that the men were worried about corporate spying and asked him to keep quiet about what was stored in the unit he was guarding. He was quite serious when he said this and became irked when my eyebrows lifted (involuntarily, I might add) at his mention of corporate spying.

"They gave me a gun," he said eagerly, "and a flashlight."

"Did they give you bullets, too?" I asked jokingly, trying to lighten the mood.

"Yes," he responded directly, "and furry handcuffs," he added, smiling.

George texted his friends and family regularly from Crete to tell them how well he was doing and that they should expect a big party when he returned. Nobody took him seriously. When he arrived home he was disappointed that his friends did not rush to welcome him. Even his mother was away visiting her sister for a few days—George was on his own. So he decided to show off the money he earned. George bought some parts for his broken car, a new mobile phone, alcohol, and a large quantity of cigarettes. He distributed the cigarettes to some older boys and showed off the phone to a number of younger kids. He gave beer to anyone who came to visit him.

Sitting beside the BMW, I asked George if he would return to Crete someday. He closed his eyes and spoke of his desire to return to work at the warehouse a few more times. On Crete, he explained, he worked with men who made a lot of money despite the actions of the state. Asked what he meant, George said that the warehouse on Crete was a business run by balamé who were not going to let the crisis stop them from becoming rich. They "found an opportunity," as he put it. Jobs like that were becoming harder to find, he explained, because balamé like the two who owned the warehouse were disappearing. He explained they were clever, well connected, and unafraid to do what they had to do to make money for themselves and their families. This, he went on, was the reason why other boys at the compound were unable to find fast-money balamé jobs: most balamé were becoming discouraged or complacent. Here my interlocutor connected the "lazy balamé" narrative that was current in the compound with the disappearance of gray areas of the economy. His claim, essentially, was that balamé who acted like Roma were both succeeding and making opportunities, whereas the other balamé were ruining the economy. I looked at my interlocutor as he talked. He was making a small hole in the dirt with his heel, eyes darting between me and the ground. George was obviously trying to have a "coming of age" experience, like his brother; but something wasn't working, and he was becoming frustrated.

The following day my interlocutor was poking around under the hood of his car when two older boys approached him from behind. They each grabbed a leg, lifted, and pushed him into the engine compartment. George twisted and yelled, eventually pulling himself out to confront the two boys, who were laughing uncontrollably. I waited for George to throw a fist, but, breathing heavily, he wiped engine grease out of his eye and offered the two boys beer and cigarettes. They sneered at him and walked away. George's reaction was considered—perhaps he was trying to communicate that he was more mature than the boys who pranked him.

Something similar occurred several days later. George and I were talking by his car when a Romani woman walked up to us and at the top of her lungs accused George of being a criminal and a sex trafficker—all those within earshot stopped what they were doing and scowled at us. I expected George to stand and shout back at the woman; however, he simply stood up and walked into his mother's house. Again, his reaction was intended to communicate his maturity, that he wouldn't be drawn into a public shouting match.

I caught up with him later that day. He explained to me that everyone at the compound had become preoccupied with trying to figure out what was being moved through the warehouse on Crete. Rumor had it that the men who hired George were "bringing prostitutes to Athens." George denied this adamantly but failed to convince anyone—it didn't help, of course, that he wasn't willing to tell them what was being stored at that location. He complained that the experience of having made money on the island was being ruined by everyone's suspicion and doubt. He blamed nearly everyone, but especially his male friends who, as he put it, spent too much time hanging out at Vasilo's house, watching TV and being jealous of those who were succeeding.

Of note, George's accusers were not wrong to be suspicious of the warehouse. As unemployment grew in Athens so too did the illegal drug trade, which had already been on the uptick in the years leading up to the official declaration of the sovereign debt crisis (see for example Kokkevi et al. 2000). During this period of growth, dealers and transporters saw the Roma population not only as customers but also as potential business partners—a trend those individuals I spent time with in Halandri resisted. By 2010 the drug-trafficking business was booming. Some drugs were being produced and packaged at various locations within Greece, but most were coming in from Afghanistan (opiates) and South America (cocaine). These drugs were moved through a handful of safe houses, including a number of houses in Roma compounds around Attica, through to Western and Central Europe. This has come to be known as the "Balkan route" (Mili and Crabtree 2014). As the expanded supply chain of drugs became established, my interlocutors noticed a new trend. Vasilo explained, "The people who are transporting drugs are now also transporting prostitutes. They treat them like animals—it's not right, it's wild." She added, "I've seen these women in the back of cars passing through here. It's a horrible thing."

There was a general perception among the Roma I knew that drug and now human traffickers were coming to operate out of squats, in part because my interlocutors thought squats had become bordellos and drug dens. They also worried that traffickers were recruiting young Romani men into their organizations by offering them opportunities to make quick money. They talked about this in terms of a risk of "decay," meaning that young Romani boys who were seduced, tricked, or forced into trafficking were becoming morally compromised and posed a threat to the community. Vasilo worried that if George became involved in this kind of work on Crete, he might bring drugs and trafficked prostitutes to Halandri. She was also worried that he might recruit others. For his part, George became tired of denying that his bosses on the island were criminals and began to redirect questions and accusations to other matters. This only raised suspicion further, prompting those who talked to him to probe his experiences on Crete indirectly—the warehouse lingered on the edge of every conversation.

All this took a rather unfortunate turn a week after George was openly accused of being involved with drug and human trafficking. In a bid to win back his friends and the respect of the compound adults, George announced that he was going to throw a party. He spent the last of his money on alcohol and pornographic magazines, which he gave away at the event. It's tempting to interpret the pornography giveaway as an assertion of George's new sense of manhood; however, it might also be interpreted, more simply, as an attempt to reconnect with his peer group, considering they used to steal pornographic magazines from local kiosks. Whatever his motivation, most people who attended the party interpreted the pornography giveaway as further evidence of George's involvement in trafficking and his corrupted morals. By the end of the night George's drinks were gone, and most of the pornography was ripped up and scattered about. George had been in two fistfights and ended up back at his mother's house, drunk and alone.

Making matters worse, someone had smashed one of the windows of George's car and threw opened condoms on the seats. When my interlocutor woke up the next morning he was inconsolable. He was hung over, bruised, broke, friendless, and his car was vandalized—the hot sun melting thin latex into old upholstery. What happened next consolidated the awkwardness of the previous night. As most people were beginning to go about their daily activities, George gathered up the remaining pornography from the night before, tossed it into his broken BMW, and set it on fire. As everyone scrambled to put out the blaze, George sat in a plastic lawn chair nearby and—with a profound sense of heaviness—smoked and texted. He was still doing this when I arrived at the compound that afternoon. Vasilo explained what happened and shook her head. I walked over, sat beside George, and leaned in. Still looking at his phone, George whispered, "I want to disappear."

The compound was established on an empty span of public and private property by a group of four Romani families at the end of the 1970s. At the time of my research there were roughly sixty families living at the site, although it was hard to tell for sure. Local authorities had been trying to evict the group since the mid-nineties, but thanks to the efforts of various advocates and lawyers, the Romani community managed to defeat each legal challenge. They were also able to fend off less-than-legal attempts to force them out. In fact, damage done by the latest thug-backed bulldozer was still visible near the northern part of the compound.

"We see bulldozers in our nightmares," Vasilo once told me. "Actually, the bulldozers are not so bad—we use trucks to block them. It's the fires. They set our homes on fire before the bulldozers move in. We always stand our ground, though. They have no power here."

The compound posed a threat to governmental authority over spacing in Halandri—it marked the edge of the political in this regard: the outside was Halandri, the inside was a distinct Romani zone where government had no power. The compound residents knew this, as did the representatives and agents of the state, and most balamé.

Indeed, Roma compounds have been off limits to non-Romani Athenians, balamé, for generations (see Panourgiá 1995, 23–33). Most Athenians I knew recoiled at the very sight of a Romani compound, fear and sometimes even disgust washing over them. This reaction kept most locals away and encouraged those who unexpectedly found themselves among the Roma to get out quick. My interlocutors would see this daily: as GPS navigation systems became commonplace, people unfamiliar with the area were frequently directed to use the thoroughfare that ran through the compound, resulting in squealing rubber and dangerous U-turns all day long. Residents joked that the only balamé who approach the compound knowingly were either advocates looking for a cause, drug addicts looking for a dealer, or thugs—typically police or the supporters of Golden Dawn—looking for trouble.

This inside/outside tension came up frequently at the compound. My interlocutors were not only attentive to how and when people and things entered and exited the compound, but they intervened or otherwise engaged whenever movements occurred. Anyone or anything permitted to stay in was "ours" or outright "Romani," whereas everyone and everything else remained balamé. Balamé people and things were permitted inside only after they were scrutinized by community gatekeepers—elders and established adults—and deemed "safe." There were always eyes on the borders: families that brought in large quantities of goods from balamé wholesalers would have them looked over before storing them at the compound; all common spaces had direct sight lines to the major points where pedestrians and vehicles typically entered the compound; young men always gathered at the borders to socialize late at night. At times when my interlocutors sensed a direct threat, they organized patrols. Monitoring the border came up in conversation in terms of protecting their ability to determine how they lived in the interior. The border was present as a source of safety, a condition of autonomy, and a limit of territorial identity—of Romani space that was different from balamé space.

While it is tempting to treat the compound as a simple "reflection" or perhaps a "manifestation" of differential belonging informed by common experiences of violence, such generalizations do not do justice to the way my interlocutors related with the place they called home. After grappling with literature from across the social sciences on collective identities and place, I decided that the most tenable approach was a concept of *contingent co-emergence*. Jacques Derrida provides a useful framing. He coined the term "ontopology" to describe the ontological value of present-being to its situation, to the *topos* of territory (1994, 82): *these people* are intertwined with *that place*—the two inform each other. Taking Derrida's lead, but with some wariness of essentializing place while reifying discrete and transparent identities and differences, I want to underscore the importance of the compound, and specifically the specter of *losing the compound*—of becoming displaced—in relation to Romani identity politics.

The territory of the compound held manifold interconnected and intersecting experiences, memories, relations, and desires. Critically, however, these were haunted by the hostile spatial politics that threatened the compound, a politics that stirred a near-constant sense of anxiety among residents—especially at times when city officials lurked about and the threat of fire and bulldozers became more immediate. The uncertain situatedness of my interlocutors' lives in the place they called home had a simultaneously reductive and totalizing effect on their sense of belonging and the identity politics that informed this. As long as the compound remained, so too did the threat of its destruction. This threat located the various lives it troubled within a common fold. The individual everyday protective actions, postures, and strategies that residents of the compound undertook to minimize displace-ability and thus stave off displacement were legible to others as part of an ongoing cooperative project of resistance.

"Don't misunderstand—we're Greeks too," Thanos explained one morning as we walked along the southern edge of the compound. "But we're different. We're Romani, and this is the problem," he added. "They feel uncomfortable when they see themselves in us. So we stay in our places and in our roles, and we hope they stay in theirs. We're all Greek, but we belong to different worlds."

In the weeks that followed the disastrous party, George continued to struggle socially. Every move he made appeared to be miscalculated, out of step, and out of touch. He would shrug this off whenever I asked him why things seemed to be going wrong—"it's mostly their fault," he'd say, meaning it was primarily the adults in his life who were acting negatively toward him. Pressed to answer *why* the adults were doing this, George hesitated. He knew they were responding negatively and even violently to his actions; he suspected his actions were being misinterpreted and his explanations were being misunderstood, but he couldn't explain why. The adults thought George's response was ridiculous, that he couldn't possibly have done the things he did without knowing how they would be taken by those around him. I found this gap very interesting. It hinted at a growing divide between the life worlds of those young people who spent most of their time within the compound among their peers, and life worlds shaped at least in part through recursive engagements with a socioeconomically unstable and increasingly austere "outside."

During the period of my fieldwork when I was beginning to note this gap, I thought it was unlikely that George and the other boys would be unaware that Romani adults were thinking differently about fortuitous employment opportunities and frivolous spending displays. Seeing that adults were struggling financially and were no longer able to make spending displays like they used to should have signaled to my younger interlocutors that talking about finding temporary work and throwing around money might be problematic at this time. It seemed obvious to me that even planning to make the public displays that adults could no longer afford might be taken as a criticism of the older generation. It also seemed obvious to me that adults would find the arrogance with which boys talked about the likelihood of finding temporary jobs annoying, and perhaps even dangerous now that quick jobs were rare in the shrinking gray economy. Yet my young interlocutors didn't see things this way. It took me some months to unravel why: whereas George and the other boys experienced being Romani in terms of a grounded identity politics still shaped by threats posed by balamé directly—a subject position that preserved the conventional meaning of "coming of age displays"—adults had become oriented to dangers posed by the crumbling balamé economy. The difference in the way the two groups perceived the risk of displacement was subtle, but produced observable differences in the way they conducted themselves and related to the physical space of the compound.

I watched George closely as he tried to repair the damage he had done. At first, he attempted to take on the kinds of obligations and responsibilities his brother assumed after he returned from Volos. He offered to be a godfather to a newborn baby, and to become a blood brother with an older boy—a move that would have gained him access to the other boy's father's still lucrative scrap metal collection business.[8] Both of his attempts were met with derision. George didn't bother trying to find a girlfriend—"I should probably wait," he said sagely. Yet, despite ongoing setbacks, George had become convinced of a change in himself and that, despite early misfires, this change would allow him to differentiate himself from his peers while healing social rifts. He started behaving differently. For one, he stopped smoking near his BMW—or what was left of it—opting instead to smoke in places where he could see the borders of the compound. This change signaled a shift from needing protection, to protecting. He would also walk along the streets around the compound, showing confidence by being alone and moving slowly. He would occasionally make eye contact with a balamé man and raise his head slightly to signal acknowledgment of the other person. These things were consciously done. George made it a point to report what he had seen and where he had been to anyone who would listen.

His behavior changed in other ways too. For one, George stopped bothering his friends and family. This was something everyone noted—although they suspected he was lying low because of the trouble he had caused, not that he was becoming more mature. I found two other changes also interesting: he would occasionally become totally recalcitrant—to the point of absurdity, really. There was a period of two weeks when he stopped answering phone calls, explaining, "Dogs respond to whistles." He also took to making deeply impassioned appeals in the face of even the slightest perceived injustice. Any provocation, from walking too closely to him to greeting someone else in a room before him, sparked tirades. I asked Vasilo about this. "Maybe he's trying to act balamé?" she offered, shrugging. Indeed, George's behavior brought to mind the stereotype circulating within the compound at the time of balamé as being stubbornly anti-authority and self-involved. Predictably, these changes were another misfire. While he was trying to present himself as a protector who was familiar with balamé, who could interact with them, and who could move easily within their spaces, the overall performance was confusing. Romani adults did not act like balamé, nor did they spend leisure time making eye contact with them. Most people assumed he was "going through something."

This bothered George, but he was not willing to give up. Over the following month the economic situation continued to deteriorate in the compound, and he kept looking for ways to win back everyone's attention and to gain the acceptance of older boys and adults. At this time, most families were struggling financially, and food and other resource sharing had become commonplace. Also, all celebrations in the compound became very subdued affairs. Everything from baptisms to weddings, which used to be occasions for big parties and lavish giveaways, came to be marked by displays of public pining by sponsors unable to play their roles and fulfill expectations. George and a few other older boys picked up on this and also tried pining publicly: George, for example, wailed about wanting to be a godfather but having nobody to christen; another boy around his age, Spiro, cried in front of a number of men because he had no money with which to buy a present for his sister who was about to give birth to her first child. These displays induced cringes among onlookers. They were definitely awkward.

Public pining made present the day-to-day experiences of hardship most all adults were living with. These public displays, which became quite regular, established a new normative narrative of Romani "life in crisis." When bad feelings resulting from daily hardship were intensified by inability to meet social responsibilities, individuals would gather the people they were letting down to admit and explain their failure. They would speak nostalgically about the time when state agents were not so involved in the economy and (Romani) work was easier to find. They would continue by narrating how the economy changed, and why their various attempts to make money despite the economic downturn were unsuccessful. These gatherings would attract other adults, who would offer similar stories and expressions of encouragement. At the end, all would be forgiven.

Nostalgia was a critical component of public pining—it verified the performer's social status, which in turn validated the performance. Older boys had nothing relevant to be nostalgic about. Rather than accepting their wailing and crying as expressions of frustration stemming from an inability to make change in their lives, adults were provoked to angry responses, accusing them of pretending to have "adult problems." By expressing pain stemming from unfulfilled desire, boys like George fell unintentionally into the established Romani cultural frame of *children who want and consume*, which contrasted sharply with the narrative establishing around the ongoing struggle against impoverishment that positioned *adults as sufferers who provide*.

"He has no reason to be upset," Spiro's mother explained. "It's the other way around. His father and I make sure he has everything. Nobody expects this little shit to buy anything or do anything."

Spiro listened as his mother spoke, his head hanging low. "I still feel sad," he said into his chest.

"No reason," she snapped back, not looking at him.

The silence in the room grew heavy. I asked, "When should he start feeling sad about things like this?" Spiro perked up. His mother stood.

"It's not up to me," she replied as she walked out. Spiro looked down again.

Thinking back, Vasilo told me she regretted not spending more time with George during these months. He was obviously upset and was growing desperate. Everything he did was disastrous. He began to spend more time away from the compound. I talked to him about this. George explained that he wasn't avoiding anyone. In fact, he said he was doing something amazing for his home, and that

"You'll see." Despite his reassurances that everything was OK, I continued to worry. He would borrow his brother's small red pickup truck at night and return in the morning in time for Thanos to leave for the farmers' market where he helped his friend sell potatoes. For a while, George wouldn't say where he was going or what he was bringing back. Rumors began to circulate that he was working again for those men on Crete.

It took me a while to work out what George was up to. The explanation requires a brief discussion of Halandri Romani architectural aesthetics. During the early 2000s, it became fashionable in the compound to incorporate pillars into the exterior of one's home. These were used primarily to hold up awnings and door-way overhangs. Most Romani homes in the compound were also painted white. Some wealthier individuals put clay shingles over the corrugated metal sheets or plastic-dressed cardboard that usually served as roofs. Others placed coffee tables fashioned from discarded pieces of marble in front of their homes. "These are our things too," an elderly Romani man once told me, "so why not, they look nice." By 2014, many of these architectural features still stood, although white-washes were fading and peeling, and some of the pillars had been replaced with pieces of wood or pipe. Most people didn't seem bothered by this. New homes followed a simpler, boxier style.

I discovered what George was up to one afternoon after helping him push the charred remains of his BMW into a ditch by his mother's home. George told me he was planning to "clean things up." He was beginning a project of exterior renovation. At first his parents were very excited about this. George would drive to building sites and, under the cover of darkness, steal any materials he could quickly throw into the back of his brother's truck. He used this material to reface an exterior wall of the family home and to reinforce part of the front door frame. A coat of paint over all this made the house look fresh, and attracted the posi-tive attention of George's friends and neighbors. However, with things looking up slightly, George decided to take it to the next level. Unknown to his family and friends, George began stealing supplies from archaeological excavations in and around Athens. He was unconcerned with the type of object he brought home—he seemed to prize only that it was taken from an archaeological site. His mother suspected something was wrong when George brought home a large angular rock and tried to jam it under a wall at the front of the house. She confronted him a few days later when he came home with burlap, a stadia rod (which he mistook as framing for a window), and a low stool. I did not witness the ensuing fight—Vasilo told me about it afterward. Actually, several people told me about it.

Upon learning that the materials were from archaeological digs, George's mother began yelling and kicking her son. As she pushed him out the door, she demanded that he remove and discard whatever he stole from these sites. George resisted feebly. The neighbors became involved. A fight broke out between George and his neighbor's son, which drew others in. When he was finally subdued, he was told to leave the compound. Vasilo explained, "It's better that he left. You never know—he might have burned the house down."

George was out of touch, out of step—out of time and out of place. The stealing and displaying of archaeological materials was a perversion of the appropriation and incorporation of "Greek" architectural forms into Romani space that was part of a visual identity politics current in the compound during the early 2000s. George was playing by the old rules of a game that had changed. As his earlier attempts to show that he was now a protector who had mastered the mannerisms necessary to liaise with Greeks failed to improve his situation, George upped the ante by demonstrating some mastery over Greek spaces and things. His end goal, simply, was to demonstrate that he was a capable young man who was able not only to safeguard, but also to improve conditions for his family. Stealing from construction sites was one way of showing he was able to take what he wanted from balamé. Taking from archaeological sites was intended to achieve something more: whereas others could only buy and make replicas of "Greek forms" to incorporate into their homes—with wealthier Roma incorporating more expensive things—George's midnight raids on archaeological sites appeared to be an attempt to demonstrate that he could go right to the source, as it were. These *more authentic* Greek objects were not only intended to improve the home, but also raise the status of his family.

"He's crazy," yelled Thanos when I asked him what happened. "He's risking our lives for old rocks. Fuck him!"

Unlike stolen construction materials, which were by most measures ordinary, archaeological materials were different—they had power. George's family and neighbors were worried that the objects would draw the attention and ire of the police and also the cultural guard.[9] In other words, they feared that having stolen this material, George had sparked a recovery effort and perhaps even retaliation. After sending him away, they took the various "archaeological things" George brought into the compound and destroyed them. The pieces that remained were gathered up and dumped in another neighborhood. Thanos spent hours washing out the bed of his truck. This episode came up again and again in conversation over the following days. There was no longer any doubt that George was corrupted on Crete: George was given a taste of money by the "traffickers," but was unable to find a regular job back home (not that George was looking, really; although nobody seemed to notice). The compound adults agreed that George became obsessed with quick cash and that this led him to make bad choices: in trying to reconnect with a fleeting feeling of success and wealth, he was doing things that put everyone at risk. Parents began to cite George when talking to their young kids about the dangers beyond home.

George hadn't returned to the compound in four days. This is when Vasilo called me to ask what was happening. When I suggested he might be at the nearby squat, Vasilo encouraged me to find out. I texted George as I left the compound. He replied almost immediately with an address. I set off to find him, and when I was halfway there, he texted again with a different address. Both addresses were nearby, so I walked to the first. He wasn't there, so I set out for the second address. I found George a few blocks down, sitting on a bench, smoking. He was staring vacantly in the direction of the compound. He looked bad and smelled like urine.

"Don't people make you want to give up?" he offered as I sat. "I can't anymore."

"Can't what?" I asked.

George looked past me, "Can't try."

"Shouldn't you be getting home?" I asked. "People are wondering what happened to you."

"Liar!" George yelled loudly. "Nobody is wondering, they all know. They did it to me. I'm going to stay here. It's better."

I didn't know what else to say to George, so we just sat for a bit and then agreed to meet again the next day. I connected with him regularly over the following week. He told me that after being chased out of the compound, he had gone to the nearby squat, where he found several slightly older Romani boys. They were sitting around with a few other people—balamé—listening to music. George felt uncomfortable, so he left. He was now living in the space between the squat and the compound, between the addresses he texted earlier. He would go to the squat to find food, use the bathroom occasionally, and connect with other Romani boys. Otherwise he was alone. George came to the conclusion that his situation was not his fault. He noted that many other boys had left as well (albeit not under such dramatic circumstances), and not because they wanted to. Again, George blamed the older generation—although this time he had an explanation. He knew they were struggling to make enough money to live, and because of this, he thought, they were doing anything they could to get by—including blocking young people from "competing with them," as he put it.

The other expelled boys I spoke with—about seven other individuals—agreed on this last point. They shared an experience of not being able to find work and being treated like children. They also expressed a feeling that the compound adults were holding them back. Most of these boys would spend their days at the squat (although not necessarily hanging out with each other) and return directly to their parents' home at night to eat and sleep. A few of them had been stopped late at night by Romani men in the compound and accused of peddling drugs and attracting police attention. I heard about the latest confrontation from one of Vasilo's sons. It was between a boy named Leander and two men who were talking by a large fire burning in a barrel. The men heard him coming into the compound through some overgrown weeds and chased him down in the dark. Leander didn't shout or struggle—he lay still as the men searched him. They then dragged him behind a nearby home and beat him. The men claimed they found drugs. Leander eventually made his way out of the compound and back to the squat. Overhearing her son telling me the story, Vasilo explained that this was not unusual. Boys who spent time outside the compound, and at the squat specifically, risked being attacked if they returned. This is why she wanted George to come home.

"He's an asshole, but I'd hate to see what they would do to him if he starts acting like an anarchist."

I nodded. "I don't think he's well," I told her. "He lost weight, and he's very unhappy." At this Vasilo began to look worried.

"They're really going to hurt him if they catch him. He's a joke." She added, eyes cast downward, shifting back and forth, "Actually, it might be best if he stays away."

The time I spent with George in the space between the compound and the squat helped me to make sense of the social constraints working-age Romani boys were facing. I began to see how two related issues came together to make life unbearable, prompting my interlocutor and others in his position to leave. First, the worsening economic situation made it increasingly unlikely that Romani boys could signal their readiness to take on new social and economic roles within the community through conventional means. Quite simply, acceptable short-term, high-paying work that Romani boys could do had become nearly impossible to find anywhere in Greece. Even if they could signal their readiness for new roles through conventional means, chances are these signals would be misinterpreted. This leads to the second issue. Romani adults who were struggling to meet their various responsibilities while searching for work and staying safe in balamé spaces came to see perseverance in the face of hardship, or endurance more generally, as a Romani quality central to community membership. This came to have normative force, in part, through repeated performances of public pining validated by expressions of nostalgia that evoked a pre-crisis economic sphere. Having no work experience about which to be nostalgic, Romani boys were unable to demonstrate perseverance and thereby claim community membership in the same terms as adults. George and others in his position were expected to stay put—often in Vasilo's sitting room. Their occasional attempts at making a change were interpreted as childish, and sometimes even dangerous.

It's easy to criticize Romani adults for denying boys' claims of experiencing hardship and, further, their desire for a different future. They were, after all, also suffering because of the economic downturn. How could adults, and parents especially, continue to shut down the attempts boys made to demonstrate their readiness for new social roles? Boys were leaving the compound—did adults not realize they were making it nearly impossible for these individuals to stay in the community? By 2015, the vast majority of Romani adults at the Halandri compound were completely consumed with making ends meet. Some were spending days away from home looking for whatever work they could get. Vasilo was the only Romani person I knew with a steady income, and even that had been reduced dramatically by recent changes to government pensions and benefits. She was also the only person I knew who was worried about the slow exit of older boys. While others had noted that this was happening, few people fretted over it. Even parents who had positive relationships with their sons assumed that spending time away from the compound, even at the squat, was a phase—something their boys were trying out.

"No, no, he'll come back," a father told me, and made a show of looking out the window, down the path by his house, and back to me. "He's a good boy, he'll find his way." He took a deep breath and itched at his graying beard. "I think about him when I can."

Of note, I heard similar talk in non-Romani households as well. Dependents were often left out of conversations and excluded from decision making, as working individuals sought solutions to constraints resulting from shrinking and sometimes disappearing salaries, growing expenses, and changes to the public services on which they relied. The changes in their lives sometimes created gaps that, in turn, activated unexpected movements that produced new distances of their own. In these examples, like in the Roma compound, as gaps deepened and widened, the modes of agency available to those who were struggling with and within the constraints of the consolidating neoliberal governmentality were differentiated from those available to individuals suffering incidental and often unintentional abandonment.

"Are they Albanians?" Takis asked, looking at a group of Romani men walking down the street toward the compound. I told him they were. "Fuck my life," he replied, "they're living there and I'm out here." Takis had left the compound some months back. He became upset when his cousin overlooked him as a possible godfather for his newborn daughter—a role Takis wanted dearly. He approached his cousin about this some weeks after what he considered to be a surprisingly quiet baptism; but not to complain—he just wanted to know if his cousin was mad at him. He was assured that their relationship was fine, but that he was just a kid who was not ready to take on big responsibilities. This didn't sit well with Takis, especially because the person who had the "big responsibility" was unable to fulfill it as expected. Takis wanted to make a change. So, knowing it was unlikely that he would find a job on his own, he offered to help his uncle at *his* job, for free. Takis thought this would be a way for him to make connections, while gaining respect within the compound. His uncle, however, refused to share his work or his contacts. The same tactic failed when he approached an older cousin, his father, and a family friend. Feeling utterly frustrated and hopeless, Takis found himself at a crossroads: he could either go to Vasilo's house, where most of his friends still hung out, or he could leave the compound when the adults did in the mornings. He chose to leave, to "try his luck outside."

Several weeks of searching unsuccessfully for work led Takis to feel disappointed. He explained, "I knew there were few jobs available, but I still thought I'd find something." As his hopefulness faded, so did Takis's motivation to continue searching. Instead of traveling great distances to find work, he began to wander closer to home, looking for opportunities. Takis's first encounter with the squat was accidental. He saw an old van parked outside—its back door propped open by a dolly. The van looked familiar. He approached, thinking he would ask whoever owned the vehicle if he could unload the van for a few euros, but froze in his tracks when two balamé stepped out of the back holding a box each. They were all too close to each other to ignore the encounter, so after an awkward beat, one of the guys asked Takis if he wanted to help them. They offered to give him a drink and a cigarette in exchange for his labor. Takis agreed.

News of Takis's interaction with balamé at the squat spread quickly within the compound. At first, my interlocutor tried to spin the encounter as a work opportunity; however, the reputation of the squat as a place where the laziest and angriest balamé went to have sex and to take and sell drugs marked Takis as someone who was becoming lost.

"I tried to tell them that the squat is like the compound," Takis explained eagerly, "that the police and Golden Dawn have tried to burn it down several times. But my friends thought I was becoming an anarchist. My father tried to hit me."

Playing up similarities between the squat and the compound—especially in terms of a spatial politics that set the residents of the compound and the users of the squat in a common position against the state—was dangerous. His mother tried to keep him from leaving again. She talked to him about becoming corrupted, but the prospect of spending another day sitting idly in Vasilo's home struck Takis as a step backward. When his parents left the next morning, so did he.

"I was not working at the squat, but I was definitely doing something more than just sitting around. I was also hoping that spending time with balamé would lead to work connections. I know a lot of the younger balamé talk about never working, but the older ones, the smarter ones, come to the squat after work. Everyone has to live."

As Takis settled into a new life outside the compound—a life his friends and family assumed was filled with drugs—it seemed to my interlocutor that life in the compound was becoming strange. The newest families moving in were Romani, but from Albania. Up until that time, Roma from other areas, and even Roma from other clans, were welcome as visitors but not as neighbors.[10] However, the two new families were work partners with an older established Romani family living at the compound. Inviting them to stay was a strategic move intended to create employment opportunities for local community members. When asked about this change, Takis's father echoed his son: "Everyone has to live."

The opening of the compound to non-Greek Roma of different clan affiliation was made possible by crisis-driven changes in the ordering categories of self-identity and broader transformations in the ethics and politics of community inclusion that followed. In other words, as the threat of displacement by eviction came to be joined and compounded by a growing threat of hunger, the ways residents experienced and maintained the compound and, moreover, imagined the collective within it, changed. This change, which made it possible for Albanian Roma to live in the compound, was unintelligible to those young Romani boys who were already displaced—first socially and then physically—from the once-familiar space.

George, Takis, and other "outside boys" whom I talked to expressed confusion and concern over what was happening "back home." They began to question the understandings of Romani identity communicated in the forms of relationality they grew up with, the supposed commonality of the experiences of exclusion they struggled with individually, and the purposes of the protective actions they witnessed and supported. This questioning led to their rethinking their memories of a whole, enclosed community and the stable identity politics on which they assumed it was grounded. One of the boys described his new perspective as a kind of paranoia: the more he thought about it, the less he knew for sure.

Within the compound, instability produced anxiety and launched stabilizing responses that evoked being-in-common. Outside the compound, instability and anxiety without the possibility of stabilization eroded the embeddedness and embodiedness of being Romani, launching multiple forms of inward and outward conflict and questioning, which in turn challenged the engrained mythologies and orthodoxies through which life in the Halandri compound took form.

Becoming stuck, then isolated, and eventually becoming separated from the compound were desubjugating: it enabled a mode of critical agency that exposed the limits of the normative (Roitman 2014, 65–66).

"I'm used to life out here, but I don't feel human anymore," George said casually when we met in the summer of 2016. "I don't know anything. My life is chaos."

He was still spending most of his time between the squat and the compound. Thanos would give him money sometimes.

"Look at everything that's happening. Balamé are begging in the streets, Albanians and Romanians and even Bangladeshis are living in Roma compounds. Nazis are everywhere." He took a breath, tears welling up. "My family thinks I do drugs. Balamé think I sell drugs. The joke is I can't afford to buy them or sell them, but I feel like I'm hallucinating all the time."

George stared at my wedding ring and fell silent for some time.

"We're all the same, you know, in some ways," he offered quietly.

"Yeah," I replied.

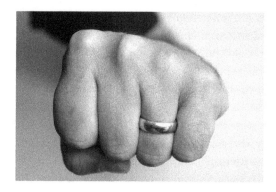

FIGURE 3. Author's fist, wedding ring. Athens, 2018. Photo by the author.

ORDINARY GHOSTING
How to Yield Stability from Chaos

Frantically scanning street numbers, I rushed along a busy sidewalk a few kilometers away from the metro station at Omonia Square. It was a hot July morning
in 2013, and I was on my way to a meeting with the administrator of a clinic
operated by a well-known local aid agency, which I'll call HMA.[1] The group's
mandate was to provide free medical care, emergency housing, and counseling
services to "all those in need"—as stated on the small banner hanging over their
front door—although their clientele at the time consisted mainly of migrants
from Nigeria, Senegal, and Pakistan.

I entered the building and pushed into a small, crowded foyer: behind me
was the door to the street, and in front of me (past a mass of people) was a narrow, winding staircase. Slowly, apologetically, I worked my way up the staircase,
pushing past dozens of individuals, inching toward the reception desk on the
second floor. There was no light in the stairwell, save the dim glow from a dirty
window partway up, nor was there ventilation: the air was hot and thick with
the odor of sick bodies. The stairs themselves, wide enough to accommodate
two people standing shoulder to shoulder, were steep and inexplicably wet—
I steadied myself against the walls and other people as I climbed, toehold by
toehold.

Three strides back from the top stair stood an imposing desk that took up
almost the entire width of the narrow hallway. Two women wearing scrubs, latex
gloves, and face masks sat behind it. They were glaring at a woman who was

trying, through gestures and shouting in a language I didn't recognize, to convey that her young son had been vomiting—a message made clear a moment later when the boy began to heave into a plastic bag. On the desk lay a tatty register, a stack of paper bracelets, and two mobile phones, toward which the nurses glanced with what struck me as habitual regularity. Behind the desk, along the hallway, was a series of wooden benches occupied by clients waiting to be seen by the staff in the offices across from them: four doctors and two counselors. At the end of the hallway stood three narrow doors. The door to the right, secured by two deadbolts, led to the storage room where medicines were kept. The door in the middle opened to a cramped washroom. The door to the left led to the office of my interlocutor—HMA's director, Maria.

One of the triage nurses noticed me making my way through the crush of people and yelled for the mass to part. A few moments later I found myself sitting in Maria's air-conditioned office. At the time, I didn't have the presence of mind to reflect critically on the various power plays that facilitated my way through the building, although I've since thought back to that stairwell with tremendous guilt.

I met Maria a few weeks earlier at a conference in Athens. She had given a polemical paper that criticized medical practitioners operating in government clinics: she highlighted corrupt practices and named names. In her conclusion, she called for an "ethical overhaul" of Greek medicine—the only hope, she posited, for a health care system in crisis. I was inspired to explore this idea further, so I approached her to ask for an interview, and she agreed to meet me at her HMA office. I took the time between the conference and this meeting to prepare by reviewing reports from various think tanks on corruption in the Greek public sector. I also scanned various reports commissioned by the Ministry of Health on the state of the public health care system and read through a number of recently revised ministry policy papers on topics ranging from Greece's use of specialized medical services elsewhere in the EU, to spending priorities on medical technologies.

The conversation with Maria began positively. She was flattered that I had taken careful notes during her presentation. I explained that I had observed several instances of what she described as "corrupt practices" in medical and non-medical spaces alike. I told Maria I was coming to think that, since these practices had become normalized over time, and now justified as "the only possible responses" to tightening budgets and depleting resources, the intervention she called for—an ethical overhaul—would be quite challenging. Case in point, I explained that one physician I had spoken with recently cast various practices, like those Maria had described in her paper, in terms of performing a kind of corrective good—corporate-focused or socially minded—that also improved the professional and sometimes private lives of those individuals or small groups who were in one way or another "breaking the rules." Looking to reconnect with her conference paper, I related my observations with her musings on morality and power. I then realized I was talking too much.

My interlocutor was leaning back in her chair, looking at me blankly. Not wanting her to lose interest in the interview, I asked her to tell me more about the cases of corruption she described in her paper. I was especially interested in a case that involved collaboration across several departments in two public hospitals. Maria hesitated. Thinking I was beginning with a touchy subject, I asked a more general question about people's motivations for breaking workplace rules. Again, Maria hesitated. After some probing, I discovered that my interlocutor had not written the paper she gave: she had hired a ghostwriter to translate her observations "into the right language." As it turns out, the ghostwriter had done more than just translate. In fact, the ghostwriter added the section on corruption I found so interesting, the section that grounded her call for an ethical overhaul of medicine in Greece. Maria shrugged this off, explaining she was too busy to prepare her own presentation and that I shouldn't get caught up in details that were "added in the edit," as she put it. Maria sat up in her chair and refocused. She explained that the paper was about the future of health care in Greece. She had very little to say about corruption specifically, or about the call she sounded for an ethical overhaul, which at the time had inspired a room full of hospital administrators, ministry staff, researchers, and advocates to clap and cheer.

"You have to find the *real* message in my paper," she challenged. "I was talking about finding a future that will be correct for everyone. You took notes. I'm surprised you missed that."

I spent the next hour in her office feeling increasingly agitated, trying to direct the conversation toward something relevant to my work—perhaps a new contact, some info about HMA's operations, a personal story about corruption at hospitals, Maria's vision for the future of public health care, anything. Maria, however, resisted my attempts, opting instead to talk about her career trajectory and hopes for a seat on Greece's National Commission on Human Rights (I made the mistake of mentioning that I had interviewed a member of the commission the week before). Of course, I knew the *what* and the *how* of what is unsaid during fieldwork interviews is also data, but I was still frustrated.

Then, at about the forty-five-minute mark—the point where I had given up trying to change the conversation, the point where I felt completely deflated—I realized something: there was complete silence on the other side of the office door. Apart from occasional exchanges between the triage nurses and the clients in the stairwell, and a few passing comments between staff in the hallway, the clinic that was bursting with people in need was almost completely silent. I mentioned this to Maria, who replied, "Just wait until the Greeks get here—they usually come later in the afternoon. The migrants are civilized; the Greeks bring chaos!"

Now, the characterization of migrants or "others" in general as civil and Greeks as chaotic or uncivilized is a well-worn trope in Greece (see Herzfeld 2005). What I found interesting, however, was the suggestion that Greeks were using HMA's services *at all*, considering every Greek citizen enjoys a constitutional guarantee to public health care. I asked Maria about this directly. She suggested mainstream Greeks were coming to HMA as a consequence of the poor public medical system—making reference, once again, to the paper she didn't write. She then tried to press the importance of her contribution to that conference and turned back to talking about her career prospects. At this point (knowing that my patience and my time with her were about to expire), I insisted rather impolitely that she answer my question directly and honestly based on her experience. Perhaps caught off guard, Maria blurted, in a rather matter-of-fact tone, that the increase in mainstream Greek clients was a result of the economic crisis, that regular public clinics provided basic medical care to those who were willing to "suffer for appointments," but HMA saw people promptly and also gave away free medications, advice for finding social services, and offered vouchers for free foodstuffs from local stores and charities. What's more, she continued, the growing population of impoverished Greeks was increasingly unable to afford the standard bribes patients pay for diagnostic services and specialist consultations—something HMA covers for its clients. I looked up from my notebook. *Does HMA really pay bribes on behalf of patients? Why had Maria not mentioned this HMA service before? And did the ghostwriter of her paper know about this?* After an awkward pause, Maria eyed her watch and the door. She stood up before I had a chance to ask another question.

I walked toward the still-crowded stairway and was about to push onto the first step when Maria called me back. She was standing with a nurse by one of the offices. As I approached, she turned away and mumbled that her staff might be better able to answer my questions. I would think of this introduction later as a turning point in my fieldwork. Maria and I had friction, and she didn't have to entrust me to a member of her staff. For this I have since been very grateful.

The nurse, Amalia, had been working at HMA for a little over a year. She also worked regular shifts at a public hospital. Amalia was obviously tired. She was in her late thirties, but exhaustion made her seem much older. We sat for a quick cup of coffee at a café across the street. Amalia had studied nursing in the UK but returned to work in Greece so she could care for her ailing mother, a widow with no other children. When the financial crisis hit in 2010, Amalia began looking for a second job, as backup, should she be laid off. She began working for HMA as a nurse manager in 2011.

Amalia was also surprised when mainstream Greeks first started to use the clinic. At the beginning, she explained, Greek clients suggested HMA was convenient to their homes; but as more and more of them began to clamber up the stairs, their explanations as to why they were there changed: some claimed that paying bribes for service in the public system had become too much of a financial burden; some explained that last-minute appointments were hard to come by; others needed financial assistance to purchase medication; and so on. With time, Amalia suspected the locals were coming up the stairs for another reason still—but we would talk about this at a later date. Of course, HMA helped local Athenians as it helped undocumented migrants and others.

Amalia made it her personal goal to ensure that one group did not get preferential treatment over the other. This did not appear to bother anyone, according to my interlocutor: "What else would they expect from a humanitarian clinic?" Amalia went on to describe countless moments of what she called "beautiful interaction" between Greeks and migrants where they would help each other, be friendly, and even commiserate at times. In her words, "A member of Golden Dawn would drop dead at the sight of HMA's main corridor. Maybe we should start giving tours."

After a chuckle, the unexpected quiet at HMA came back to my mind. I mentioned it to Amalia. I wondered if she had noticed it too. She had.

"You know when you're in a crowded room and there is noise everywhere? You know when all of a sudden everyone stops talking at once, as if someone flipped a switch? That happens a lot at the clinic." Amalia ran the tip of her ring finger along the lip of her coffee cup. "I wonder sometimes if there is a rhythm . . . you know, something human? Maybe we become more in sync when our bodies are sick and our minds are unsure."

I left our first meeting thinking about spreading silences, vital connections, and synchronicity.

From 2010 through 2016, governmental and economic institutions in Greece rolled out troika-mandated austerity policies that decimated public services while eroding the possibility of economic self-sufficiency for most Athenians. In rapid time, large swaths of the population became increasingly subject to what scholars have called "precariatization": a biopolitical situation in which populations are gradually acclimatized to insecurity and hopelessness, typically through the normalization of temporary labor and the depletion of social support, coupled with attrition of social democracy in favor of entrepreneurial modalities (Lorey 2015). Rapid precariatization pressurized HMA. As impoverishment spread and supports were eroded, Amalia saw more and more people in increasingly dire states of health. These individuals pushed their bodies, and/or the bodies of those for whom they cared, to the ends of their abilities as they struggled to remain economically active, let alone competitive. Examination rooms became awkward spaces where patients would often employ a new moral language of *economic ability* grounded in neoliberal capitalist narratives of individual self-management when describing their medical problems, which effectively positioned medical staff as gatekeepers of their capacity to work.

So, whereas HMA's corridors appealed to Amalia as "beautiful" sites of connection, the confidential spaces where patients were examined, diagnoses were made, and treatments were decided troubled my interlocutor. Amalia would eventually tell me that she did not know how to position herself in the room when requests for what patients regarded as immediate solutions, like pain relievers and antibiotics, were denied by doctors, and their ensuing explanations were in turn rejected by anxious patients. My interlocutor came to think that this relatively greater potential for negotiating with HMA staff, which allowed patients to avoid a slow-moving and expensive public system, was the other reason Athenians had begun to use the clinic.

She came to contrast the occasional silences in HMA's corridors, which for her made present both the vulnerability and the struggle against further deterioration that her patients shared, along with the shouting, crying, and pleading for help that often took place in the little rooms that ran along its length. These occasional silences and charged negotiations became more common as the government continued to roll out austerity measures and HMA became more consistently jammed with sick and injured bodies. I came to think of the rhythms at the clinic in terms of diastolic quiet and systolic noise—the accelerating pulse of something coming.

In the following I will explore Amalia's becoming involved in injurious situations that moved her from frontline *observer* of the human effects of governing through crisis management, to troubled *participant* in the struggle she witnessed every day at HMA and beyond. Specifically, I will argue that a series of awkward encounters between my interlocutor and a migrant girl, and then with this girl's father, made the multiple violences to which Amalia was a witness visible and legible as a quality of a coming situation of which she too was a subject. I show that her response to this coming situation, with others, rendered legible an alternative terrain of the present defined by compassion and inessential commonality that challenged neoliberal governmentality. Further, I will suggest that this co-emerged terrain resettled the sense of continuity inherent in the ways Athenians imagined and lived their lives, producing an unsettled and unsettling stability.

Amalia was tall with short dark hair that gave off a hint of red in bright light. She was soft-spoken but not shy. Talking to her was easy. We met several times over the following weeks to discuss her work at HMA; specifically, I wanted to learn how a humanitarian medical clinic operated alongside the public and private health care sectors in Athens. HMA was one of a proliferating number of humanitarian organizations operating in the city, including informal unlicensed pharmacies, registered aid groups, and informal neighborhood rehabilitation programs. As Coutinho has noted, these organizations came to play a critical role in crisis-era health care (2016). With private health insurance and thus private health care services out of reach for the majority of the population, and with endemic problems in the public health sector exacerbated and multiplied by cuts to government spending, medical humanitarian organizations like HMA filled a growing need, especially among the increasing numbers of Athenians who were in deeply precarious situations and who were sacrificing their bodies to remain economically active.

As Ticktin observed in her work on humanitarianism in France, medical NGOs have become involved in a transnational system of governance tied to the demands of capital and labor, a national-cum-transnational biopolitics primarily concerned with maintaining a ready supply of informal labor (2006, 2011). Before the crisis, HMA did the same work and contributed to the same biopolitics. However, as mainstream Greeks started to use the clinic more regularly post-2010, HMA also began to contribute to broader European biopolitics. While HMA supported a supply of informal labor in the form of undocumented migrants, it also tempered the everyday injuries inflicted by the troika-mandated neoliberal austerity agenda. This humanitarian organization, HMA, simultaneously maintained laboring noncitizens and precarious laboring citizens—both groups positioned within the profitable, carefully monitored and maintained economy of abandonment (Povinelli 2011) that was in many ways blurring the distinctions between them.

HMA's director, Maria, did not see things this way. She had become preoccupied with finding ways to leverage HMA's growing importance within the local health care scene with a view toward furthering her career. As the number of sick bodies crowding the waiting room grew, Maria began to seek opportunities to expand, both the clinic's operations and her personal influence over health care policy (and spending). Unlike the multitudes of people in deeply precarious situations who were struggling with impoverishment, shame, and competition, Maria, like many other wealthy Athenians in stable life situations, remained critical of austerity policy but had also become caught up in the neoliberal fantasy of the market-oriented "good life."

This contrasted sharply with the way Amalia talked about HMA. Whereas she too felt her position in the organization was relatively secure, and although she had a second job at a local public hospital, Amalia was overworked and was feeling increasingly uneasy. Tension was growing between staff and management both at HMA and in the hospital, leading Amalia to feel unsupported and at constant risk of disciplinary action. She was alarmed by the increasing regularity with which staff at both institutions were having to make difficult, often morally fraught decisions about patient care—decisions that usually led to acting against one's professional better judgment and clinic regulations.

"You know that feeling you get when you miss your connection, that sinking 'what now' feeling? I feel that way every time I come here or even think about this place—" Amalia gestured toward the HMA building. "Things are changing, and it's become expected that we just adapt. But it upsets me. I'm doing things, but I feel like I can't see in front of me."

Maria and Amalia experienced the present moment differently. This difference marked a growing gap between those poised to benefit from the crisis and those who struggled within and against it—the precariat—for whom precarity became more than an economic and political condition: it was now a way of life. So, whereas Maria was using the changing situation to springboard her career, the same situation, and Maria's actions, were fixing Amalia in an increasingly difficult place. Amalia had become absorbed in the work of adjusting or, as Berlant has described it, "jostling and inventing new habits of being and relating in space" (2011, 206). This adjusting was progressive, or perhaps cumulative. It occurred little by little in response to unexpected situations, challenges, and encounters. It involved writing an "experience of the present" that slowly pulled away from the past, from what Amalia remembered and thought she knew (Koselleck 2004, 259). That feeling of having missed her connection captures this pulling away of the familiar, of one's ability to have a sense of things, of the disruption of continuity and the imperative to find a way forward without being able to draw on experience to anticipate. Amalia, like so many other Athenians caught up in consolidating neoliberal chaos, was finding herself in an increasingly worrying, small place out of time.

I had several meetings with Amalia over the course of the next few days. I became particularly interested in a case she told me about of a young Senegalese woman who had brought her toddler to HMA, and then to the public hospital where Amalia worked. The woman's daughter, Nefeli, was born in Athens and lived with her parents in Kypseli, a neighborhood that had become popular among more economically stable migrants. Nefeli's mother worked as a house-keeper for a family in the suburb of Mets (about an hour away by public transit), and her father had steady work at a property maintenance company as an office cleaner.

Nefeli's mother was her primary caregiver, since her father worked unpredictable hours. Most office buildings were cleaned nightly, meaning he was usually away from home between seven in the evening and three in the morning; but he was also on call should customers make special cleaning requests. After 2010, these special requests began to come more frequently—a result of an explosion in graffiti writing and an uptick in homeless people sleeping in sheltered storefronts. Nefeli's father came to be in and out of the house rather irregularly. He was always tired and slept a lot. Nefeli's mother kept the house in order. Before leaving for work, every morning she would leave a plate of food for her husband in the fridge, tidy up, and prepare her daughter for drop-off at a neighbor's apartment, where Nefeli would spend the day with eleven other children. Amalia suspected that this is where Nefeli contracted tuberculosis—an infection that complicated a previously undiagnosed congenital disorder.

This story was difficult for my interlocutor. She told me that the police had taken Nefeli's father to the notorious Petrou Rali migrant prison on the edge of Athens a month before her mother brought the little girl to HMA. He, apparently, did not have the papers migrants require to remain safely in the country (Cabot 2012). He would later explain that "life got in the way" of his chasing papers. Amalia told me that a doctor at HMA prescribed aggressive medications for Nefeli, which she took every day, but her condition continued to worsen, prompting the doctor to recommend Nefeli be taken to the public hospital. She told Nefeli's mother to look for Amalia, as she would be able to facilitate Nefeli's admission. Amalia told me that Nefeli's mother had grown increasingly desperate as their savings dried up and Nefeli's condition continued to deteriorate to the point where she had to be tended to constantly. She told me that Nefeli's mother, unable to balance longer and longer work hours and care for her daughter, followed the HMA doctor's advice and arranged to meet Amalia at the public hospital so Nefeli could be admitted. She put Nefeli in Amalia's arms. Amalia found a friendly doctor who, with the help of a sympathetic administrative assistant, fudged the paperwork (Nefeli had no ID) and admitted the little girl. Nefeli's mother kissed her barely conscious child, pressed her against her heart, and told her she would come to find her up on the ward after work. Amalia took Nefeli upstairs, settled her in, and watched her closely as she stabilized over the course of the next few days. I met Amalia during the second week of Nefeli's hospitalization. My interlocutor had never dealt with a situation like this in the past.

Amalia was charting new territory on two fronts: first, in dealing with the growing numbers of migrants desperately seeking help at public hospitals, and second, in dealing with the growing numbers of Athenians in need of regular care at HMA. For Amalia, Nefeli brought together the reinvention of care work being done at HMA with the reinvention of care work being done at the hospital. This little girl put these fronts into conversation. Like compassionate individuals working in all manner of aid spaces around Athens, Amalia had become a "moral pioneer" (cf. Rapp 1999). My interlocutor described recurring moments of uncertainty in which she found herself within confused situations, evaluating options, weighing consequences, and following through with concrete actions that seemed right. Of course, she was not alone. Amalia made decisions with others. She participated in teams that felt their way through challenging moments together, and she took part in reflective conversations in which staff looked back on their decisions to identify strategies or "informal policies" to help guide them with future patient and institutional difficulties.

At HMA, informal policy and the discussions leading to it came easily, even if the situations requiring disobedience were sometimes very difficult. Whereas migrants and other regular users continued to present with conventional concerns—illness from viruses or bacterial infections, difficulty with chronic health issues, and so on—Athenians were now coming with much more acute and sometimes strange concerns. It was not uncommon, for example, to see patients suffering from injuries they would leave untreated for much too long, or who were suffering from infections that were now causing fevers and other terrible complications. Amalia shuddered as she described one man who came to HMA with an infection from a gash on his left foot that had festered to the point where he was unable to walk.

"At another point in his life I'm sure he would have gone to the hospital. . . . He would have taken a day off work, weeks earlier, to have it looked at. Not anymore. Work until you drop," she said earnestly. Then she wrinkled her nose, "The smell was horrific."

The staff at HMA tried to persuade this man to go to the hospital, but he wouldn't leave. He pleaded until they treated him. Amalia wouldn't tell me what they did, only that it went well beyond what she thought was possible (and safe) at the clinic. The patient left at the end of the day with a bag of antibiotics and painkillers. His friend picked him up. They never saw him again.

"I wonder if what we did was illegal. It felt illegal . . . or bad at least," Amalia explained. "I don't know anymore, and it doesn't matter really. We did the right thing."

Despite knowing that some of their decisions pushed the limits of safety, best practice, and sometimes exacerbated resource scarcities, staff at HMA rarely encountered resistance from the administration—from Maria and her deputies. Amalia suspected her superiors were turning a blind eye. This situation caused her a lot of turmoil. On the one hand, she was happy to have the freedom to work with the team to help patients who needed their expertise. On the other, she felt that the situation had become compartmentalized and, thus, purposefully rendered invisible for the benefit of those who were in charge of HMA. This dilemma—a moral dilemma—was disorienting.

Things were not better at the public hospital. Those in charge were very concerned with "the budget"—an opaque and in some ways mysterious object that changed regularly, was often out of order, and could be summoned, usually with urgency, by low-level directors and supervisors to support their demands and critiques. They closely monitored Amalia's use of supplies, reviewed her patient assignments with the intent to identify "inefficiencies," and were always at odds with her nurse managers who saw it as their mission, at least in part, to protect their staff from interfering higher-ups.

"It's about women, really. They exploit women's labor," Amalia explained. "You see, we're all in on it—doctors, techs, cleaning staff—but nobody else in the hospital is targeted like nurses, who are almost all women." She was clearly agitated.

Amalia's comments hinted at gender politics that extended well beyond the health care space, and certainly well beyond the current crisis moment. The women and girls I knew in Athens bore most of the weight of holding their households in order—against all odds—as livelihoods were depleted on multiple fronts. As neoliberal restructuring squeezed families, my interlocutors described a shifting, or reordering in some cases, of the relations of responsibility. These changes turned on women's labor that was seen as sustaining, reserve, or adaptable. My interlocutors experienced new stresses, worries, anxieties, and fell into numbing habits of indifference as they repressed their desires and delayed dreams. Thinking with Berlant on becoming adjusted to the precarious present, I came to understand that these women were responding to a new gendered regime of daily struggle produced by neoliberal restructuring, in part by cultivating a condition of suspended affective transaction so as to continue on despite uncertainty and insecurity (2011, 211). This, however, did not play out as one might think in the public hospital space.

Like the case at HMA, Amalia and her colleagues at the hospital were faced with increasing pressure to care for more and more patients and their families; however, unlike at HMA they were expected to work unpaid hours, with drastically fewer resources and supports, and with increased monitoring. In other words, nurses were expected to do more and more care work with less of nearly everything except interference from management. To be sure, this was another effect of the state's neoliberal program of structural adjustment, continued economic decline, cuts to social services, and the sedimentation of the competitive neoliberal capitalist imperative to "reduce waste" and "find value" filtering through public structures of management. However, instead of producing anxiety, apathy, or depression, as one might expect, the intensifying economization and monitoring of nurses and other medical professionals charged with caring for increasing numbers of desperate patients under deteriorating conditions produced something unexpected: at moments when their patients' needs became critical—at times of crisis—Amalia and her colleagues cooperated to throw off or otherwise counter the individuals with clipboards who lurked in corridors and who snooped around nursing stations.

Anthropologists have observed that crises provide conditions of possibility for the coalescence of supportive networks—specifically, networks of actors who do not necessarily know each other or are otherwise connected or committed to each other, but who nonetheless become part of cooperative social formations in response to external pressure (De Genova and Peutz 2010; G. Feldman 2005; Inda 2006). Gregory Feldman has referred to these social formations as apparatuses (2011). Apparatuses do not work through top-down rule, but rather through activations of logics, norms, and moral narratives that disparate actors share, and from which they can draw authority in their respective domains of work. When Amalia was faced with a crisis on her ward, she knew she could act in ways that would be supported by others she had never met, despite her violating hospital procedures, management directives, or even Ministry of Health policy. As these disobedient actions became more frequent and regular, and as the supportive actions of others across the hospital became predictable, Amalia began to refer to an informal structure of joint hospital regulation. She explained that this structure produced, in her mind, a number of informal policies:

- Everyone was entitled to medical care; intake procedures were modified, and the requirement to record a patient's family history and national ID card details was dropped.[2]
- Medicines, regardless of cost, were offered freely to patients staying in hospital, including to patients with no ID cards and no insurance.
- Family members and close acquaintances of patients, having received a minimum of training from a floor nurse, could administer medication, including medications administered through IV setups.
- All medical samples were sent for testing individually to expedite processing—a change that altered the rhythm by which workers and human materials moved through the hospital, machines were operated, and which, no doubt, cost the institution more.

- Patients who hired private nurses received less attention from floor nurses so floor nurses could concentrate their efforts on those patients who could not afford private care within the diminished public system.
- The very young would be attended to more quickly and more thoroughly than the very old.

Amalia explained that her colleagues understood what they were doing in terms of a responsibility to their patients, and to their professions. They talked often about growing restrictions on their practice as a consequence of crude budget cuts and out-of-touch policy. Nurses, doctors, and other hospital staff talked about their actions as "the right thing to do." For their part, the few members of management I was able to interview seemed aware of what one individual described as a "problematic culture of noncompliance" on the floors. This same individual also described feeling like he was trapped on a sinking ship.

Amalia broke many rules as she cared for Nefeli. While the little girl was at the hospital, nurses and doctors did everything to help her. Members of the custodial staff would spend time with her before and after their shifts. The administration, on the other hand, seemed to actively try to block my interlocutor at every step. Amalia spoke with failing self-restraint.

"I had to have conversations with coworkers every time she needed something. We'd start by asking if we could do what was necessary, knowing all along that we were going to do it anyway." Amalia's voice trembled. "These conversations were about agreeing to take a risk together. Is a little girl's comfort . . . her health . . . worth a job? Can you imagine having to have this conversation!"

I met Amalia over the course of the next few weeks to discuss her take on acting morally, and on the broader implications of systematic disobedience among public-sector health care workers. We talked of little else. She recounted case after case where nurses, doctors, staff at various desks, floor managers, custodial workers, and sometimes even patients and their families would decide how things should work on the floor. In these discussions, she often referred to the hospital administration and "the state" interchangeably, and on many occasions equated the broken hospital with the broken city. Her "hospital as state" analogy was compelling. She came to suggest that what she and other frontline health care professionals were up to was a form of protest against inhumane government economic policy trickling down "on their heads" in the form of swelling numbers in emergency rooms, dwindling resources, and tightening restrictions. She often evoked the kind of morally inflected age-old Greek tensions between "the people and the state," or *ethnos* and *kratos*, described in detail by Michael Herzfeld (1985) (and Campbell before him, 1964).

Greek hospitals have been sites of political resistance in the past (see Panourgia 2009, 148). The prospect of following along as workers became more systematically organized against austerity measures was very exciting to me at the time. I asked about processes of building consensus on the floor. I was interested in learning how people were recruited or included in informal policy making. Had this become routine? How did people know what to do, how to partici-pate, how to initiate the kinds of discussions Amalia described? I began to see the parallels between what was happening on the floor at the hospital and what was happening among advocates and others on the streets of Athens. I began to think about sociopolitical microcosms and patterns of collectivization. Amalia participated actively in these discussions, and we made plans for me to visit her workplace.

All this came to a stop, however, during our eighth meeting. Actually, Amalia didn't show up to our eighth meeting. I was worried and texted her. She replied the next morning, and we rescheduled. She came to our rescheduled meeting looking terrible—she hadn't slept in two days. She sat and, without a hello, told me directly that Nefeli had died. Amalia opened her mouth to say more but found no voice. She closed her mouth, swallowed, sat silently looking at her hands, then over to mine, then to the ground. Rousing herself out of whatever memory cap-tured her during those few seconds, Amalia smiled at me and offered to recount what happened. I listened. She described the scene: a little pink toy truck loaded carefully with a handful of stickers on a nearby chair, a doll Amalia had brought for her sitting on the nightstand beside Nefeli's bed. Ventilation equipment puls-ing rhythmically in the background.

I put my notebook and pen back in my bag. There would be no discussion about reinventing the *polis* within the clinic, no back and forth on improvised responses—in that moment none of that really mattered, and clearly it was inappropriate to take notes during this conversation. I felt my philosophical concerns becoming inconsequential, like those playthings at the bedside of this deathly ill child.

Amalia took me back to 9 p.m. two nights before our meeting, when she had turned off the lights and stood by the window in Nefeli's room.

"At this point," she recounted, crossing her arms tightly, "Nefeli was still with us, but her suffering was ending—I could see death was coming just as fast as it could."

The little girl died five hours later, in the nothingness of a darkened hospital room just after 1 a.m. Her father was in detention at the migrant prison. Her mother never came to find her after dropping her off nearly three weeks earlier. Amalia held her hand as the world became a little emptier.

Nefeli's body was removed from the room by an orderly and a custodian. She was wheeled to a lower floor, washed and prepared for burial. Truth be told, however, Amalia wasn't sure what happens to the bodies of dead migrants, even locally born migrants like Nefeli: unlike the bodies of Orthodox Greeks, which receive religious rites and transparent processing to a funeral home, migrant bodies are disposed of more mysteriously by state agents.

Amalia quit her shift early, intending to find Nefeli's father at the Petrou Rali prison on the edge of Athens—the city's very own zone of exception (Agamben 1998). Arriving by taxi at 6 a.m., she was stopped short of the door by a police officer demanding to see her identification, then was harassed in the hallway by another police officer who accused her of working for a human rights NGO; but ultimately she was permitted to see the man she sought. She told me that the encounter was awkward. They cried together. At first, Amalia cried for Nefeli, but then also at the sight of this man—emaciated, hopeless, now unmoored from any meaningful human connection in his life. Amalia recounted, "I can't imagine what he was thinking. This sadness will stay with me, as it will stay with him."

Amalia returned to the migrant prison once again to tell Nefeli's father about his daughter's final weeks of life. Months later, after his release, he brought sweets to the nurses who worked with Amalia at the public hospital. He asked to see Nefeli's room. Amalia, a few other nurses, and a member of the custodial staff stood with him and felt his pain as this man closed his eyes. He knew they had done everything they could for his daughter and that she didn't die alone; but this gave him little comfort. *Did she glance at the door? Did she ask for him?* With nowhere else to mourn, he returned to the floor regularly and sat silently by the room in which his daughter took her last breath.

I spoke with this man only once, and with Amalia present. While allowing me to tell his daughter's story with reference to his wife, he asked me to not name him in my work, in any way: no pseudonym. He told me that he had never wanted to go away from his family, that they (meaning the police, I assumed) took him. He also explained that he missed his wife and that he did not know where she went. His old neighbors didn't know either. He assumed she had been taken too, so he asked a friend to inquire with the police. This friend—a Greek citizen—reported back that the police had no record of her. This news led Nefeli's father to assume his wife had died somehow.

"We held on to each other so tightly. We had nobody else in Athens. No family, I mean. Just us." He showed me his clenched fists as he said this, then lowered them to rest on the floor where he was sitting. "I cannot let go. If you have a daughter, and she dies . . . a wife, and she dies too . . ." He took an unsteady breath. "Do you stop being a father? A husband?" His mouth contorted momentarily. I asked if coming to the hospital helped him cope, somehow, with his loss. He replied, "I think my wife's spirit was here with my daughter when she died. I join them now. We're together again, in a way. . . ." He shook his head, looked at the floor, and said nothing further. The conversation was over, and we left him to mourn.

Walking down the hallway toward the exit, Amalia whispered that she thought this man held out hope that his wife was still alive and that she too would return to the hospital to look for her daughter. We walked into the bright afternoon sun, leaving the hospital behind. Amalia's eyes were bloodshot. We sat on a curb, and I began to look through my notebook for a blank page.

"He carries so much guilt . . . it's heartbreaking." Amalia continued: "We all hope his wife will come, but we suspect she won't. It has been too long."

I found a page, but it resisted my pen. I remembered him asking me to not name him in my work.

"It must be so heavy . . . and for you too," I said, drawing a horizontal line on the paper, then making a series of little lines through it. "I mean, he must remind you of Nefeli. Of that night."

Amalia nodded her head and reached into her bag for a pack of cigarettes and a lighter. I wrote the word "hospital" under the doodle and then crossed it out. I did the same with "mourning," "hallway," "waiting," and "spirits." I noticed Amalia's eyes dart toward my notebook as she lit her cigarette. I began to feel self-conscious. I went to write the date above the doodle and the crossed-out words but just stared at the page for a moment before I put the notebook away. Although I thought my scribbles on the page were pointless at the time, they have taken me back to this scene over and again (Taussig 2011). The tension between the doodle and the crossed-out words—incomplete attempts at capturing something; messy renderings—have brought to mind my unresolvable desire to connect with this man who could not, and to understand his world.

Like the patients in the waiting room at HMA, Amalia and Nefeli's father occupied different but co-emergent worlds. They were feeling their way through various, multiple crises, orienting meaning and action to shifting realities and to the phantoms in their lives, along with countless others struggling to make sense of the clamorous neoliberal-fed chaos of the emergent ordinary. As I spent more time with Amalia, I became interested in the instances of co-emergence in her life—specifically, the times when hospital and clinic staff came together to resolve critical situations, and when Nefeli's father would come back to the floor. I was curious about whether these recurring instances structured, or were otherwise generative or evocative of, something novel in reference to Amalia's relation to the social world. Were these repetitions producing difference? Amalia also began to pay attention to these instances—maybe because I kept asking about them.

The returning of Nefeli's father to the hospital was uncomfortable for my interlocutor. He brought his situation to her mind again and again, making present powerful memories of his daughter and wife well beyond the normative parameters of biomedicine's hospital-based therapeutic time. With each subsequent visit, Amalia was seized by this remembering—she, quite literally, stopped in her tracks at the sight of him. Amalia questioned how this man was living outside of the hospital. She began to worry about his future. She worried about Golden Dawn, the police, and the various other dangers this man faced in the worsening world beyond the hospital. With every returning, this man blurred the frames of the hospital scene. He became a switchback of sorts between the realm of her work and the conditions of life in the city. He concentrated realms of care and processes of depletion.

The repeated coming together of hospital staff to resolve critical situations also evoked the tension between care and depletion. As the austerity measures continued to create shortages, as management continued to monitor and inter-fere, and the risk of disciplinary action seemed to grow, Amalia and her col-leagues continued to take risks for their patients. She chalked this up to their compassion for others, for fellow human beings in difficult situations, and to not being able to stand by and let someone suffer to "save the state a few euros." The tension between care and depletion would spill onto the streets, occasionally, when nurses went on strike (for example in July 2013, May 2015, June 2016)—times when, for my interlocutor, worn-down frontline workers called for an end to what they saw as a war on compassion. They called for a return to care work as it once was. These strikes were times when the apparatus operating just below and sometimes against the procedures and policies set out by hospital manage-ment became at least partially visible as a traditional political form: bare compas-sion becoming shared passion.

As Amalia oriented to the new connections and realities in her life, as work and life bled into and out of each other, as she struggled to make sense of instances when her work life became a public life, my interlocutor was coming into a new ordering milieu and a new terrain—a new playing field shaped, in part, through responsive action to the threats and realities of structured uncer-tainty. As I will discuss below, this was not revolutionary ground; that is, Amalia was not on a footing to take on what we might describe as traditional resistance action intended to disrupt neoliberal governmentality. She was angry, fearful, and disappointed, but felt no impulse to be disruptive beyond her support for the occasional large-scale protest actions in Athens—and even then, she saw this support as the "only possible option," as a default for anyone with self-respect and a sense of self-preservation. Rather, Amalia's new terrain was defined by an impulse to sustain. In this, my interlocutor was not unlike countless Athenians whose lives were upended by austerity, who—against all odds—struggled to care for themselves and their loved ones as they used to do, while their livelihoods, life chances, pleasure and desire, were systematically depleted.

Sustaining, for Amalia, came to center on doing what she knew was right, although this did not always *feel* good. Nefeli's father's returning to the floor over and again brought back painful memories and difficult worries, but she continued to spend time with him. She took risks to help vulnerable patients, or to support colleagues who were doing the same, that created uncertainty and spiked fears. She stood in protest with other nurses even though this exposed her to scrutiny. All this—like her occasional participation in anti-austerity action—achieved for my interlocutor her re-inscription as a moral subject, a human soul of a familiar sort (at least to her), on a shifting terrain. All these repetitions of sustaining action signaled to Amalia that although her world was being changed, she had not become lost. Austerity tinted her actions with worry and sadness; yet insofar as these feelings related to actions that were *hers*—the results of her choices in a life that had become stretched between care and depletion—Amalia took the negative feelings emitted from her interactions with leaking spaces, invisible connections, and ghostly presence as affirmation that she remained, even if her familiar world had not.

When Nefeli was brought to the hospital after her unsuccessful treatment at the HMA clinic, Amalia began to compare what was happening at HMA and what was happening on the hospital floor. At first, my interlocutor saw positive continuity between one site and the other: HMA stood in for primary health care, and the hospital continued to serve its purpose of treating those with more acute needs, albeit now with the risk-taking and creative interventions of frontline staff. It appeared that the crisis had simply produced a structural change. However, as Nefeli's condition worsened and as HMA pressurized, Amalia began to see things differently. She began to suspect that the connection between HMA and the hospital had become "wicked" (to use her word). She put it in poignant terms:

"HMA keeps unhealthy bodies moving. The hospital pushes broken and breaking bodies into the grave more quickly." Amalia raised her eyebrows and shook her head.

She was tracing the contours of a consolidating necropolitics grounded in a neoliberal capitalist valuation of the subject's worth.

"They still complement each other, but I see things more clearly now. Greed is at the root of all this."

Asked who she thought was profiting from the expansion of humanitarian clinics and the dismantling of public health care, Amalia hastily named the troika, then she specified Germany and France, and finally added "rich Europeans": a popular catchall category for European elites with financial interests in the neoliberal experiment playing out in Greece. She insisted that "these people" had no regard for human life.

So, on the surface (and like the clinic itself) my interlocutor's efforts at HMA appeared to be complementary to the actions she was taking with her colleagues at the hospital: two aspects of the same human drama resulting from crisis-driven austerity, uncertainty, and injury among the growing precariat. Thus, just as the clinic appeared to play into the consolidating neoliberal biopolitics, so too could Amalia's impulse to sustain be seen as supporting a regime that was downloading responsibility for primary care to clinics like HMA while cutting expensive emergency services and complex and long-term care for those individuals who had become less productive. But when conditions worsened—when the impulse to sustain came more regularly and urgently, ultimately becoming a project of care against depletion—something changed in my interlocutor that would trouble interpretations of her work in terms of capitulation to the new biopolitics.

The actions Amalia and others took at the hospital reduced profitability for those with a stake in cutting public health care costs. Operations at clinics like HMA might have allowed the state to cut public health care funding, but these cuts produced responses within hospitals that reduced savings and produced friction between frontline staff and management. So, as clinics like HMA supported the dismantling of public health care, they also—albeit indirectly—contributed to conditions that stirred various multiscale alternative projects motivated by and grounded in compassion, that were supported by protective apparatuses, that ultimately challenged neoliberal logics at the heart of new austerity health care policy. Thus, Amalia's new perspective marked an important moment for my interlocutor: she was aware that restructuring of health care in Greece was shaped by a neoliberal biopolitics of abandonment benefiting the elite at the cost of the health and sometimes the lives of the precariat; but she also developed a sense of herself as someone who was opposed to these efforts and willing to act accordingly with others and thus, like others, somehow spun out from, or differentiated by, the forces and structures of neoliberal mainstreaming.

Amalia, in her unsettled and unsettling commitments to the work of HMA and the public hospital, her relation to patients, their families, and her coworkers, actively practiced and encouraged something else, something radically immanent to neoliberal biopolitics, something off the grid. This *something* grounded in commitment, in sustaining, in a sense of familiar self on unfamiliar terrain, was not a politics, by which I mean Amalia's actions along with those of others had not been gathered under the sign of political identity, consensus, or type, and were beyond subjectivity, and ideology (Ngai 2004). So, whereas the restructuring of health care in Athens was producing something radically immanent to the neoliberal biopolitics that drove it, something that troubled the logics and effects this biopolitics followed and sought to bring about, it did not spark a traditional resistance movement as such.

Asked why she thought this was the case, Amalia shook her head, saying she didn't know other people's commitments and, anyway, didn't have time or the energy to be part of something more coordinated. She went on to say that politics wouldn't work anyway: the problem was that money was being siphoned away from care spaces, and she believed that no form of protest could bring the money back without regime change—which seemed unlikely to happen. Amalia also balked when I suggested she and her colleagues, along with patients and their families, were acting in the spirit of solidarity. Amalia rejected this idea, which she characterized as "activist-speak" for the same kind of efforts others termed corruption. Instead, she insisted, people were working together not for the explicit purpose of challenging or troubling the state, but according to what they knew was right. This seemed to me to go against what she said earlier about the wickedness of those profiting from neoliberal governmentality: How could she not see her actions as a form of resistance against the "wicked forces" of depletion? Amalia's response changed my thinking about cooperative action: "You have it wrong. I hate what the government is doing to us . . . and I protest. You know I do. You've seen me out there! But I'm not political in that way all the time, especially when I'm at work. I'm me."

Amalia signaled that being herself had become a form of protest, an act of resistance. The world had changed in ways that made pre-crisis selfhoods, commitments, and modes of relating to others based on non-neoliberal codes of the human tantamount to resistance in certain spaces. She was not acting in solidarity with others, nor was she colluding with others in networks of corruption and noncompliance. She was holding on, like others, to commitments and practices that marked a better life, even if this meant ducking the forces and conditions that structured the normative direction of things around her, from the space of the state's hospital or the NGO's clinic. My interlocutor and others like her became an echo, or perhaps a haunting that created floating borders, which appeared and disappeared, and along which the *what might be* of a coming situation emerged.

One of the lessons Amalia asked me to take away from HMA's waiting room is that when accelerating vulnerability becomes apparent—when sick bodies sit side by side—the normative distinctions between people, and peoples, become less absolute. She was careful to point out that this did not imply that the waiting room made people the same; she was simply pointing out that within the *special space* of the waiting room—behind the murmuring and rhythmic silences—something was happening. The way she talked about this context led me to think about the recognition of co-emergence. We might say that vulnerability comes to constitute a condition of sociality that renders visible and affirms what individuals have undergone (their past), are enduring (their present), and seek to achieve (a future) and, in this, sustains by revealing vital connections without necessarily forging commitments. Individuals become encouraged by circumstances into awkward intimacy.

Some weeks after I met Nefeli's father, Amalia began to notice that he was becoming unwell. He was losing weight, and she could see a rash on his chest whenever his shoulders fell forward, causing his collar to droop away from his skin. She offered to accompany him to HMA. Of course, this man was familiar with HMA and resisted going. Amalia thought he feared the memories the clinic's corridors would evoke. My interlocutor didn't press the issue, although this new development made it easier for her to be with this man who now, she decided, needed her help. Amalia kept an eye on him as the days wore on. She hoped he would accept her offer before his health became much worse.

"We can probably treat whatever he has at HMA. If it gets worse, he'll end up here or at some other public hospital. It will be a lot easier to help him at the clinic. I hope we're not watching a slow suicide attempt."

This new situation helped Amalia to feel more comfortable around Nefeli's father. Before this, she felt a connection to this man but didn't understand it. She couldn't relate to him, really, and didn't really know how to interact with him. She was not invested in his future but worried about it. She never held a conversation with him that went beyond Nefeli. Their occasional interactions were always sad, and at times Amalia expressed a wish that he would move on from his loss, and move away. Yet, again, she felt connected to this man—an "awkward" connection, as she once described it.

"Every time he comes, I feel happy to see him, but I don't know what to say, and my world falls apart. I become obsessed with people who are gone, absent things, and with impossible situations. . . . I don't want to be dramatic, but I go through a kind of small crisis of my own whenever he sits there."

In seeing Nefeli's father Amalia also saw a broken everyday, a personal state of affairs inverted and hollowed out by austerity. Her experience of the negative changes happening in the city, together with her connection to a life lost, a life disappeared, and a life ruined, troubled my interlocutor. Amalia kept turning the situation over in her mind. She thought about how she and her colleagues had done all they could within the hospital, but that the situation remained tragic because of the circumstances Nefeli's parents faced. Amalia remembered the shape of Nefeli's face whenever she looked at her father's; and of course, she remembered Nefeli's tears. These reflections, realizations, and recognitions marked the awkward connection between them with traces of intimacies my interlocutor did not intend. Until, that is, this man became unwell. His deterioration lessened the awkwardness of the intimate relation lingering from their co-emergence within a chaotic Athens. As he became sicker, she began to feel more familiar: more like a nurse.

Amalia met him at HMA on a Wednesday morning. He was given an antibiotic cream, some vouchers for meals at a nearby community kitchen, and was instructed to return a week later. He returned, as directed, for his follow-up. The rash had largely cleared up, and he looked better, although not well per se. He was still thin and looked terribly tired. Amalia considered his treatment a partial success. Before he left the clinic this second time, my interlocutor darted into the office, took another handful of food vouchers, and, as she handed him the stack, asked this man to visit her at the hospital again soon. He promised to do so and left.

This interaction did not go unnoticed. Maria chastised my interlocutor for giving him too many vouchers and for making a "public show" of her relationship with this patient in the corridor. Amalia was enraged by her manager's words but kept quiet. Maria knew the staff gave food vouchers away to people who could use them. She also knew that staff bent the rules to help people in need. The problem, it seemed to Amalia, was her doing so in the corridor rather than the private space of the examination room. Her manager appeared to balk at the possibility of one of her staff becoming friendly with a patient—an apparent breach of Maria's take on HMA's ethical standards. The sudden policing was grating:

"We can break all kinds of rules in the examination rooms—and she knows we do—but not in the corridor. . . . There are different rules in the corridor, public rules . . . for others to see. She's hiding behind her finger."

It appeared Maria was playing politics as usual, but the game was beginning to generate friction as the pressurization of HMA led the renegade actions of compassionate staff to leak out of the containments Maria cultivated through tactical ignorance. Maria instructed Amalia's coworkers to "watch her," warning that her "display smells of corruption." Amalia's coworkers indicated that they would keep a close eye on my interlocutor—something they laughed about later in the protected spaces of the examination rooms.

Amalia began to see further similarities between HMA and the hospital. These two spaces seemed to perform different health care functions, and the divide between management and staff at each space was formed by different interests and pressures; however, both spaces were being shaped in relation to neoliberal logics, austerity policy, and modes of regulation, and both spaces demanded excesses from staff. By accusing Amalia of flirting with corruption, Maria evoked the imaginary line between HMA and the hospital in which she was invested and on which she was staking her career advancement—a line my interlocutor, like many other staff at the clinic, troubled by working in both spaces. This line became present when staff was reprimanded for acting in ways that suggested the other space, but it remained invisible otherwise. Maria's comments implied that HMA was a different kind of care space—we might say a different ethical domain (Faubion 2011)—within which staff behaved differently than staff behave at the public hospital: a demarcation that appeared to reflect the aspirations of management at the clinic, but not the realities of care work being done at either site.

This is not to say that staff at all clinics and hospitals in Athens, including those that can be identified as "humanitarian" or "solidarity" clinics, were at odds with neoliberal-minded management. However, Amalia's experience in this instance reveals something important about how apparatuses in care spaces operate in general: apparatuses can become activated not necessarily around acts of compassion for patients and their families, but also to preserve the possibility of acting compassionately. Amalia knew her colleagues would protect her, not necessarily because they were in solidarity with each other, but because they participated in a cooperative social formation from which Maria was excluded and which Maria activated when she singled out Amalia's act of compassion for disciplinary action. The apparatus was activated by the existential threat Maria posed.

As I came to understand the relations among people in these care spaces without deferring to the ready explanations we might find in reference to biomedical frames, moral frames, and without defaulting to overdetermined terms like "solidarity," I observed that Amalia was becoming more comfortable with Nefeli's father. She cared for his daughter, and now she was caring for him. They were not necessarily comfortable around each other, but Amalia no longer felt panic every time she saw him. They had history. When this man came back to the hospital, as Amalia had asked, he did not sit in his usual spot: he took to cleaning the space. At first, he simply arranged hallway chairs against the wall and picked up a few random pieces of garbage. Later, he brought a small bag of cleaning supplies: some general-purpose surface cleaner and a rag. He sprayed cleaner on the rag and wiped the frame of the doorway that led to his daughter's room, the doorknob, and the plastic room number sign that was glued to the wall. Amalia asked the cleaning staff to leave a broom for him to use in one of the storage closets.

This man came a couple of days every week. Sometimes three. The spray he used left a sweet smell on the surfaces around the room. Amalia remarked that the area "wanted" this cleaning (*to íthele*), that it was therapeutic. The area and the room itself still evoked sad memories for my interlocutor, but this sadness was sweetened, somehow, by the traces of cleaner in the air. Like the flowers that appear at a place where someone tragically lost a life, the smell of Nefeli's father's cleaner marked the corridor in the same way: a mark of innocence on a wound, it signaled where a particular episode of loss had occurred, and evoked a sense of what had been taken away. In this, the smell brightened as it made legible and present Amalia's role, along with that of Nefeli's father and the others who cared, despite the risks they faced and the scars they lived with—both legible and present relative to a world that inflicted wounds on the vulnerable.

"I told him I liked the smell of the cleaner he uses," Amalia said, gesturing toward the corridor. "He said he mixes it himself. He thinks it works better than the cleaners we buy at the supermarket." She shrugged. "It's the same cleaner they used in their home. I guess Nefeli and his wife, wherever they are, would recognize the smell."

Niko from chapter 1, George from chapter 2, and Nefeli's father sustained deep injuries as the neoliberal regime consolidated around them. Niko became isolated as his political world unraveled, rendering his impulses harmful to those with whom he wanted to align himself and those he sought to protect. George became isolated as his social world turned inside out, leaving him completely dispossessed of a sense of his past, future, and self in the present. Nefeli's father was taken, held, and he lost his wife and daughter. In this he lost his sense of self, or, to borrow from Judith Butler, the ties by which *myself* and *you* are differentiated and related (2004, 22). He became isolated too, but not for long. Amalia and I marveled at this. Whereas this man could have resigned himself to his situation and moved on, alone, to compete in the struggle to survive "out there," instead he continued to return to the hospital. At first it seemed that this returning allowed him to establish a new rhythm, to regain a form of momentum that helped him deal with the ghosting he suffered of all meaningful content in an already precarious life. Eventually, however, I came to realize that in refusing to make a go at a life on his own—in continually returning to the hospital—Nefeli's father was trying to make stability, to sustain himself by pursuing something, something that felt right.

Nefeli and her mother mattered. The man they left behind found a way to reconnect with them by maintaining the last place anyone had seen Nefeli. In this he also became open, with those who cared for his daughter, to new possibilities of formation in relation to the normativities ordering the sustaining apparatus of which Amalia was a part. By returning to the public hospital and engaging in sustaining work of his own—work that allowed him to remain connected to those taken from him—he held his vulnerability in a way that evoked and affirmed vulnerability, past and present, among those who cared for his loved ones. In this shared but separate condition, Nefeli's father and the members of the apparatus conjured an inessential commonality: the act of maintaining oneself by way of sustaining action grounded in, and informed by, a commitment to care. Allowing others—victims of the present moment—to matter, and in this to put yourself at risk, structured a possibility of togetherness within injury and depletion.

There are many apparatuses that come into formation around crises in Athens. They are hard to pin down, describe, and observe, in part because they are always shape-shifting in relation to new threats and the conditions of their emergence. These apparatuses, these cooperative social formations, are not traditional political collectives, nor do they operate as such. They are something more elemental, complex, and responsive. They encourage resilience insofar as the participants seeking to sustain themselves in these formations come to utter: "In this moment I can let others take from me, and I can take from others."

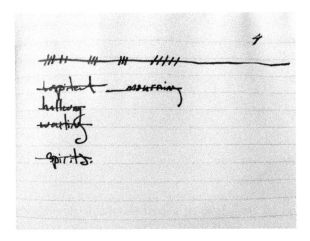

FIGURE 4. Field note. Photo by the author.

COMMON MATTERS

How Awkwardness May Create Possibility

He became nervous every time he walked into the neighborhood bakery, even though he looked forward to doing so. The woman who worked there on the days he came by knew him by now, knew his "usual"; but Samba still felt a pang of nervousness when he approached the door. He was nervous she might forget him, confuse him with someone else, or overlook him if the bakery was crowded. Being overlooked was perhaps the worst possibility. Being overlooked put Samba in the awkward position of having to signal his presence, of somehow having to draw her attention. These worries came to his mind as unhappy playthings, as charged scenarios he would rehearse on his way into the bakery and up to the counter. Most days they disappeared the moment he walked in and was greeted by the woman in the apron. Other days, however, when something unexpected would occur, the tensions in these scenarios would creep down to his heart and then back to his mind and double the bad feelings, which in turn seemed to fuel new, terrible scenarios.

Walking in, Samba scanned the space behind the glass display case, then, spotting the woman he knew talking on the phone near the cash register, he moved forward cautiously, gazing directly at her. He was moving his lips slightly. Someone else came in behind us. Samba stopped, glanced at me and smiled, then shifted toward the glass display case and pretended to inspect the tiramisu. I had no idea what was going on with him at the time, but his behavior struck me as odd. Why would he not simply approach the cash register? Why was he staring at tiramisu? Why were his hands in his pockets? He never put his hands in his pockets. The situation began to feel awkward for me too, although I didn't know why.

The woman noticed me first and the other customer, who had moved toward a freezer. She returned the phone to its base on the back counter and, turning around, saw Samba. She smiled. Samba, however, hadn't noticed that she saw him. He was crouched down and rocking back and forth on his heels as he looked at the tiramisu. The woman greeted him loudly as she reached for tongs and asked if he wanted the usual. As if woken up, Samba snapped straight, turned his head, smiled, and quickly said "yes." The woman asked if I wanted what he was having—a sausage wrapped in flaky pastry—but having already eaten, I said no. Smiling at Samba, I asked if I could buy him a piece of tiramisu. He laughed and said no, that it would make him "slow." The woman behind the counter proceeded to bag Samba's lunch and then moved to the cash register. She and my interlocutor exchanged some joking words about overeating and the dangers this posed to productivity. Samba put his coins on the counter and grabbed the paper bag she had placed there. We walked out into the sun.

The awkwardness that felt so heavy a moment ago had disappeared the instant Samba knew the interaction was going to go the way he expected—when the casual relationship he thought he enjoyed with the woman behind the counter was affirmed by her actions and words. At the time, this exchange and the moments that preceded it seemed to me to be, if not normal, then unimportant. Samba acted strangely. We all act strangely at times. I dismissed it easily. However, after getting to know my interlocutor, I realized that this situation held something more (as these ordinary situations often do). I came to understand that Samba's awkward behavior before he was noticed by the woman behind the counter expressed the visceral imprints of violence, dispossession, and abandonment on an individual who has suffered a lot in his life. It also confided a painful question: Will you see me as I expect you will see me?

This question was reverberating out of an uncertain although perhaps consolidating selfhood provoked by a situation that flipped normative presuppositions back over happier expectations cultivated by experience, albeit momentarily. When answered by the woman behind the counter, this reverberation produced a progression of synchronized, albeit now bent, sounds: risk-laden but smiling words, dirty coins on a counter, the snatching of a paper bag—affirmation of a different sort of encounter.

Samba was taking a break when I met him that day. His work partner, Taj, was sitting in a rusty old pickup truck parked around the corner from the bakery. The back was heaped with scrap metal. Taj was texting on his phone when we came back out. This was the end of the first part of their workday. After Samba had a quick bite, the pair would head back to the depot to unload what they had collected before setting off into the streets of Athens looking for more. The early morning was for searching industrial areas, and the afternoon was for searching residential areas.

Collecting scrap metal was not a new business in Athens. Besides licensed businesses that operated in this space for decades, small informal groups were also active across the Attica plain and beyond. Among those informal groups, some were more organized than others. The less-organized groups— sometimes just a few individuals—would operate occasionally, and usually whenever an opportunity to make money by collecting and selling scrap presented itself. These opportunities were sometimes tied to other labor activities those involved pursued or had ties to—often construction. Others worked more consistently along established routes that would yield enough material to sustain those involved. These groups would often consist of individuals who, for one reason or another, were unable or otherwise disinclined to find other work. Scrap collecting was difficult, expensive, and sometimes dangerous. Samba and Taj would talk at length about the weight their bodies bore and the damage this was doing. They would talk about their investment in the truck they relied on but did not own. They also talked about turf wars, stealing materials from derelict buildings and building sites, their visibility and thus exposure to police, and other dangers. Scrap collecting was a high-risk undertaking, but the rewards could be great.

My interlocutors came to this work from different directions. Samba traveled to Athens from Mauritania in 2007, and Taj arrived from Afghanistan in 2013. Samba was trained as a police officer, and Taj worked as a laborer in construction. The men had both spent time at a migrant reception center: Taj had just arrived in Athens, and Samba began to drop in looking for someone he knew. They struck up conversations with a Greek man who was volunteering at the center. They discussed the sovereign debt crisis, the still-sinking economy, and the lack of jobs available for migrants in Athens. It turns out that this man was a recruiter, of sorts. I never met him, but my interlocutors claimed he was very charismatic and approachable but quick to anger when challenged, although not prone to violence. When they first met him, this man used the language of economic decline they were hearing in relation to the crisis to convince them that finding work would be difficult. Samba was especially drawn to this talk, as he had spent years in the city barely making ends meet. This man cast his struggle in terms of a general trend of inopportunity and deepening insecurity tied to Greece's economic decline.

"I felt better about myself after talking to him. He made me think my situation wasn't just a newcomer's situation, but a Greek situation," Samba recalled.

"He told me I wouldn't arrive at a solution to my problems by acting like a migrant. I had to act like a Greek. He made me see things differently, and I began to trust him."

Taj told a similar story: "At the time, I wanted to travel to Germany, but he convinced me to stay and try things out in Athens." Taj squeezed his left shoulder gently with his hand. "I have a problem with my shoulder from an old injury. He told me I could get help for it more easily in Athens than I could in Berlin. He said this was because of the crisis. Things could be done more easily here if you know how."

He offered my interlocutors work in his scrap metal collecting business. They had been working for this man for several months when I first met them. They talked positively about their employer and their collecting work. I struggled to make sense of this man's activities and relationship with these individuals. It seemed to me that his interest in them and influence over them wavered between care and violence: a wavering I was beginning to see as characteristic of various Athenian spaces described to me by those who were involved in them in terms evoking "potentializing solace." This wavering confused and reduced things. Wavering spaces were ambiguous in that they were not easily located within established projects or relative to high-level moral narratives. They were awkward. These spaces imparted an understanding among those individuals who were drawn to them that the vicissitudes and variety of their lives could be distilled into one or two aspects, a couple of bare needs: for sustenance, explanation, shelter, medicine, love—whatever. Once involved, individuals tended to become entangled with each other and invested in these potentializing undertakings. These wavering awkward spaces incubated relationalities that evoked what we might call a *reductive becoming*, a becoming irreducible, with others.

Samba sat between me and Taj in the truck and began to open the bag the woman at the bakery had given him. His arms rubbed against mine and Taj's as he ate. We cruised around the Halandri neighborhood scanning curbs and empty lots for scrap metal. It wasn't long before we found something along a narrow residential road. Taj downshifted sharply as we approached an old cathode ray television sitting on a curb next to a dumpster. The engine revved noisily and the truck shuddered. I braced myself against the dash. Taj applied the hand brake when we came alongside the television. The truck stopped dead, and he opened his door. I began to open mine, but Samba reached over and held it closed. He handed me his bag from the bakery and jumped out behind Taj, who had already made his way to the back of the truck with the television. Understanding that I was to stay in the vehicle, I watched in the rearview mirror as my interlocutors broke the casing of the television, tore out a thick wire, something that looked like a cone, a circuit board, and a few other parts. They placed the salvaged pieces into a plastic box in the truck and tossed the remains of the television into the dumpster.

"A good start!" Taj exclaimed as we set off again. "Copper, steel, aluminum, some transformers . . . that's all money—about two euros."

Samba resumed eating his lunch.

"How much of that do you keep," I asked offhand.

"We keep it all," Taj replied sharply. I glanced at Samba, who had finished his meal.

He shook his head slightly. "No," he said, "you misunderstand, Taj. Our anthropologist is asking if we are being exploited."

These words made my stomach drop. Whether or not they were being exploited was on my mind, and this was indeed what I was asking—but it was not my way to ask so directly. I began to apologize for not being more honest but was interrupted by Taj: "We keep everything we make, but we pay to use the truck, the mobile phones, and we pay an administration fee. It's not much, really. We still make a living." He stopped the truck and jumped out with Samba to collect a number of old folding lawn chairs.

"This is life," Taj continued as the truck lurched forward again. "It's our life," he added, correcting himself.

Samba nodded. "Look," he said, as he grasped my hand. He held up my palm like a fortune teller and ran his index finger across my skin appraisingly. After a beat he said, "Your past was great, and your future will be great, too. Why not?" Taj laughed, and Samba let go of my hand. He showed me his palms like he was being arrested. "This is not our story," he said with a smile. "We've been brutalized."

The truck shuddered to a stop again, but only Taj got out. He loaded part of a bed frame into the truck. Samba continued: "If you're trying to understand us, don't bother asking about exploitation and violence. Those things were done to us, but they do not belong to us." Taj opened the door and took a swig from a plastic water bottle lying behind his seat before jumping in. As the truck lurched forward again, Samba added, "What we have is trust. This is something we came to ourselves."

In this chapter I will discuss how, as economic opportunity continued to disappear and precarity intensified across Athens, many of the most vulnerable members of the Athenian precariat responded by turning to sites of "potentializing solace." These sites differed in terms of the forms of potentialization they cultivated, the number of people involved in them, their location, and the modalities of solace they fostered; yet these sites were all awkward in that they exposed and thus challenged normative schema of various sorts. In this, awkward sites brought together, even if only initially, feeling awkward (as we saw in chapter 1), being awkwardly out of place (as we saw in chapter 2), and coming into awkward relation (as in chapter 3). The forms they assumed, the contents these sites drew together, and the directions they put into motion were out of step with what one might expect or anticipate, but in line with the ethic of cobbling together an advantage out of the ruins of various lives—they were both the products and the effects of finding oneself on a map that had changed. Individuals I knew who became involved in these sites probed and challenged the limits of the normative on various fronts, which in turn encouraged hope as it discouraged belief and, in this, I will suggest, created new possibilities along alternative terrains.

The possibilities I would like to consider, the possibilities I saw cultivated within awkward sites of potentializing solace in Athens, have to do with finding ways—not necessarily ways out of precarity but, more generally, ways to continue living on: ways of living a meaningful life that were not possible before. These ways became visible when participants in awkward sites connected with others in these spaces, regardless of who these others were. These connections created what might be considered social anchoring points: relations that could be known and were predictable in spaces that were full of the possibility of hope but otherwise uncertain and unpredictable. They also enabled the emergence of what Berlant has called consensual rubrics (2011, 225). These connections provided a space where individuals made sense of what was happening, of the present situation, in relation to their engagements with and investments in the hopeful, awkward space itself, rather than the various narratives they had readily available to them. These rubrics produced a satisfying sense of knowing otherwise that enabled living on; but—and this is where I move away from Berlant—in so much as they challenged the normative principles that would form subjects within established relations of power, these rubrics ran beyond the limits, boundaries, and constraints that made the realities and truths that each individual struggled with what they appeared to be. Again, Foucault has referred the undoing of normativities and the new perspectives this enables in terms of a process of desubjugation (1997). In this chapter, I will consider the coming to consensual rubrics and the edging toward desubjugation this enabled as a site of the animation of new possibilities of life with others: of becoming-in-common.

I should note that the connections I observed in awkward spaces differed from the relations built on cooperation among strangers who participated in the familiar spaces of established projects of various description—spaces where ways were rarely found, but taken. Working together that occurred in awkward spaces held different potentials from working together in established spaces— spaces already determined as sites of solidarity. I am not proposing that awkward spaces necessarily brought diverse individuals together, or that these individuals always entered into transformative relation. I am critical of romanticizing sites that trouble normative cultures. They were, after all, unpredictable sites where various trajectories, interests, and commitments intersected and produced various effects. Yet the ambiguities of awkward sites, their anti-foundationalist evocations, and the tensions between hope and uncertainty they held, provided conditions for a radical becoming-in-common that the being-and-doing-together of participation and cooperation in established projects did not afford.

Samba and Taj were very different men, with different interests, talents, and very different personalities. Until they traveled to Athens, they lived vastly different lives, spoke different languages, and identified with different histories. In Athens, they both experienced, in their own ways, individual and institutionalized racism, poverty, fear, the thin camaraderie of their expat communities, doubt, and regret. Yet scrap collecting in Athens—work to which they both turned in the hope of stabilizing and perhaps even improving their lives—did not evoke or otherwise signal these histories and experiences with any regularity, predictability, or coherence. This lack of, or ambiguous, referencing, coupled with the work-related imperative to navigate new and unexpected social terrains, effected an un-structuring that set the stage for my interlocutors to come to know each other not in terms of the shared, similar, or at least comparable aspects of their worlds, experiences, and beliefs, but in the process of feeling their way toward the futures they hoped to realize.

The notion of trust also runs throughout this chapter. Samba mentioned trust when talking about his connection to Taj. He talked about trust as something the two men came to, that was the foundation of the connection between them. Trust, it seemed to me, followed allowing oneself to become open to relations not grounded in traditional things: kinship, friendship, community, belief, common investment or experience. The possibility of trust also appeared wherever there was shared possibility of hope, or at least optimism. It was expressions that gestured toward hope and openness which, again, provided the conditions for the finding of new ways and possibilities. Trust held people together. It provided an anchoring point in awkward space. What's more, and as we will see in this chapter, trust was also instructive. It revealed and nudged. It corrected. In the past, anthropologists have considered the notion of trust in relation to knowledge management, systems and cultures of responsibility, and in contrast to cultures of suspicion and spiritual ambiguity (Corsín Jiménez 2011). Here I consider trust as a pre-political social form that animates and energizes relations in awkward spaces where the precarious become irreducible. In other words, I consider trust as a catalyst of radical non-normative subjectivities.

We turned toward the depot some hours later with the back of the truck stacked high with scrap. My interlocutors told a story about how they lost a refrigerator on a road near where we were: the result of a sudden maneuver to avoid a pothole, and a broken rope. They laughed as they recalled the mayhem this caused behind them.

"It was like a cow jumped out onto the road," Samba said, snickering. "Cars swerved everywhere!" He moved his hands around wildly and made screeching noises. This set Taj laughing, "We didn't know if we should stop or take off!"

"We stopped, though. We had to so we could re-tie the load anyway," Samba continued, "but we moved faster than we ever had before! A few people were shouting, but we got the thing loaded without trouble."

"Too bad it didn't hit a car," Taj said, smiling. "Scrapping a car might give us enough money to quit scrapping."

Samba and Taj had about an hour of unloading and separating ahead of them. They dropped me off near a metro station so I could get home. I offered to buy them each a pack of cigarettes and a beer to say thanks for taking me along. Samba walked to the kiosk with me.

"It will be my birthday soon," he told me as I opened the door to the fridge. I grabbed two bottles and closed it again.

"Oh, yeah?"

"I always went home to have a cigarette with my father on my birthday."

"What's your brand?" I asked as we walked around to the front of the kiosk. "Camel," he replied. "Taj the same."

"So how will you celebrate this year?" I asked. "What can I get you?"

Samba laughed. "I'm not telling you this to arrange a present for myself . . . although if you're thinking of me next week, buy me a phone card."

"Done!" I said happily. Samba always wanted phone cards. He talked to his sister regularly.

"My birthday reminds me of how long I've been here," Samba continued as we walked back toward the truck. "I arrived around this time of year."

I was surprised to hear Samba make reference to his journey to Greece. My earlier attempts to talk to him about it made my interlocutor uncomfortable, and he had told me so. I knew general information—where he traveled from, that he took a big boat, that he arrived at night—but that was it. The story of his journey remained a blank space until I got to know him better and began to notice what I suspected were its imprints on Samba. The more time I spent with him, the more I began to see—although not fully understand—traces of a difficult experience expressed in his revulsion to bodily smells, attempts to avoid crowded spaces, and his compulsive habit of checking the time. The memory of the journey remained, for him, ineffable; however, his preferences, intuitions, and habits provided glimpses.

I didn't pursue the matter of his journey that day, but I brought it up again the following week. We were sitting at a park bench in the evening talking about his sister and her kids. This was a happy topic for Samba. He had just wired money to her from a nearby store and was very excited to talk about what she might do with it. Perhaps she would buy his nephew the shoes he wanted, or a new phone charger she needed. Alternatively, she might save the money. She was very responsible. He pulled out his phone and played for me the birthday message she had recorded for him with her kids. I asked if he missed them. He nodded. After a moment of silence, he looked up at the sky and said that it was getting easier now that his life was a little more stable. I asked if it was harder when he first arrived. He said no, that it was hardest when he was on the boat. I took this as a cue to ask about his journey. This is what he told me.

He set out on a clear November night in 2006. The boat was laden with fifty-three people from various parts of northern Africa. He expected the voyage from Senegal to the south of Italy to take four days. Samba was twenty-one years old at the time, as was his friend and traveling companion, Jigo. The two men were desperate to escape the poverty, uncertainty, and racism they suffered at home. A month earlier Samba had quit his job, paid nearly three months' salary for passage, and was looking forward to what he thought, based on the stories he heard from friends and family, was going to be a promising new life in Europe. Once loaded with its human and other cargo, the boat slipped away from the port of Dakar, unimpeded.

On their second day at sea the captain informed the passengers that the ship was entering heavy weather typical of the Mediterranean that time of year. Everyone was to stay below. Samba and Jigo waited hopefully, but the days passed with difficulty; the small hold was becoming inundated with the stink of human waste, sweat, and other filth. Most passengers began to run out of food, were having trouble sleeping, and began to miss their homes and families; others were becoming restless. My interlocutor had remained quiet, hoping the close quarters would not rouse baser human instincts among the passengers: the tales of rape and murder on these ocean crossings were well known to him and, no doubt, to the others as well.

With the passing of time concern began to grow. General consensus among the passengers was that the trip was taking much too long. Making matters worse, the captain had ceased communicating with the cramped mass, as too had the small crew of four burly sailors. Speculation circulated within the hold that the boat had been sighted and was forced to detour; others wondered whether the captain was lost. Finally, after what seemed like almost a week at sea, one of the crew came down to announce that they would arrive that night and instructed everyone to prepare. A mixture of relief and angst gripped the passengers.

Well after sundown, at nearly ten o'clock, the passengers were instructed to move to the deck. In the distance, Samba and Jigo saw a small cluster of lights faintly illuminating a gray landmass, the borders of which blended seamlessly into the surrounding darkness. As the boat moved closer, they removed their identification papers and some money from the duffle bag they shared and placed them in the pockets of their coats. Lack of sleep and hunger helped the cool ocean air penetrate Samba's body; shivering, he waited with his friend. According to the instructions they had received in Senegal, a small boat was to meet the group offshore to ferry them to land, where another contact would lead the group to safe lodging for the night. Excitement grew on deck, although the captain and his crew members looked stern and drawn—all five of them remained in the control room, staring fixedly ahead.

Without warning, at about eleven, the boat came to a stop some distance from land, well away from the lights and well away from the shore. All eyes turned to the distant beach for any sign of a boat, but it was too dark to see. What happened next was seared in Samba's memory. One of the crew appeared on deck holding a handgun and instructed everyone that the contact was not coming, and the crew couldn't risk getting closer. Samba realized what was happening: he would have to swim to shore in the icy water, without his belongings, and would have to fend for himself once onshore. After some delay, and fierce shouting and crying, the captain agreed to take them closer to the beach; but eventually all the passengers, including some younger children, were forced overboard. At this point, Samba became separated from his friend Jigo in the water. Samba did not recall how long he swam, but when he reached the beach he lay numb and shivering on the sand, frozen and unsure if he would survive the night. He had a little money, no passport, and no idea where he was, but he wasn't going to wait for the authorities to find him. Forcing his frozen limbs into action, Samba began to move.

That night was a blur. Samba and another man from the boat—a tailor's apprentice from Senegal—lumbered to the main road and walked until they spotted a small shed in a field nearby. They forced their way in and slept huddled together on bags of what seemed to be cement mix. At daybreak they moved on, following the road at some distance to avoid being seen until they came to the town they had observed from the boat. For the first time Samba and his companion spoke at length. On the outskirts of the town they discussed their shock, fear, and a crushing sense of helplessness. They longed for the people and places they left behind. They walked closer to town, still unsure what they would do when they got there.

Later, sitting at the port, Samba and his companion ate a loaf of bread they had purchased from a bakery. Once again silence sat heavily between them, until, finally overwhelmed, Samba began to weep. The suspicion he had fought since arriving was confirmed when the baker did not understand his rudimentary Italian. The captain had cheated them all. Samba was on the island of Lesbos, Greece: an island in a country on the periphery of the Europe he imagined—that migrants traveled through, not to—where he had no contacts, no knowledge of an expat community he might contact for help, no sense of the terrain.

This story came out all at once. I scribbled down quick notes when I got home that night, but had many opportunities to ask questions and seek further details in the following weeks and months. With every retelling of the story Samba changed some of the details. For example, in subsequent conversations, he said the crew of the boat had locked the door to the part of the hold the migrants were kept in. Later he said the boat made several scheduled stops where other travelers disembarked. Another time he told me it was raining and very windy when he and the others were forced overboard. Sometimes he talked about helping another migrant reach the beach; and other times he said he swam alone. This bothered me at first. His story seemed to lack concreteness (Potter 1996). With time, however, I learned to recognize my suspicions and discomfort as evidence of my own subject position and turned to listening closely and recording new and revised narrative elements carefully whenever these uneasy feelings arose.

It is important to maintain particular defining narratives of one's life history, for various reasons—but this does not mean keeping them unchanged. The travel story Samba shared with me changed from time to time, certainly because time itself erased some details and created new ones, and certainly because memories of traumatic events can be fraught, but also because the recollection of memories can reflect one's active ordering and reordering of things—a making sense of the world or, similarly, of trying to locate one's self in it, as we will consider in more detail in chapter 5. While certain core elements of his narrative did not change, different experiences, pressures, moods, and situations my interlocutor faced produced subtle revisions: sometimes he recalled details that cast the journey as more violent, or planned but uncomfortable, or typical of a particular group. This revising of one's travel story in relation or response to new pressures, situations, and shifting conditions in one's life was typical among the undocumented migrants I met. These revisions indexed the vagaries of migrant life in Greece.

These revisions were made not only to the content of one's travel story, but also in the way of its telling. For example, many of my interlocutors who were newly arrived to Greece described their journeys as a series of places where particular things happened to them: a departure beach at night where they were given no lifejackets; a boat where they were crushed between people; sinking into shallow water when the smuggler cut holes in the rubber boat so islanders could not push the group back to sea from the beach. Taken together, these places provided an account of motion, of crossing space over time (Bal 1997; Mikkonen 2007). This mode of telling—of recounting place and event after place and event—communicated a lack of agency: it cast movement as tantamount to fate. Later, however, these interlocutors changed the way they told the same story. Although the core content of their travel narratives did not change, references to place were made in relation to doing: arguing with smugglers before deciding to board the boats without lifejackets; pushing for a place to sit on the boat that was not too close to the outside; calling out in the water to others. Doing connected places, sketching a path taken. The sense of being carried along by fate, chance, or by other people's actions that was prevalent in the narratives of new arrivals was replaced in their later telling by a feeling of agency that came from action taken—even if this agency was limited or hemmed by particular circumstances.

As I recorded more of these narratives I came to think about this particular change in the way of their telling, this subtle revision, as evidence of a fundamental repositioning of the teller's relation to a sense of causality: from some happening beyond one's control, to an occurrence that was in some ways within the realm of the teller's scope of influence. This revision reflected, to my mind, a shift in the experiential frame in the teller—a move from seeing oneself as someone who had been moved along by other people's doing, to someone who despite what was happening was able to affect one's own, perhaps small at times, happening. This shift did not accompany a major change in the life circumstances of my interlocutors: it did not occur in relation to the gaining of stability, or new hope, or options. Rather, this subtle revision occurred, it seemed to me, as an effect of telling and retelling one's story to someone else—as a consequence, at least in part, of having a listener.

Some held their arrival stories close, not sharing them with anyone. Samba, like many others, however, came to tell his story "at the right times," as he put it. Asked what he meant, my interlocutor joked that he was normally very off-putting, and that his arrival story helped him to make friends. Having arrived in Greece via some illicit pathway—regardless of whether or not one shared the story—appeared to mark an individual. Wayfaring to and through national borders by utilizing smugglers, sensing and following safe pathways, and by other unconventional means, leaves what I have called imprints on an individual: subtle signs in the form of, for example, unusual attunements, habits and preferences. We can take these arrival stories as a kind of disorganized minor literature (Deleuze and Guattari 1986), as a narrative milieu belonging to undocumented migrants who had not yet come to see themselves as a community or collective. This disorganized minor literature grounded in these changing stories that were shared in groups with hard edges but fuzzy centers, groups that were always in processes of aggregation or disaggregation, was *imminently* social—a gesture toward the collective. These stories evoked a sense of shared experience and, in their revision, narrativized the subjective work of making sense of and making one's way in the present situation, but they did not foster a sense of traditional community.

Samba told Taj his travel story shortly after they met, and Taj had told him his. They had also talked about what they sought to gain from scrapping, about their current living arrangements, and about their medical troubles. Taj had trouble with his shoulder, and Samba complained about his back. When things became boring in the truck and at other quiet times they also talked about their lives before they arrived in Greece. They found some commonalities, but not many. He wasn't really curious about Taj's past life, Samba confessed to me; rather, these were conversations intended to probe and communicate values and commitments. Samba suspected this was also the case for Taj. These conversations were about the possibility of establishing familiarity and trust.[1]

The connection between Samba and Taj was fundamentally different from the other relationships in Samba's life. Shortly after my interlocutor arrived on Lesbos, he and the man he met on the beach were approached by local volunteers of an informal aid organization—one of several that have operated on Lesbos for decades. They gave the men some basic supplies, advice, and sent them on their way. In Athens, Samba left the man he met on Lesbos, who had made contact with an acquaintance and decided to try his luck crossing to Italy from Greece's western shore. Samba was hopeful that his friend Jigo had survived the swim to Lesbos and, figuring Jigo would eventually make his way to Athens, turned his mind to trying to reconnect with him. With survival and reconnecting with Jigo his primary objectives at the time, Samba sought out other Mauritanian or Senegalese migrants in the city in the hope that they might offer some support—or at least a place to stay.

Unless they already had established contacts in the city, or were able to quickly make new ones, many newly arrived undocumented migrants lived in Athens in small, often interconnected groups of other newly arrived undocumented migrants. These small groups were loosely formed around nationalities, as a result of allegiances or friendships established en route, or by chance as newcomers met and helped each other on the streets. Small groups were also formed within reception centers, prayer spaces, squats where individuals found shelter, or in other locations where new arrivals found support. It was common for individuals to come and go into and out of relation with others, forming and dissolving these groups according to work opportunities and other factors such as the threat of violence or the opening of opportunities elsewhere. In this way newcomer groups were very unstable, while providing newcomers with a fleeting or at best temporary, often fraught, stability.

Samba was afraid to register with the authorities or to ask for help from NGOs or other humanitarian groups or take help from generous Athenians, so he made his way to Victoria Square, following the advice he was given on Lesbos. He arrived at the square not knowing what to expect but soon understood why he was advised to go there. Samba encountered a number of migrants in the neighborhood around the square. One of these people showed him a safe place to sleep that night. He spent a few days hanging around the neighborhood, talking to whoever would listen.

"I thought being quiet would be a death sentence, you know, like fading away," Samba explained.

One of the people he met—a Nigerian man who had been in the city for a few months—had asked around and told my interlocutor where he might find Mauritanians. Samba hadn't encountered any other Mauritanians up to that point and, realizing they were likely few in the city, followed this man's directions.

"I needed help. I needed help the moment I agreed to step foot on that boat in Senegal—to be sure—but I really needed help in Athens. My situation was getting worse." Samba crossed his arms and looked up. "The only thing I had at the time was my name and my nationality. I needed to find people who would place some value in them."

My interlocutor eventually connected with other Mauritanians. This group—really just one slightly more established family and a few of their friends—provided him with shelter, food, and connected him with their social networks. They provided the conditions for Samba's becoming more stable and moving toward hopefulness.

As he settled into a slightly less precarious situation, he began to turn his mind, once again, to finding Jigo. The men had known each other for years and had traveled far and endured a lot together. Samba was certain that if he himself was able to swim to the beach, his friend must have been able to do the same. (On this, I later discovered, Samba was correct.) So, as my interlocutor made his way, day by day, earning what little money he could, he also took whatever opportunity he found to ask about his friend. He asked other migrants, trusted employers, and he sent messages to Jigo's family and friends back home. Samba also asked around in the place where he took free language lessons: a safe place where migrants and others were welcomed and supported in the city. During this time, Samba also began to reflect on his situation. The fate of Jigo pinned Samba's life onto Athens. This was at once a lingering question—a point of thoughtful returning—a labor, and a reason not to move on. Despite poverty, uncertainty, and fear, Samba could have dedicated himself to amassing whatever resources he needed to move on, and then done so; but his absent friend kept him in place. Samba was stuck.

Being stuck, my interlocutor had time to figure things out. He had time to find opportunities, to learn where dangers lurked, and to interact with others. Being stuck afforded Samba the opportunity to become familiar with the social space of the city and to find a life for himself within it. It also afforded him the opportunity to rehearse the distance of time from the beach on Lesbos to the coming familiarity of Athens. He began to see stress points, crucial intersections, and began to draw up explanations and stories with the resources he had access to. This work of figuring things out, of finding one's way, was also the work of self-authoring: of writing one's self relative to some consolidating sense of the situation. Until he started scrapping, Samba saw himself as a migrant who, like so many others for their own reasons, became stuck in Athens and was starting to sink in.

Taj was less willing to talk to me about his journey to Greece and passage to Athens. We were friendly, but I had the impression that he didn't trust me. Taj was sudden and quick to anger—I was always cautious around him. Whenever we talked about his past, Taj would offer whatever he wanted, and I'd listen. I'd rarely question him or ask for more detail, and I'd never ask Samba to fill in blanks, even when he offered. So, when Taj told me he came to Greece from Turkey, I didn't ask how long he was in Turkey or if he came to Greece by the northern border or by sea. Then, when he told me he took a train to Athens, I surmised he crossed in the north and made his way to Athens to meet someone or, perhaps, to take up some prearranged labor or pursue some opportunity. In other exchanges, Taj mentioned paying a group of smugglers, walking to reach the point where he crossed into Greece, being wet on his journey, being threatened, never losing his things. He also mentioned feeling a sense of great disappointment when he arrived in Athens.

I found it interesting that Taj intended to travel to Germany but ended up staying in Athens, especially as he arrived at a time when violence against migrants was on the rise and the economy was still worsening, meaning many migrants were losing their jobs. Even if he found a lead on a job, why would Taj decide to stay in Athens? Why, with Germany's reputation at the time for being a safe haven where migrants were treated humanely and were finding both economic and social opportunities, would anyone decide to stay in a city in obvious rapid decline? Again, many new and settled migrants—regardless of their status—were leaving Greece between 2011 and 2014 when the country's northern and western borders were still relatively passable. Why would Taj stay? Thinking his decision to stay was far enough away from the story of his travel and arrival, I asked him about it.

"I came to Athens to join friends who had been here for a few years and were planning to move on to Germany. One of them had been beaten by the Golden Boys, so they all decided to leave." Taj looked me in the eye when he mentioned the Golden Dawn, or the "Golden Boys," as many migrants referred to them. He spoke carefully. "I couldn't go with them, though, because I ran out of money. I didn't think the smugglers would take so much."

His story was beginning to make sense. We were sitting on a curb. The sidewalk behind us—like many sidewalks in Athens—was broken where tree roots had pushed up and cracked the pavement, forcing walkers onto the street. There was a long scrape in the road in front of us: something heavy had been dragged. Beyond the scrape was a car mostly covered in an old tarp held down by bungee cords hooked underneath it. The rim of the rear driver's-side wheel had sunk through the flat tire that surrounded it and into the pavement below. Feeling encouraged that he had answered my question, I asked another one: "Why travel south to Athens from where you crossed? Why not continue north to Germany? You could have met your friends in Berlin instead of Athens. Wouldn't this have been quicker, easier, and cheaper?"

Taj shook his head. "You've never made a journey like this. You use airports and pass by border guards; people like me walk, swim, and hide in the back of trucks. We live in different worlds. I *was* going directly to Germany, but my route was through Athens."

He wouldn't elaborate beyond this, which I found frustrating at the time. All the other travel stories I had heard told of difficult, but rather direct pathways to Athens. Taj was the only undocumented migrant I had encountered up to that point in my fieldwork for whom Athens was not an intended destination or otherwise obviously "on the way" to somewhere else. I couldn't help but think he was hiding something—a suspicion I returned to, time and again, whenever his response to my questioning of his chosen route would pop into my mind. It wasn't until months later, after talking further with Samba and others about their journeys, that I began to consider another possibility.

The routes migrants took to and through Greece were contingent and constantly shifting in response to and in anticipation of social, legal, economic, and political situations and processes within which those making the precarious journey were embedded and subjected. In other words, migrant routes were not simply a matter of start and endpoints, but rather accumulations of tangible and situated engagements (see for example Cossette 2016; Ingold 2007, 2011; Jackson 2013). My question to Taj was ignorant of this. By stating that he *was*, in fact, going directly to Germany, my interlocutor challenged the teleological, sedentarist, state-centric perspective on movement I unwittingly voiced by asking him, implicitly, why he detoured through Athens (Malkki 1992; Nail 2015;

Papadopoulos, Stephenson, and Tsianos 2008). His response and my later conversations with others challenged me to see the possibility of a mode of movement informed by attunements (Stewart 2011, 452) to a world that spun individuals out onto topographies fraught with danger and uncertainty. Continuing onward in the most direct way possible sometimes meant joining other migrants who shared one's perspectives, understandings, and imaginaries, or seeking intersections of other migrants, things, and circumstances that held the potential of opening passages.

Athens was along Taj's direct route to Germany insofar as directness was not determined by normative mainstream navigational sensibilities but by one's willingness and ability to continue moving toward some desired future elsewhere. Tim Ingold has described the ability of a migrant to maintain movement in terms of *wayfaring*: a skilled feeling-tinkering practice guided by one's own past experiences, limitations, and practical knowledge of the world, as well as one's ability to improvise and to creatively adapt and respond to different situations as they emerge (2000, 219–20; 2007, 162; 2011, 154). By questioning Taj's route, I was unwittingly critiquing more than just a travel decision: I was effectively questioning his wayfaring, which, as I suggested above, was an elemental component of undocumented migrant narratives of self, narratives that marked individuals as having something in common with other undocumented migrants. This questioning must have stung, considering Taj went to Athens so he could continue with others toward a better future but was ultimately left behind by those individuals when he came without the resources required to continue wayfaring. Taj's relation to migrant collectives was fraught from the start, it seemed, and asking why he did not go directly to Germany was tantamount to blaming him for this.

The relation between undocumented migrant pathways, the narratives they grounded, and the forms of sociality they made possible played on many factors. If Samba's relation was bolstered by his becoming stuck and actively seeking out others to whom he could relate, based in part on having arrived by illicit pathways, Taj's relation was troubled by his having newly arrived and having been left to fend for himself. Together they represented, to my mind, opposites of a field of possibility for the grounding of collective in the sensibilities and sentiments fostered by traditional becoming-in-common, simply because Samba was actively seeking to improve his life through the making of connections with others, while Taj was isolated and appeared to want to remain that way. Both were pursuing projects that would improve their lives, projects in response to violence and other forms of subjugation, projects that were bound up in conditions and relations of power that made the prospect of their efforts becoming part of some collective undertaking—a communitarian or even co-emergent proceduralist action—unlikely. This changed, however, when they began scrapping.

Samba's only request of the recruiter was for a small fan to plug into the cigarette lighter of the truck. I could see why a fan would be nice in a hot truck, but why set conditions? Why give the recruiter a reason not to hire him? My interlocutor replied, explaining that this was a test of sorts. The friends he was staying with had told him horror stories of extreme exploitation. Other undocumented migrants—especially those who had taken work in the agricultural sector—were being treated like slaves. Even migrants working around Athens in comparatively more comfortable jobs like carpentry, dishwashing, and installing air conditioners were being exploited. One young man Samba knew had worked for a handyman and his brother, at first for what he thought was a fair wage, but then without pay for two months. When he threatened to quit, they gave him twenty euro and told him to stay quiet, keep working, or they would call the police or Golden Dawn. They told him they were withholding his pay as reimbursement for the space he took up in their vehicle on the way to jobs and for the use of their tools. The young man was too frightened to fight back. He continued working for them for a week or so before he disappeared.

"There are many tricks. Many, many tricks! Greeks are very good at tricking desperate people," Samba told me. Taj nodded his head. He had been warned about this too. Samba continued, "The bosses always make you pay for something you need for the work you do, but the price is as high or sometimes higher than what they pay you. It's a trick. A trap."

I had heard about this before, about tricking workers into unrepayable debt situations, from another interlocutor (Alexandrakis 2015, 39). It seemed that, in the wake of the sovereign debt crisis, some struggling Athenians had become adept at the invention of personal debts, the assigning of obligation, and demanding of repayment. Samba was trying to figure out whether the man who had approached him about scrapping was trying to trick him.

"I didn't know anything about this work, but the deal sounded good. He told me how much the rent for the truck would be, plus his percentage, and the rest was up to me. How much money I made was up to how hard I worked." Samba looked over at Taj. "How hard *we* worked," he corrected himself. "But we didn't know we would be working together at the time."

"So, the fan?" I asked.

"Yes, I asked if he would provide a fan, because I wanted to see if he would treat me like a human being."

When Samba showed up to begin his first day of scrapping, he found a fan screwed to the dash of the truck. Its wire led into the glove box. When he opened the glove box to find a plug that would go into the cigarette lighter, he didn't see one: the wires were dangling bare. When he asked about this, his employer told him that the fan would work, but it was up to him to find a way to power it. He could wire it directly to the car, or salvage a plug that would work with the lighter. He could bring a battery. Whatever he wanted. Samba took this as a good sign. Like the success of this enterprise, it was up to him.

Taj joined them that afternoon. The recruiter drove around what would be the core of their territory. He showed them where to look for scrap to gather and how to expand their area. He then spent a few hours with them back at the depot demonstrating how to break down appliances and instructed them as to where to take the metals. At the end of the orientation, the recruiter gave them papers. They were given papers for the truck, papers for driving, and other papers. A few days later, before their first trip out scrapping, he gave them a few more papers—ones with their names on them. He explained that some of the papers were forged, but forged well enough, he assured them, to confuse municipal police or the odd traffic cop. He suggested that, if questioned, they should simply hand over all the papers in a stack. This would perhaps overwhelm the officer, or at least slow things down enough that the officer might become impatient and simply let them go. The recruiter told them that the more complicated the arrest—the messier it was—the less likely the officers would be to carry it out.

If other undocumented migrants were consumed by the nearly impossible task of amassing the correct papers to secure their safety from detention and deportation (Cabot 2012), my interlocutors were now in a markedly different position. They suddenly found themselves on the outside of a governmental rabbit hole. Although they knew the documents they were given might not protect them, they also knew bona fide documents might not protect them either—so why concern themselves with chasing paper? They had documents that were as good as any others. This thought made plain a public secret (Taussig 1999): government paper was just paper. With this, they rethought the value of government documents, which had been communicated to them by NGOs, humanitarian organizations, and by other migrants. The small assemblage of documents they kept in the glove box—their disobedient archive—exposed the hustle to stay safe from state violence, which drove most settled undocumented migrants to chase hard-to-get government papers, as a mode of state domination itself.

"We are visible in the truck and on the streets when we work, which is why we take precautions," Taj explained the first time we went out together. "We usually go out midday when it's quiet, or very early in the morning when it's still dark. We go on the same roads. We move fast."

Asked if they thought the documents in their glove box would keep them safe if they were stopped, Samba replied, "I don't know. Nothing's sure. I don't think about how to stay safe anymore. I think about making money. The papers let me focus on the money."

Taj was nodding his head. "Before they left, my friends told me to find work and hide from police and Golden Boys. But I can't do that. Safe jobs make you stuck. Fuck police and Golden Boys. Fuck that life."

Samba slammed his hand on the dash of the truck. "Yes" he said assertively, then set his jaw and looked out the passenger window.

Scrapping disrupted my interlocutors' lives in many ways. The disobedient archive that came with their new work was just one source of disruption. It nudged Samba and Taj away from the normative thinking among undocumented migrants about the issue of safety. They no longer looked to the papers they possessed, or did not possess, in relation to staying or becoming safe: the kind of survival auditing that frequently consumed individuals struggling to access state resources that might stave off various forms of precarity. Realizing that papers were just paper—that a forgery in hand, and under the right conditions, was just as good as the "real thing"—made a new critical perspective possible. My interlocutors would more fully realize this perspective as other aspects of scrapping disrupted their lives further and, as this disruption deepened, they began to feel awkward around other undocumented migrants.

Samba got the fan working on their fourth time out. He pulled some wires that led to the hole in the dash where a stereo would have been and used twist-on wire connectors he saved from a discarded light fixture to connect and disconnect the fan to them. This made life in the cab of the truck much more comfortable, if a little noisier. Taj was also becoming more comfortable behind the wheel. He soon mastered the truck's clunky gearbox and worn-out clutch, which freed him up to think about the route and how to navigate alongside, and despite, the other cars on the road. He told me proudly that he had never hit another moving car—parked cars were a different matter—or become stuck in the city's narrower streets. In fact, moving the truck along came to him rather easily. Stopping, on the other hand, was more difficult, and after spending a day with my interlocutors on the road I understood why.

During my first hour in the truck I learned two important lessons: the feeling of uncertainty that comes with riding in a vehicle that does not have seatbelts can ease quickly after a few blocks of smooth driving; and dropping one's vigilance, allowing one's body to assume comfortable postures, and falling into habits of inattention that have been cultivated in safer vehicles are mistakes when there is nothing between you and the windshield. The moment my interlocutors spotted scrap, the truck would stop dead. After a few bumps and some teasing from

Samba, I learned to keep a hand on the dash and would tense my back instinctively whenever one of them yelled "*ep!*" This was no substitute for a proper seatbelt, of course, but I avoided smaller bruises. I also became more aware of what was happening outside the truck. Besides scanning for items that might cause Taj to hit the brakes, I began to monitor other drivers more closely. I wondered if the occupants of the truck were not only in danger when it was in motion, but also when it was stopped.

Confronted with a scrapper's truck skittering to a halt, most drivers would apply their brakes too, and wait. Others would stop but also lean on their horns and shout, or both. Some more aggressive drivers would try to swerve around the truck. Occasionally, the stopped truck and those stuck behind it would attract the attention of pedestrians. Most people simply looked on but did not become involved. Other times, according to my interlocutors, they would shout and maybe wave their arms in disapproval. All this made Taj nervous at first. He worried someone would attack him. Over time, however, he realized that this was unlikely. My interlocutors described acquiring a sense for how others would respond to them, and for how to behave, by unlearning key messages they had picked up from other migrants and in the established spaces of rest and care.

"The first time we blocked a road and cars lined up behind us, I thought we would be killed!" Samba shook his head and laughed. "I was ready for a fight, but nothing happened." Samba turned to Taj. "I don't know about you, but I was surprised."

"Wait," I interrupted, "you thought doing this job would lead to you getting beaten up? Why did you do it?"

Taj answered. "OK. I thought I could do it safely, you know? I had seen other migrants digging through garbage bins by hand and thought I could do the same . . . work quietly . . . maybe at night. I didn't realize I'd be in a truck all the time. I also didn't realize that making real money meant chasing down every piece of scrap on the side of the road." Taj and Samba laughed.

Taj continued, "We've only been in one fight, but it was with other scrappers. Some Albanians. The Greeks don't bother us, really. They just sit in their cars and wait. Sometimes they yell. Same for the people on the street. Mostly people just look at us." Samba added, "I'd yell too if some assholes in a shitty truck blocked me from going to the shops!"

We joked for some time about what the people behind the truck could be missing, but eventually returned to the question of learning to read and, more to the point, anticipate their reactions. "I had to learn to look up," Samba said, lifting his chin slightly. "I realized I was always looking down before. I had to look up when they were around. When I began to look, I understood them more. Looking was hard, though—especially when I was out of the truck."

Similarly, Taj described a shift from being prepared for the violence he thought would come to becoming curious about how those around him were reacting when his preparation was met with nothing.

"I'd make fists whenever I heard beeping or people on the street talk loudly nearby. I was ready to go, you know? I'd turn to look for an attacker, but there was never anyone there, so I'd wait for a second, looking around. I was wasting my time! Samba started telling me to focus on what we were doing, so I did. He learned what Athenians would do faster than me—but I think this is only because he knew I was ready to beat someone's ass!"

The recurring lack of nonviolent reaction—and in many cases, no reaction at all—that my interlocutors experienced on their scrapping routes troubled what they expected and what they had seen in other spaces. As they caused disturbances by making noise or blocking traffic time after time, and were never harmed—even on occasions when police officers were held up or drove by when cars were stopped behind them, but did not intervene—Samba and Taj found themselves on unfamiliar, and certainly awkward, ground.

So, every day my interlocutors drove their rickety truck along the same set of routes within and around Athens, collecting discarded metals to sell to scrap dealers, who in turn profited from moving these materials into various global flows of recyclables for processing and selling back into manufacturing processes. From the interstitial spaces of the city (Lovell 2007, 317–21) to global markets, the network between my interlocutors' local circulations and various global circulations contributed to the rhythmic pulse at the heart of a non-mainstream yet familiar economic space. This economic space was immediately intelligible to my interlocutors who came to scrapping with pre-established understandings of the prominent codes employed in this space: euros per kilograms; buyers and brokers. Less intelligible, however, were the social dynamics along Athenian curbsides.

Samba and Taj found themselves in a position of having to navigate the tensions of an unexpected social field brought into formation by their work-related circulations, a social field that challenged the normative meanings, narratives, and understandings by which they had, up to that point, come to know Athens and their lives in it. As Taj explained one afternoon, "We knew where to go, but didn't know how to get along." Ultimately, my interlocutors turned to a strategy I came to think of in terms of *social wayfinding*: a mode of figuring things out by tuning in to the social effects of willful acts of being-in-place activated by unexpected differences in the social field. Social wayfinding was a way of probing the social topology, the underlying meanings and order of things. The way my interlocutors pursued social wayfinding, specifically by looking up and by consciously going about their business as others went about theirs, created moments of being present—moments of becoming grounded in which the normative edifice of self and place cultivated in other migrant spaces was slowly re-formed.

"Looking around and just doing our work was hard at the beginning," Samba reflected. "It felt like we were challenging the Greeks, you know. Inviting them to attack us."

"So, do you think you two were just doing what you had to do, or were you ambivalent about what might happen?" I asked, hoping to put him in one of his philosophical moods.

Samba lowered his head and pulled on his earlobe thoughtfully. "Maybe both? But, no, not ambivalent. I think determined, or resigned. We were trying a way to be because things were weird, and we didn't understand."

Trust made social wayfinding possible for Samba and Taj: Taj trusted Samba to look up, and Samba trusted Taj to have his back. Within the awkward context of scrapping, trust became a possibility in part because the demands and processes of the work structured conditions and situations that troubled the normative codes of the human produced and regulated through the intersecting powers of capital, nation, gendering, and racialization that in turn structured the condition of "becoming migrant" in Greece. The relationalities and the modes of trust that emerged within the spaces of scrapping did not follow or otherwise evoke the social norms and familiar logics by which undocumented migrants typically sought to create stability, safety, or the possibility of continued mobility with others. So, unlike the accounts of trust I recorded among undocumented migrants in other settings around the city—accounts that typically centered on mitigating vulnerabilities, or, more specifically, allowing oneself to become vulnerable in particular ways so as to establish or strengthen bonds that could lead to better, safer, futures—my interlocutors talked about trust in terms of activations, the same activations that enabled their social wayfinding.

For Taj and Samba, willingness to trust became a response to a shared sense that something in the world was not as they expected it to be: trust became one of my interlocutors' responses to unexpected difference. There was no tenderness in this trusting, no call to nostalgia or other feelings of familiarity. This trust, between two people who had become irreducible, who shared the same objective and had little else to lose, was about finding new ways to get things done, and to get them done together. If one of the two saw things differently, there was no trust, and the other was forced to take another look—that is, to reflect. In this, the repeated call to trust was a recurring site of formation of sorts, or, more to the point, a space of subjectivation. So as unexpected situations came up and my interlocutors worked to figure them out, they were coming into non-normative subjectivities: subjectivities formed on the outside edges of the normative. This was echoed in the way my interlocutors talked about the warnings they heard from friends who were concerned that their trusting one another was unwise. Taj was especially bothered by this.

"Fuck them. All of them. The ones talking from Germany know nothing about my life here, and the people who are here can only see trouble." I asked Taj what he told his friends when they warned him about Samba. He replied, "I asked them why they think this way. They always say something about him stealing from me or using me. They can't see past this. I think about that a lot."

Having worked with Samba for some time, Taj was not willing to listen to what other migrants had to say about trust—about the connection between him and Samba. To borrow from Judith Butler's reflection on Foucault's essay on critique (1997), he was not concerned about whether or not the opinions of others were correct per se, but about the very framework of evaluation itself (2002, 214). *Why were their opinions always the same? Why couldn't they see things in a different way?* Taj's concerns were radically immanent to the normative narratives and codes that regulated the enactment of migrants into being within particular relations of power.

After breaking down the objects they gathered on their first collection run, my interlocutors had them weighed, and then got paid. Taj didn't remember what he did with his share of the money, but Samba did: he bought sweets for the family he was living with and used the rest to buy vise grips and a large hammer. He brought the tools with him in the truck should they need to disassemble something curbside; however, they were most useful back at the depot. Taj used the hammer to break down large objects, and Samba used the vise grips to loosen and separate metals from fasteners and enclosures. Dealers paid more for isolated metals than they did for bulk scrap. Pulling things apart was worth the effort. Samba explained that the more effort he put in, the more money he would receive. This is how scrapping worked at the depot. On the street, it was all about speed, strategy, good eyesight, and, of course, luck.

Taj agreed with Samba's description of things. Appreciating how much more quickly they could operate with the tools Samba bought, Taj contributed two pairs of work gloves and a heavy pry bar some weeks later. With these tools, and more experience, they saw their profits grow. By the time I met them, they had the collection, stripping, and selling of metals down pat. They made several stops on their route to sort through what they had and weed out less valuable bulk. This made space in the back of the truck, reducing depot runs. Watching them break objects down roadside was mesmerizing: they smashed and stripped electronics and appliances at speed, flung around coils of wire and tangles of broken patio furniture, bent antennas and other awkward objects with ease; all the while they passed tools back and forth without saying a word. My interlocutors agreed that they were making more money than they thought they would when they first began. This, however, did not mean that they were satisfied with their income. They knew that the man at the depot was giving them a bad rate on some metals, and the rent they paid for the truck was unfair. They also begrudged having to pay the recruiter every week.

"I know that this is good. I mean, I *still* know that this is good," Samba explained. "It might not seem that way to others, but I know this." Samba's tone was flat—he was not trying to convince me. He was simply stating something he knew to be true.

"It's a little unfair, though," I interjected. "Other people make more money for the same work, don't they?"

"Yes, but we are in different situations. They're not migrants. All *we* can do is work and find ways of getting things done." Samba paused, then added, "Anyway, we're not all doing the same work. Others collect scrap to sell to a buyer. We collect scrap for a scrap collector who gives us access to his buyer, for a cut."

Taj, who was sitting nearby trying to balance a cigarette box on his finger, nodded his head, adding, "It's different."

The differences ran deep, and along clearly defined racial and socioeconomic lines. Taj noted that other scrappers—"Greeks and Gypsies," as he put it—could go door to door to ask for high-value items like old TVs and appliances, or could drive around neighborhoods offering, over loudspeakers, to clean people's cellars and storage spaces.[2] Samba and Taj could not. They were also missing out on the broken machinery, vehicles, batteries, and other items collected by scrappers with lucrative agreements for access to factories and other businesses. Many spaces were off limits, and most interactions were off the table for my interlocutors. So while "Greeks and Gypsies" found and exploited new economic opportunities, Samba and Taj were restricted to collecting mainly at the curbside. In this, they were more exposed than other scrappers: physically in terms of their visibility on the streets, but also economically, in that they had very little means of hedging against fluctuations in the price of scrap. My interlocutors were on the outside edge of this economic space, and they knew it. According to Taj, "Prices go up and down. Sometimes we find scrap, and other times we don't . . . but we always have to pay for the truck, and we always have to pay something to [the employer]. He always makes money, even if we don't."

My interlocutors were quick to point out that they still considered themselves lucky. However, they were also aware that they did not have the same access to the scrapping economy as other players. They worked hard and appreciated the pay they earned—and Samba repeated to me that the recruiter, now employer, was a good man who treated them as fellow human beings—but they knew what was going on. Contrary to what he told them when they first met, my interlocutors knew that scrapping was not a stable economic space in the context of a tanking national economy: various domestic and international factors dictated the prices of different scrap metals, and their truck was often in need of repair, meaning their take-home pay fluctuated considerably, even day to day. They also came to see through this man's suggestion that inopportunity and insecurity were tied to crisis-driven poverty. As Taj put it, "Having a few more euros in your pocket and a job to go to in the morning won't stop a Golden Boy from beating you."

Again, life was better for my interlocutors now that they were scrapping—they were making money, new connections, and were gaining access to new milieus of possibility—but the histories and conditions that structured inopportunity and insecurity for migrants in Athens remained.

When I met him, Samba was talking about scrapping with Taj as an occupation between scavenging and collecting: an awkward space of multiple social and economic in-betweens. Although they were hired by a recruiter who was a member of an informal association of truck owners and scrap depot administrators looking for an additional revenue stream—an extension of their established operations—the recruitment of migrants into this work produced an awkward frame, if not for anyone else but for the migrants. I thought back to the conversation we had about exploitation and, more specifically, to Samba's insistence that I must stop thinking about exploitation. His reminder that the things done to him and Taj did not belong to them stayed with me. We all operate within fields of power, and our actions are always already dependent on power; but I came to understand that *who they were becoming* within this field, within the terrain of scrap collecting in Athens, was in many ways radical to the context in which they labored.

This became very obvious to me one afternoon when I was talking to Samba and Taj about my grandmother's storage room. She had moved from a beautiful old home in Halandri to an apartment in the northern suburb of Vrilissia some years earlier. The storage room—a cellar, actually, where I had found the bundle of love letters years earlier—contained items left and forgotten by various friends and family members over several generations. Some of these objects were well over a hundred years old. In the process of cleaning out this space, I came across a number of small icons and crosses in various drawers, suitcases, and boxes. Some of them appeared to be souvenirs from visits to religious sites, others may have been gifts given at baptisms, others may have been kept in cars as protective objects, while still others may have been purchased or gifted for display in homes. Not knowing what to do with them, I began a small pile, which eventually grew to fill a box. Whereas most other objects were easily dealt with—old clothes went to the theater, furniture to an antiques dealer, the piano was given to a family nearby—the box of icons and crosses posed a problem: throwing them out was taboo, and nobody I knew wanted them. This was likely the same reason these items ended up in the storage room to begin with. Our solution was to take the box to the local church.

Taj scoffed when I told them this: "The priest probably scurried away with the box so he could strip the silver from the icons!"

Samba punched him in the shoulder. "I wish I knew you then," he said to me. "I collect things like this."

It turned out that Samba collected many things: watches, small toy cars, discarded keys. Icons, however, were his favorite. He reached into a black fanny pack he kept behind the passenger seat of the truck and handed me a small icon: an image of a saint. Samba didn't know the saint's name. I didn't recognize him either.

"It's nice, right? It's old, and someone used to care about it."

Taj rolled his eyes, "Don't be naïve: some people have icons because they believe, and others have icons because they're expected to have icons."

"Whatever," Samba replied. "It's still nice. I like how it looks."

Anthropologists have written at great length about the histories and multiple personal and collective significances of sacred objects. The disposal of these objects, however, has received considerably less attention, in part, perhaps, because of the myriad methodological challenges this topic raises. Yet here I was: someone who effectively disposed of something that was not meant to be disposed of talking to someone who collected discarded objects that were not meant to be discarded. This was an awkward interaction that quickly became a site of bonding between the two of us. We talked about doing something that was socially unacceptable, about treating these objects differently, about allowing objects that came to a secret not-mattering to matter again in new ways (Taussig 1999).

Samba handed the icon to me. I had seen hundreds of similar icons in my lifetime: small wooden rectangles fitting neatly into the palm of the hand. This one featured a balding man draped in purple robes with a long white beard. Like all the others I'd seen, the image on the wood he handed me was rendered in the Byzantine style. I couldn't tell how old the object was or how it was used before it came to be in Samba's fanny pack. The figure looked out and to the right as I looked down on it. I asked Samba how he got it.

"This one was given to me. I never find the wooden ones in the trash. I find paper ones though. In the garbage. I have a stack of them at home. I keep this wooden one with me in the truck and the paper ones at home. This old man brings me luck!"

Taj scoffed once again, then admitted, "Really, I don't know if it's your picture or something else, but this is working. It shouldn't, but *this*"—he gestured back and forth to himself and Samba—"is working." I handed the icon back to my interlocutor. He rubbed the saint's beard with his thumb.

Samba smiled, "You like having grandpa in the truck!"

Taj cracked a rare smile. "Why do you think I stop so you can check the garbage around churches, you ass! We've never found a piece of metal there, but you've hauled away loads of paper, haven't you!" Looking at me, Taj added, "People ignore us when we scrap in front of their homes, but they think it's strange when we're stopped in front of the church. Why shouldn't Samba collect these things? He likes them. This is a way he makes life better for himself. We can't do only what other people want us to do."

It's easy to explain away my interlocutor's collecting icons and other things as a hobby echoing his work life, or perhaps more cynically as a sign of his becoming stuck (once again) in someone else's designs. Yet, the time I spent with my interlocutors both in the truck and curbside led me to see things differently. Samba and Taj's collecting, and the collections that related to their work, created ambiguities that raised questions and opened the potential of possibility. To my mind, Samba's personal collections—and especially his collection of icons—extended their perhaps quiet but consistent troubling of normative cultures and expectations, stretching what was the potentializing space of critical intelligibility that developed in relation to their work to their lives beyond scrapping.

Like other Athenians who were coming to benefit from unexpected and perhaps unlikely but positive interactions occurring at sites of solace dotting neoliberalism's contact zones of abandonment, Samba and Taj were nurturing a relationality that gestured toward an inessential collective politics grounded in becoming radical. Critically, my interlocutors helped me to understand that at these sites this politics was not necessarily grounded or motivated by experiences of shared hardship or some sense of community, but was activated and catalyzed by the possibilities and perspectives produced by the multiple disruptions of having become irreducible and the promise of finding new ways created by trust. What I didn't expect was the reverberations these sites produced beyond their immediate spaces—the other activities and conversations in both public and private spaces—reverberations that synched up at unexpected moments. Seeing these reverberations helped me to recognize that some awkward sites, like the daily ritual of an Athenian bakery worker exchanging smiles and kind words as she hands an undocumented migrant his lunch on his way to work, were related and, more to the point, produced a kind of polyphonic interlacing and refrain that exceeded the codes of its constituent parts (Deleuze 1995; Guattari 1996).

When we parted ways that year, Samba gave me one of his paper icons. The one side had a print of the archangel Michael in the usual Byzantine style. The paper was glued to a piece of tinfoil: Samba's handiwork.

"You're flying away, so I'm giving you one with wings!" he said with a smile. I put the icon in my bag and thanked him. "I will be in a better place the next time you come." He said this with determination.

I nodded. "I'm sure of it."

I reconnected with my interlocutors in 2016. They were still scrapping, but things had changed. While they worked for the same man and drove the same truck, they were now beginning to collect nonmetal objects too. These they sold to other collectors—newly arrived Bangladeshis, according to Taj—who in turn sold them to recyclers. They also kept their eyes open for items that could be upcycled and sold in the growing number of secondhand and trendy handicraft stores across Athens, and online. They had another buyer for these.

The ecology of scrap collectors and scavengers had expanded and diversified. There were even small informal sellers' conventions, of sorts, organized over group chat—where collectors could sell their finds to potential buyers. Some Syrians had organized the one my interlocutors frequented.

"We're talking about making pocket money," Taj explained, adding, "but it's better to make some profit than leave something you know has value behind on the curb."

"So are these Bangladeshis and Syrians, like, partners now?" I ventured. "You all help each other?"

"No!" Taj laughed. "Fuck! What do you think is happening here? We don't know each other! I don't care about them, and they don't care about me! There's very little trust."

"Is it more like business contacts then, like a kind of agreement to work together?"

"Maybe, but not really. I see that they're doing something like us. Not collecting, I mean surviving. We're all surviving in this shit." He explained, "The scrap thing is just a common language. So there's something there, and we're looking at it."

Samba said again that there was no trust between them and these other collectors. He was also adamant that I understand they did not socialize with these other scrappers. Nothing like that. Furthermore, he made clear that this was not a "migrant thing," as he put it. Greeks were surviving too, and they were involved in this scene. They had called a Greek collector instead of the Bangladeshis when they came across a discarded collection of what looked like classroom maps: those large, colorful maps that rolled down from above a blackboard when the teacher pulled their string.

"I wanted to give them to the Bangladeshis for paper," Taj recalled, "but Samba thought this guy Takis might pay more. I would never have thought of selling to him until recently."

Samba agreed. "Something is changing."

FIGURE 5.   A collection of rolled-up classroom maps, Athens, 2018. Photo by the author.

RADICAL POSSIBILITY

Why Some Solidarians Believe
Solidarity Doesn't Matter

Niko began to refer to his social media silence, his self-distancing from anarchist collectives in Athens, and his general lack of a social life during 2015 as his "monastic period."

"Everyone takes time to fucking find themselves," he told me over a bad phone connection. "Maybe it took me so long because I have more shit to work through than other people. Maybe I'm more complicated. Don't worry, though," he continued, "I'm back."

I didn't know what he meant. Back in the fight against Golden Dawn? Back with the collective? Back to recruiting? To street action? I tried to ask, but he was already on a tangent.

We met some weeks later, on his home turf in the Exarchia neighborhood. We drank beer and talked about the "new Niko." He told me he was completely disillusioned with anarchism and collective action. He no longer believed he knew what was going on and was not interested in pretending that he did. At this, he asked if I could explain things to him: "You're supposed to be an expert—what the fuck is happening?" This was not the first time I'd been asked this question by an interlocutor; yet I was caught off guard to hear it from him—a man who generally knew everything. Maybe Niko *had* changed.

It was the summer of 2016. Anthropologists had been thinking and writing for some time about crisis as a distinct assemblage of power, knowledge, and subjectivity (Roitman 2014) and, critically, how crisis was being deployed as a mode of neoliberal governmentality—especially bluntly in the context of Greece. A number of compelling works focused especially on the growing sense of suspension, abandonment, and disillusionment that was spreading among Athenians (Knight 2015b; Theodossopoulos 2013; Panourgiá 2016; Papailias 2011). Greece's more recent crisis, the so-called migrant crisis, had renewed scholarly focus on the country's still-failing social security system and the ongoing struggles of citizens and now noncitizens alike (Faubion, Georges, and Van Steen 2016). This work raised new questions about precariousness, dispossession, and the possibility of political response. I was also exploring these themes in my own writing at the time (Alexandrakis 2016b), although I certainly did not pretend to understand "what it all meant." Realizing I was taking too long to respond, I simply said, "I don't know if there is one way to characterize what's happening. I think we should stop talking about what bankers and politicians are doing and just think about everyday people relating to each other." Niko's eyes lit up.

"Yes," he replied, "you're talking about solidarity. But what is solidarity? This is another thing I used to understand but I'm not sure about anymore. I'm playing anthropologist, though! I'll let you know what I discover."

In this chapter I will consider my interlocutor's desire to return to some kind of social action and his eventual participation in the daily life of a shelter for migrants. I come to focus on a conflict that simmered and popped between my interlocutor and a resident named Hassan as the shelter came under threat of attack by Golden Dawn. I locate this conflict within what I understood to be a more general register of small disagreements and misunderstandings that perpetuated bad feelings running just below the surface of many relations between and among solidarians and shelter residents. I show that with time, and increased external pressure, what had been regular but passing moments of tension within the shelter became land mines. As small explosions became frequent, they made legible a growing catalog of sociocultural incommensurables tied to formative subjective experiences and commitments that individuals refused or were unable to compromise, alter, or disregard. As pressure from the Far Right showed no signs of abating, and life chances for residents were steadily diminished by national and international political maneuvers aimed at managing the "migrant crisis," my interlocutors began to question if the shelter was sustainable. I will argue that this questioning marked a critical moment for my interlocutor—a coming to a working understanding of the political grounded in the experiences of solace that defined the new social terrain of his life.

I will argue that unlike accounts of collectivization and commoning that suggest that projects like the shelter promote coalescences, this site—which was under constant threat, and where all participants endured varying degrees of exposure to various forms of violence—can instead be understood as a site of practical co-cooperation. Conceptualizing the site in this way, we gain critical purchase on established understandings of such political forms as *solidarity* and *community* opening space for more grounded interpretations of such sites. Across Athens, various iterations of practical co-cooperation had rooted and spread since 2010, encouraging novel, potentializing critical engagements without necessarily leaving ideological imprints on participants. These co-cooperative sites, grounded largely on an ethic of finding ways as explored in the previous chapter, encouraged an understanding of oneself as having become involved in a co-emerged methodology of action that facilitated continuing on, despite things, toward a better life. They may have been rooted in places like the shelter I consider here, but they were also more diffused and less certain in identity: methodologies unfixed in form and content, feathering into and out of various sites at various times. Thinking with Jasbir Puar, I saw these sites as coming to form an assemblage within which intersectionalities produced intensities of various kinds (2007). Sites of practical co-cooperation like the shelter can be taken as interwoven with other sustaining and potentializing acts, encounters, processes, and spaces—both past and present—insofar as these touched the daily lives of individuals struggling against erosion, depletion, and the crisis-driven sense of uncertainty. The present case demonstrates that co-cooperation at sites of intersectionality can be world making in a way that is not reductive, not totalizable or essentialist. Subjects come into relation with practical truths that relocate the social, effectively providing new terrain for a remapping of the political. As Niko discovered, this remapping can be a radical experience.

In the months leading up to our meeting Niko had become restless again. He felt "the itch," he said. There was too much happening in the country, and he couldn't sit idly by. He tried to tune it all out at first. He told me he thought about deepening his silence by leaving the city. He thought about building a small house and growing a garden on some vacant plot of land. Although it seemed odd to hear Niko—a man who once showed me how to rig gas canisters to explode—talk about escaping to some quiet pastoral paradise, he was not the only one. Dozens of individuals I knew, including anarchists, leftists, and young people with no clear political leaning, described the same dream: a small house with a garden, far from politics. The initial and then spreading and deepening mass impoverishment that came with neoliberal austerity measures had driven a movement of people out of urban centers like Athens to family homes in Greece's rural villages. Now, it seemed, deepening feelings of disorientation and hopelessness sown by what many individuals saw as the surreal politics of 2015 were pushing too. A second wave, this time voluntary, appeared to be forming.

Ultimately, however, Niko stayed in the city. He explained that moving to the country required "a great deal of sacrifice," and anticipating that he would find himself in conflict with whatever neighbors he found there—neighbors he assumed would be supporters of the political Right (or worse)—Niko decided to scratch his itch by getting back in touch with some of his friends. These individuals were not the few who were involved in his violent and ultimately short-lived "protection campaign"; instead, they were involved in the food-sharing scheme he dropped out of shortly after joining. He learned that the scheme had fizzled, and the members of the old collective had drifted for some time: some tried to revive the collective, while others found other things to do. Among this latter group, some individuals were working at a shelter that served as a temporary residence for migrants. This was not one of the bigger occupied sites in Athens but a small space that housed only a handful of families. It was not in the Exarchia neighborhood, but closer to the seedier part of the city. Niko decided to help because, he explained, he identified with the migrants living there.

"The poor people living in that shithole became stuck when the border closed. One day they were moving, and then, because of the actions of some elites, they were unable to do anything or even speak. The same thing happened to me." The corner of his lip betrayed an effort to suppress a smile as he said this. He seemed to be proud of himself.

I couldn't hold back my disapproval. There was no way that Niko—by most accounts a very intelligent person—saw the events that shaped his life, not to mention his present situation, as equivalent or even comparable to the lives lived and conditions suffered by migrants fleeing war with barely more than memories, uncertain futures, the weight of endless life-or-death choices for them and their families, and whatever they could carry across perilous borders, on overcrowded dinghies, and then on foot across the fields and down the sweltering highways of a foreign land. There was no way this man who lived in an upscale apartment, who didn't worry about money and who could travel freely, thought he could identify with a family that was out of choices, forced to rely on the kindness of the anti-authority activists who had given to them a tiny space to live in, with others, down the street from a brothel. Was he back to his old tricks? Was Niko trying to be charismatic?

I lifted an eyebrow and said, "Seriously?"

Not missing a beat, Niko replied, "I just think we felt the same thing. We both felt panic. Panic reduces things. We both felt that."

"When were you panicked?" I asked. "After the vote?"

"It was a slow panic. It came on with my disorientation. It lasted a long time. I almost lost my mind."

Niko went on to talk about drinking every night in an attempt to blunt the feeling of building anxiousness that gripped him when he lay in bed to sleep—a condition that worsened as his world stopped making sense. He talked about poring over his social media accounts when panic attacks started coming during the day, as if the digital archive of his work for the collective could reinscribe meaningfulness and order onto his life. Being reminded of past campaigns, going over blog posts on protest strategy and skimming messages from various supporters and followers, calmed him. He also talked about a critical turning point when this strategy stopped working, when the archive failed to make things better. He talked about becoming obsessed with looking for evidence of his "poor judgment" in particular exchanges and "hidden meanings" in the words of his supporters and followers. Eventually, he became suspicious of the archive itself. *Had someone been tampering with it?* He described feeling as though everything was unraveling before his eyes. As with the "outside boys" from chapter 2, Niko found himself in a state of becoming undone, desubjugated, and not yet able to critically engage with the exposing limits of the normativities in his life.

As the panic attacks worsened, he reached out for help—or at least this was my interpretation. Before joining his old comrades at the migrant shelter, he spent time reconnecting with two of them offline. They talked about the old days, the common desires they expressed but now questioned, and the projects these commonalities made possible. He felt relief with these friends. He could be himself—his new uncertain self. The panic attacks didn't stop entirely, but he felt again a sense of belonging, albeit a sense of belonging grounded in the coproduction of a re-forming perspective on their shared past.

"I don't think it bothered them as much as it bothered me," Niko mused. "We were all disappointed and confused, but *they* weren't losing sleep over it! Fucking anarchists!"

He placed his beer bottle on the table in front of him and, with his index finger, pushed it back just to the point of tipping—then released it. The bottle wobbled upright.

"They found something to do . . . ," he continued, "something to fight for." He took a deep breath as he sat back in his chair. "I felt I needed that again. I had to get involved with something."

Niko was invited to present himself at the shelter's next general assembly: a gathering of residents, anarchists, and others with antiestablishment views and sentiments who were working there—a group that called themselves "solidarians" (*allilegyoi*). Niko snorted when he told me this. The term was not new but reentered popular discourse with the rise of social solidarity actions in Greece, across Europe, and around the globe from 2008 onward. Niko himself had used the term in his public communications, as he put it, "to appeal to a broader audience." However, to hear this word again at a time when he was questioning what he knew about solidarity—a time when it seemed to him that everyone, from political elites to young schoolchildren, claimed to be acting in solidarity with someone or everyone—made him uncomfortable. "Solidarian" had become a word, he suggested, that glossed particular forms of engagement and modes of relationality that were reminiscent of the action-activating work he and his comrades used to pursue; but, he continued, "solidarian" had also come to be used to deploy a valence of *ethical certainty* that eroded critique in conversations about the neoliberal uses of cooperative social action.

His objections to the term echoed the so-called "communist argument," as Theodossopoulos described it: an increasingly popular position among antiestablishment actors that framed social solidarity initiatives—and volunteer and informal humanitarian aid initiatives more generally—as simultaneously exploited by the state and not-for-profit organizations while also absolving state inaction and leaving the structural inequalities that perpetuate poverty in society untouched (2016, 169, 179). Niko's cynicism toward the term "solidarian," and the promises of social solidarity more broadly, had been fed by his confusion, isolation, regret, and perhaps resentment. Yet, he was willing—however awkwardly—to allow others to identify him as a solidarian so he might be permitted to participate in this space and perhaps ease, if not resolve, some of the bad feelings in his life.

Despite being caught off guard by some of the language he was hearing, and some of the more critical conversations he was not, Niko was comfortable in the assembly: it felt familiar. He greeted everyone and proceeded to talk about his greatest achievements as an organizer. He then talked about his various undertakings in support of migrants, riled everyone up with stories of following neo-Nazis to their meeting places and participating in street fights, and then asked for collective permission to join in the daily operation of the shelter. Niko was immediately welcomed by the solidarians, who mostly new him or of him already. This was notable as unlike other, larger anarchist-run squats and shelters where solidarians sometimes clash because of differing ideological commitments; here the solidarian side was rather uniform in terms of their vision for the project and the ideologies that informed it. One resident asked if he was planning to use the shelter as a new base for his political work.[1] Another resident asked if Niko knew how to repair appliances. A third resident asked if Niko was willing to accompany residents to their appointments with doctors and government officials. Niko said that he was not organizing anymore, had no idea how to repair appliances, and was willing to accompany people wherever they needed to go. A quick vote later, and he was in.

It didn't go well. Niko spent the next few weeks at the shelter doing nothing. The space the group had taken over—one of over a dozen such sites in the city— was dirty and run-down, but he didn't think he'd be much help cleaning, explaining to the residents that his talents lay elsewhere. His repeated deflections when asked for help led to one of the residents asking him—in front of everyone—why, exactly, he was there. He told Niko to either fix something or clean something like the other solidarians, or get out. Niko described this as a moment of intense personal conflict. He was embarrassed and angry. His impulse was to hit this man. He wanted to shout that he was an organizer, a communicator, and a fighter—that he knew more about collectives, occupying buildings, and acting in solidarity than any migrant at the site. Memories thundered in Niko's mind as his heart pounded in his ears. Yet he simply stood there, silently vibrating, unable to mount a meaningful response in this moment. He found himself in a new, unexpected intersection in his life with few resources to help him navigate. Indeed, like the residents and solidarians who undertook to create the shelter before Niko's involvement, my interlocutor was challenged with feeling his way through an unexpected situation. However, unlike everyone else at the site, he failed.

Niko left and didn't return to the shelter for a long time. He grew increasingly angry at what he considered to be the residents' boldness. He also noted that nobody came to his defense. Once again, he became suspicious that something was going on. He started thinking back to his interactions at the shelter. He stopped answering his phone and messages. He was panicking again and growing increasingly restless. When his friends came to find him, Niko was drunk and violent. He took a swing at one of them in the hallway outside his apartment, missed, and fell. They helped him back into his unit, put him on the couch, and left a note inviting him back to the shelter when he woke up. This bothered Niko. He believed they were taunting him. The bad feelings in his life redoubled, and my interlocutor began to reexamine, again, the archive: the emails, the texts, the social media posts, websites. He focused in on the latest messages to and from solidarians and the few he had received from residents. Nothing stood out to him until—in a moment he later described to me as "unsettling"—he glanced up to see the paper note his friends had left, now tacked to the wall above his computer. The word *xipnisis* (wake up) held his gaze.

Niko began to see a troubling trend. He was losing friends and becoming increasingly agitated and unhappy. Distance had grown between him and the people he cared for—other members of the anarchist collective, fellow organizers, and various supporters who followed him on social media and joined him on the streets when asked; people he used to talk about when we discussed resistance and solidarity—from the time when he broke with the collective to fight neo-Nazis, through to his becoming silent after the 2015 referendum and election, to lying on the couch in his spinning apartment with a bloody forehead. Now some months after his break from the shelter, as he was sitting with me at the café, Niko talked eagerly about this distancing. He referred to it as a kind of "necrosis," a deadening of his ability to connect, let alone relate to others. Every time Niko felt this distancing he turned to an increasingly panicky inspection of the interactions and relationships that gave form and direction to his "pre-crisis" world.

As we sat and talked about social necrosis and deepening isolation, I began to hear echoes of conversations I was having with countless other Athenians also struggling against the injuries, depletions, and uncertainties that were worsening everyday life at the time—individuals who felt awkward about, or even within, new sustaining socialities that were coming into formation as life became more difficult (cf. Cabot 2016). Niko experienced this worsening and articulated this awkwardness most clearly, and personally, in relation to the troubling of his understanding of solidarity. To be sure, Niko was well aware that social actions and collective responses were proliferating in Athens—and the term "solidarity" was being used by most involved to index their undertakings as a response to state violences and depletion; however, as his ability to mobilize action and orchestrate responses diminished, he regarded these diverse actions with deepening cynicism as social crutches propping up the neoliberal state. It all looked rather obvious to him, until he became involved and then confronted by someone with a very different perspective on the meaning of solidarity and collective response. He felt this confrontation very deeply. What was this man's problem? Niko had not done anything wrong, had he? Why could he not find words in response?

Niko was now playing with a loose string on his cuff. He told me he continued drinking in his apartment until one of his brothers found him. The two of them talked about what had happened at the shelter. They talked about the past few years and the state of Niko's life. Then his brother told Niko that everyone was hurting in their own way. He told him to accept his pain: to allow himself to feel it. I pressed Niko for more details of this conversation, but he shook his head. He didn't want to talk about his family. He pulled the thread a few times, allowing it to slip through his fingers. Then, tucking it back under his cuff, he said his brother changed his thinking. Everything had been shifting around him, and he was being shaken apart. He said he began to think that perhaps he was becoming isolated not only because of his dogged commitment to his political fundamentals, but also because of an increasingly desperate, and ultimately destructive searching for personal redemption. Like so many other Athenians who were unable to counteract the effects of austerity, Niko was struggling with shame, and, in his own way, he was becoming isolated.

When Niko went back to the shelter he was determined, he explained, to make himself useful. He wanted to do something—anything—so he began to clean. He cleaned day after day, even when the shelter was tidy. He would clean in places where people were socializing. He would clean loudly, and complained bitterly when asked to stop. Everyone began to refer to him as the rude janitor.

"I told myself every day, 'OK, I will not think about 2015. I will not think about last month. I will not think about how things should be.' And I didn't. I made it my challenge to just work near other people and not talk and not think, just have company. It was amazing."

Niko still liked when I recorded his words in my notebook. I was more obvious about it too: a small form of reciprocity. "You know what I mean," he added, smiling. "But then everything changed, again. At least this time, I was ready to go with things."

Niko was on the metro when his phone rang. He reached into his pocket but didn't get to it before the vehicle moved on and the signal was cut off. Seeing it was one of the shelter solidarians who had tried to reach him, Niko exited at the next station. One of the shelters in Athens was under attack. He tore through the streets as fast as he could run.

It was a simple, cowardly attack. A car sped up and skidded to a stop in front of the building. Someone leaned out of the rear passenger window and threw a Molotov cocktail through an open window. Solidarians and residents swarmed out to confront the attackers, but they had already fled. The fire did some damage but was quickly brought under control. Sitting with Niko in Exarchia as he told this story, I was transported back to when I first met this man. He was animated and passionate—captivating. He told the story as if he were there. I later discovered that most of the details he so passionately conveyed were incorrect, but this didn't matter at the time—or at all, really. At least not to Niko: the imprint of this memory was rhetorically powerful and self-justifying.

In the weeks after this meeting, I interviewed and spent time with some of the residents, as well as with Niko and a few of the solidarians—although I should be clear that I did not volunteer at the shelter. Volunteering was my intention, but tensions were running high at the site, and new people were not welcome.

Through interviews, however, I came to understand these individuals as differentially positioned subjects whose motivations to cooperate at the shelter were based on presumptions of being-together that were informed by disparate histories, experiences, political logics, and commitments. This led me to rethink what was until that point an admittedly totalizing presumption that the people living and working at the site composed a single community. In an attempt to gain a more nuanced understanding of the relations at the site, I turned my attention from easy interactions to moments of disagreement and agonism: interactions where people were doing the work of maintaining the relationalities that made the place possible. Yet, I found it difficult to think beyond simple framings of "community."

Right from the beginning I thought friction was creating opportunities for the performance of small forms of reciprocity. Regular acts of reciprocity, I assumed, served as the basis of ongoing cooperation that contributed both practically and symbolically to the social construction and maintenance of the site. This rather classic line of thinking led me to suspect that these interactions were productive of what Irene Peano (drawing on Marx) described as a "self-organized composition," meaning a collectivity of diverse subjects based on encounters that create flows of affect and desire, which in turn cultivate subjectivities that may ultimately overcome divisions (2016, 63). Continuing on this thread, I began to think of the site not as a commons per se, but as a coming commons or a work in commoning: a kind of multiple space holding countless unfixed thresholds or passages that promote connection (Stavrides 2016, 5). At the time, my thought was that perhaps life at the shelter encouraged generative encounters—that is, encounters that promoted a sense of being-together and having-in-common on which community and a traditional solidarity project could be built. I had, effectively, gone around in a kind of conceptual circle.

I began to feel uncertain. This uncertainty intensified whenever I spoke with anyone about how the shelter should be protected against the threat of a Golden Dawn attack—a topic of discussion that was still on everyone's minds weeks after the attack. Niko, along with many of the solidarians I met, talked about the firebombing not only as an attack on the shelter but more broadly as an attack on social welfare, anticapitalist and antinationalist spaces of compassion, sites that supported unregulated human movement and, generally, forms of social reproduction that challenged the nation's sovereignty. Hassan—the man who challenged Niko prior to the attack—as with most other residents I talked to, did not understand the attack in these terms. They surmised that Greek and European elites were sponsoring violence against vulnerable populations to maintain an exploitable group. Hassan and the others argued this was a universal phenomenon: politics as usual. They would remain at the shelter so long as living in this place was better than leaving. My interlocutors' understandings of the attack differed greatly and pointed back to the differential situatedness that inspired me to rethink my assumptions about community and solidarity in the first place.

The next assembly centered on the question of how to harden the site against outside attacks. Disagreements at the squat were becoming more frequent and increasingly volatile. One solidarian suggested that making the central discussion issue that of a potential Golden Dawn attack was strategic, as this was of common concern to everyone at the site. She suggested that those calling the assembly were hoping to use their common enemy as a rallying point around which everyone could come together and tension could be diffused. However, the assembly was a disaster. If, as Rozakou has astutely observed, assemblies were rituals that constituted political lessons of "solidarity" and of "being collective" (2018, 199), the lesson about to be learned by everyone was at the very limits of these concepts. There was strong disagreement over the significance of the Golden Dawn threat and what should be done: residents accused the solidarians, who wanted to establish a neighborhood patrol coupled with a public information campaign, of playing politics with their lives; and solidarians accused residents, who wanted to carry on as usual, of not knowing how to behave properly, in solidarity, with the solidarians and with the attacked shelter. Tempers flared, and the conversation shifted sharply from "what should be done" to "what are we doing here?"

A number of hotheads got angry and threatened to abandon the shelter. Four solidarians left the assembly promptly thereafter—an unexpected turn of events that triggered appeals from both sides for everyone to calm down. At this juncture, Niko told me, his heart was pounding: he felt as though another collective expression of solidarity and resistance might fall apart. Yet, it—"whatever *it* was," Niko mused—did not. When things calmed down, both solidarians and residents spoke passionately about how the shelter addressed or at least eased various bad feelings and aspects of uncertainty in their lives. Taken together, these comments sketched the contours of the Athenian context within and against which the site was situated: a context defined by multiple, or rather plural, differential forms of precarity.

As I reflected on the exchanges at the assembly, I began to see my interlocutors' efforts in maintaining the shelter less in terms of growing coalescence and more in terms of a co-emerged methodology of action against a complex topography of power. While this action pushed directly against the various state-sanctioned forces of abjection and precariatization that diminished the lives of both solidarians and residents, the activations by which this methodology consolidated and was actualized did not articulate some shared ideology, just as they did not necessarily gesture toward a single resistant collective form. I began to understand my interlocutors' relations as an "indirect politics," that is, a mode of political activity whereby individual actors communicate across the exclusionary forms by which their communities are established so as to bring about—although, critically, not determine or direct—collective response (Alexandrakis 2016a, 278). I began to understand life at the shelter as one of many manifestations of resistance I was seeing around Athens, through which various agents attempted to bring about their ambitions and desires by engaging in microsocial (inter)actions that enabled others to undertake action of their own.

Indeed, through everyday interactions, residents expressed their exposure to multiple forms of weariness and violence, as well as their need for sustaining sanctuary, while solidarians expressed anger with the forces of regulation and economization that structured the multiple injuries of abandonment and demoralization to which they were exposed. Put simply, the expressions of residents encouraged solidarians to resist, while the actions of solidarians supported residents. This enabled a connection between groups that evoked normative definitions of solidarity but was not based on a common identity, history, or shared condition; rather, this connection was based on the communication to others of one's state of affairs—communication that encouraged members of the other group to act in ways that nurtured one's own. Together, this defined a space of co-cooperation that became the shelter: a form of simultaneous response that created multiple possibilities, maintained and promoted by small but regular forms of communication that produced indirect connections between diverse groups with compatible albeit differing interests, fears, and ambitions.

Unlike collective political action grounded in identitarian forms, the actors that produced the shelter did not do so by appealing to a shared sense of being or having-in-common; indeed, the solidarians' attempt at the assembly to define a commonality nearly ended in disaster. The shelter was not a traditional ideologically coherent collective project undertaken by actors with a shared vision of the future, even though it expressed social cohesiveness and demanded change. The shelter was a co-emerged multiple front of different but related and interwoven cooperative projects that enabled my various interlocutors to sustain themselves against the multiple forces that threatened to worsen their lives. In doing so, the shelter encouraged among each actor a sense of *practical edging* toward a future that was different—albeit largely uncertain—but likely better. Critically, this edging also preserved the groups that co-cooperated.

Although they appeared to break along a clear divide within the squat, internally, these groups were multiple, interlaced, and variable. Within the awkward space of the shelter—a taken space where diverse individuals on different paths came together—the individuals of each group found ways with others of different but compatible backgrounds, plans, and hopes, others whose life situations evoked compatible milieus. The social anchoring points these in-group connections provided generated the multiple situated meanings of the space. With few exceptions—usually involving translators—these connections rarely crossed the resident/solidarian divide, forming instead two related territories of coming through injury. As ways were found that advanced their interwoven projects, and as social anchoring points were reinforced and cumulated, over time these "found ways" gestured toward groups grounded in more closely related senses of what was happening, in the present situation, in relation to their engagements with and investments in the hopeful, awkward shelter itself. These groups slowly churned alongside each other, producing intensities that sustained each correlate, keeping the site alive.

Niko was not one of the solidarians who got up and left. He stayed in part because he wanted to break the pattern of disengagement and distancing he worried was coming to define his life. He also stayed because he liked being there, despite ongoing friction with Hassan. He liked that the shelter provoked Golden Dawn. He also liked being involved in an activity that helped people. He admitted that his involvement would be a lot easier if Hassan left him alone; but he knew this was unlikely to happen. It was clear that Hassan enjoyed antagonizing Niko. Hassan was ill-tempered and popular with the other young men at the shelter. Picking on the guy who presented himself as a Nazi-fighting hero—they guy who demanded respect while doing very little of any use to anyone—was one of the ways he showed off to his friends.

Following the assembly, Niko eased up on the cleaning. Instead, he took to walking the hallways, checking the locks on doors, and testing the bars on windows. He installed a deadbolt on a back door. These activities worried some of the residents. Hassan took it upon himself to express what he described as "everyone's concerns" to Niko, stating plainly that residents feared he was inviting violence by making a show of securing the site. Niko rejected this, saying he was not putting on a show, and he was not inviting violence. He was just making "logical upgrades" to the shelter. Nobody outside the shelter knew what he was doing, unless—he added—Hassan was talking about it. Niko's account of the exchange ended there. Others told me that the two men had to be restrained. Following this, residents began to look suspiciously at the actions of solidarians, and solidarians began to keep more to themselves.

The heightened tensions at the site produced negative space between residents and solidarians where before there had been communication at the heart of the indirect politics that held the shelter together. It is not that the two groups ceased to communicate, but rather that suspicion and cynicism interfered with the reception of these communications. This space—a space generated by residents and solidarians themselves—forced attention onto the contours defining each group rather than the connections between them, effectively threatening to pull the shelter apart from the inside. Yet, while the site was tensed, it did not break. Residents remained, and solidarians continued to show up day after day. I noted that the connections nurtured within groups up to that juncture kept my interlocutors together. They trusted individuals in their own groups and remained committed to shared undertakings with them. What's more, it struck me that past co-cooperation between groups left positive residues on the space itself. My interlocutors often reflected on sustaining actions and expressions in relation to these positive residues. Even when things were tense at the shelter, various surfaces and objects—a repaired washing machine; a stack of coloring books left over from a children's program; ingredients from a shared meal in the cupboard—encouraged positive feelings.

The affective temporality of these sustaining intensities—the in-group dynamics and positive residues—was forward and backward looking. This held in check the negative space of the current situation, discouraging bad feelings from slipping into the affective terrains of hopeful futures and nurturing pasts. This dynamic was evident in the latter part of the explosive assembly when solidarians and residents spoke passionately about how the shelter eased the multiple differential forms of precarity against which they struggled. This talk bookended the present situation with memories and hopes that sketched co-emerged actions and directions, effectively diffusing tension or at least temporarily preventing it from worsening. This dynamic of containment also encouraged an unfixed sense of worth not defined in relation to some ideology, narrative, or project. Rather, this sense of worth was an echo of the containment of the tensions that corroded co-cooperation. Specifically, containment—continuing on despite the regular emergence of difficulties—produced a refrain of sustainability. Sustainability, coupled with the positive affects nurtured at the shelter, meant to my interlocutors that their projects in this space, as well as the space itself, was worth pursuing. Although there was no certainty or general agreement as to where the shelter might lead, or agreement on how it might get there, or why this coming situation was desirable, my interlocutors simply had a sense that the shelter and life within it were worthwhile. This sense—so long as it remained strong—made the shelter durable against the forces that would undo it.

Again, this is not to say that life at the shelter was easy during this time. Niko shook his head when I asked him if, despite the tension, he felt good about being there. He didn't, declaring, "Hassan is an asshole. I hate that fucking guy. . . . Also, I still don't understand the politics of the shelter, and that bothers me. Are we in solidarity with each other? No, not really. But also, yes? I don't know. I feel like I'm in solidarity . . . but it's a kind of unrequited solidarity! Maybe it's about resistance? Just resistance? A bunch of people pushing in the same direction? But really, we can't even agree on that! Does agreement matter? I don't know."

Niko was frustrated. Over our next few meetings I tried to tune in to that frustration, to understand it. Niko was game. We went over his experiences and thoughts. At first, I suggested that the place held radical possibility, that it was seeding a coming ethics and politics that were not yet coherent. This excited my interlocutor, but I immediately began to feel uncertain. This suggestion came too easily. Was I, again, making the shelter into something it was not? Niko didn't see it this way. He was excited to continue thinking along these lines. I realized later that my suggestion resonated with his ongoing reckoning with unreconciled commitments and past experiences. In gesturing to the possible coming of a familiar politics, I further fixed the stuck and sticky matters of his history that had caused Niko so much trouble.

Being at the shelter and spending time with solidarians didn't resolve the break he suffered in 2015. Indeed, just as his poring over old email, drinking, and isolation didn't fix anything, participating in a new action among solidarians also failed to make 2015 make sense. The revolution didn't happen. The government didn't fall. The people did not rise up. He still went over every detail and wondered how he could have misunderstood things. He still thought back to that brief moment at the protest and wondered how he could have been so hopeful. He still convinced himself, sometimes, that the people would remember that moment and take to the streets at the next provocation. Again, being at the shelter didn't stop all this, and my suggestion fed right into it. Specifically, my suggestion fed into the feeling Niko held on to that it was possible to return to some coherent, understandable politics. This possibility of return made Niko feel worthwhile: that the pieces of his identity would come back together, that all those wasted years of his life would eventually begin to fade when his political reality made sense again.

This realization led me to stop thinking about the shelter in terms of a project, or in terms of traditional solidarity. The shelter was evocative of a coherent undertaking, of solidarity's sentiments and commitments, but slipped solidarity's baggage of community and commonality. The shelter was evocative and remained that way. It was nurturing, and remained that way. It held people together in sometimes comfortable and sometimes uncomfortable, easy and awkward relation. The shelter was a space of solace that produced political force; but it was a multiple and unfixed force. The shelter was an incubator. It kept things alive and encouraged growth, but it did not determine form. It produced unfocused reverberations: the outputs of a mutual interlacing that preceded the effects of becoming together or becoming-in-common, that gestured toward political possibility by providing terrain emerged from the work of finding ways.

It was raining when Niko got a call that an attack on the shelter was imminent. He was in a nearby neighborhood, a short distance away. A solidarian from another shelter had sounded the alarm: they noticed a vehicle driven by a known Golden Dawn thug prowling the streets around the shelter. Niko felt a painful sensation in his chest.

"I read part of the message when the notification came up on my phone, but didn't open it. Then the group chat blew up. My phone kept buzzing in my hand, and I was shaking . . . you know? But I wasn't excited. It was something else. It became hard to breathe. I kept thinking about the deadbolt on the back door. I don't know why—maybe it was instinct, but I bent down and picked up some rocks from the street with my free hand. I put them in my pocket and instantly felt better."

Niko found Hassan standing on the street with a few solidarians and residents by his side. It was dark. Hassan was smoking, not talking much to anyone. Someone told Niko that Hassan's younger brother was in the shelter. He had just fallen asleep. Niko stayed with the group. Most faces were illuminated by mobile phone screens. He stood there for hours listening to other people's conversations. He was also aware of Hassan shifting where he stood, tapping occasionally on his phone, cracking his knuckles. Eventually, most people went in. Nothing happened. False alarm. Niko left at four in the morning. The remaining solidarians were passing around a bottle of whisky someone had brought.

Niko kept the stones in his pocket. He said he liked how they felt there: "Whether I throw myself into the ocean or join a firing line at the next protest, I'll be ready," he mused. We were talking about four stones. Not really enough to make a difference, given either scenario. Yet, he kept the stones in his pocket. He fidgeted with them at times. As months passed, the skin and oils from his hands made the stones darker. He would sometimes take a few stones out and play at stacking them when he drank or smoked. Niko's half-joking comment about the stones stayed with me. Whatever he thought of them (or perhaps at some point he stopped thinking about them, but kept them out of habit), I began to see the four stones as representative of some teetering between death and action. Over many years of thinking about Greece, I have come to pay close attention to stones. Stones, as Panourgiá has stated so eloquently, were substantive matter of modern Greek *Bildung* (Panourgiá 2010). Insofar as they were used in construction and thus the transcendence of ideality, in torture and resistance, in the coding of self and *topos*, they were elemental to the cultivation and self-cultivation of political subjects. Niko's stones were of the same stones Panourgiá described; they held the same possibilities and potentials, albeit unactualized. They were in-betweens. Blank. They were negatives that—as they were churned and churned in one man's hands—began to evoke something else, another phase, another significance. In this they were meaningful not merely as raw materials, but as something as yet *unfulfilled*. They were at once a reflection and a symptom of life in the current crisis moment.

Thus, the shelter was not unlike the stones Niko initially thought to use in its defense—stones that became stripped of particular meanings, worked, and reworked in time; stones that evoked multiple futures but realized none. Life at the shelter came with one's regular returning to tensions: in-betweens that evoked but did not demand, that invited a sustaining churning but not formation. Niko echoed this sentiment some time later in 2017. I had asked him to meet me at a park near the apartment where I was staying. We had fallen out of touch for a number of months, and I wanted to reconnect. He showed up with a friend from the shelter—a solidarian named Anitsa—whom I hadn't met before. As usual, Niko skipped the pleasantries. "Remember the discussion we were having at the shelter, about solidarity? You remember me telling you about that assembly, right? Then the fighting? I think I've made progress. I think I get it." Niko looked at Anitsa and smiled. She looked back at him blankly.

"Who I am now is different from who I was before the crisis. It's a matter of ideology versus reality. Austerity and 2015 made a strange world, and my politics couldn't explain it. This led me to the shelter, like the other solidarians who were there. As I tried to figure things out—as we *all* tried to figure things out—I took everyone else's broken politics and held them with mine. This created a jumble in my head, but I came to something."

He paused, I suspected, for dramatic effect. "Austerity achieved a kind of political sterilization." He smiled. Anitsa glanced in my direction. Her look suggested she had heard this from him before.

I took the bait and asked about sterilization. Niko began talking earnestly, as if trying to convey ideas before they evaporated from his mind. It was all a bit jumbled. He talked about his still ongoing conflict with Hassan, about residents and solidarians coming and going, about the persistent threat of an attack on the shelter. He described finding a more comfortable role for himself at the site, about new challenges and about the happenings at other shelters. Anitsa interrupted him.

"He asked about sterilization," adding, "remember?" She spoke with a slight accent I couldn't identify.

Niko was a little put off, but he focused. "It's simple," he said. "The elites waged a bloodless economic war on the people because we were out of step with their designs. We were becoming dangerous. They attacked the things on which we built our lives by making them meaningless. We couldn't organize or mount an effective response because the world was turned upside down!"

"But people did respond," I reminded him. "There were many, many responses—like the community kitchen and the shelter!"

"Right," he said, sitting a little taller. "These were survival responses. That's all. Regardless of how people talk about them now—back when they started, they were about survival. Not resistance or solidarity or whatever. We weren't able to think about politics. We were living through a massacre, a slaughter."

This is what he meant by sterilization. Political sterilization, really: action dissociated from thoughts of political responsiveness, undergirded by feelings of anxiety and need, oriented primarily toward matters of survival. I nodded, then turned my attention to Anitsa.

"Do you agree?" I asked. Niko fought the urge to continue talking. He shifted uncomfortably were he sat.

"I have a very different perspective," she began. "I don't think like Niko, because I haven't lived the same things. He's talking as a person who wanted to change the world—I don't get that. It's all too *masculine* for me." She smiled as she pushed at a crack in the pavement with the tip of her shoe.

"I know you agree with me," Niko spurted. "We talked about this!"

"OK, but wait," she said, nudging him sharply. "I'm just saying that you were a street fighter—but there are countless small places where people make a difference against terrible things. People like you don't usually care about these places!"

Niko was bursting now, but Anitsa continued. "The small stuff became disorganized, too. I used to do things a certain way because I believed it was the right way. You know? I started making different choices when my father lost his job and the money disappeared. This was a kind of sterilization too. It made me a person I didn't recognize. It hurt at first because I didn't know who I was becoming or what my choices meant for others, but I had to get used to it."

Niko seemed content with her conclusion and went on talking about desperate (politically) sterilized individuals coming together. As he talked, I thought more about what Anitsa had said. She noted that life could be skinned of political meaning in subtle, intimate ways. She knew small choices were important. They were ordinary, but not insignificant expressions of self and self as political subject—Anitsa's blurring of this line was productive. The mounting injuries and poverty of choice she came to suffer as her economic resources were diminished reoriented her engagements and the possibility of self-determination and expression through particular actions previously coded with political significance. With time, this state of affairs increasingly troubled her ability to continue interacting with the world in ways that were consistent with the political sense and agency she exercised before the crisis, edging her uncomfortably toward some other self.

As they talked, I thought further about the idea of political sterilization. With what Anitsa had just said in mind, the expression seemed extreme to me. They were talking about a kind of widespread reorientation of engagements driven not by ideology but something very elemental to the human condition: vital reworkings that come with the exigencies of bare need. The effects of this austerity-driven reorientation numbed the possibility of critical response at the level of both informal microsocial actions and resistance as a cohesive movement against the political system through which the crisis regime was implemented. Yet, this was far from sterilization or some kind of complete erasure of one's political sense and impulses. Rather, Niko and Anitsa were describing a kind of social disintegration—an individuation where the ongoing work of self-formation suddenly came to weigh on the side of contemplation over interaction. Political sterilization was the wrong expression. They were describing an experience of the subjective edged away from collective predispositions, agreements, or effects of action. They were describing the experience of a shifting political sense of self that was less fixed, if not necessarily freer, in terms of relationality and agency. Again, this was not sterilization per se, but perhaps radicalization insofar as the individual edged away from the familiar and the normative, and the possibility of their becoming open to new interactions and intersubjectivities intensified as the pressures of everyday life persisted and worsened. This was a painful experience, to be sure; but this was also an experience that could stir and activate in unexpected ways.

As I turned my eyes to Niko at that moment, my mind stayed with the idea of becoming "radical." Beyond simply a descriptive term for individuals and actions that aim to disrupt political fundamentals, as Niko had once suggested (see chapter 1), this take on "radical" gestured toward a being and doing that was not intentionally disruptive but was disruptive as an effect of having found ways to live a life worth living beyond various normative limits. That is, insofar as radical life carved out spaces, widened cracks, crossed barriers, and ossified traces that unsettled established projects, it held disruptive potential. As I now looked at Niko and Anitsa together—two individuals who found their way to something good through injury and disorientation—it became clear to me that the disruptive potential of this radical life could not be gathered up under the sign of the political. It belonged to the register of vital reworking and bare life. This form of radicalization was pre-political: it persisted in the messy background of fading, slipping, and shifting projects, of trying and finding. This form of radicalization occurred as things continued to worsen and quiet down.

When I tuned back into the conversation, the two of them were talking about the shelter again. Hassan's name had come back up. Niko was saying that despite what he thought of him, Hassan had given him an important gift: he had reminded my interlocutor that he still had the capacity to choose, to determine his actions, even if the conditions of this choosing were poor. He always chose not to fight, or not to leave the shelter again. He chose to continue on, to whatever end, despite this belligerent man. Anitsa agreed with this, saying her time at the shelter had taught her to look forward to the next choice, the next intersection: to crave it. Although she was living a large part of her life in a place she never expected, in a way that her old self would not have recognized, she was taking new steps toward something different, something better. Maybe even in a direction she would never have considered before. There was always a chance to pursue something that mattered—small or big—over and over. "There is still a future," she said, smiling at Niko.

Before we parted ways, I posed a challenge. In the two hours the three of us sat together talking, Niko never returned to the idea of solidarity. I suggested to him that he hadn't really figured it out and that he should perhaps discuss his thoughts with Hassan. This made Niko laugh—but he said he'd try. Indeed, my suggestion must have excited him, because he texted later that night: "I have risen to the challenge! I asked Hassan but he has no idea. He's just an asshole."

I wrote back: "OK, but what did he say?"

Niko replied: "H: solidarity is a European idea that people like me use to manipulate others. Fucking ass!"

I wrote: "So solidarity is still a mystery?"

A few minutes passed before Niko wrote back: "No. It just doesn't matter."

This was unexpected. I arranged to meet Niko the following week. This time he came alone. Straight off I asked him what he meant by solidarity not mattering. He explained very plainly that for him, once, solidarity meant the support by like-minded individuals. Anarchists and others who sympathized with what he called the "anarchist agenda"—others whose politics and interests aligned with his, including leftists and some communists but also, more generally, people who were limited or otherwise victimized especially by the political Right or elites in general—coming together to communicate their objection to the present politics, or, to use his term, the "status quo of oppression." Since joining the shelter, however, he began to see things differently. There was the solidarity of people coming to your side when called upon to do so; and then there was the solidarity of people who came to your side before you knew you needed them. In his experience, this was a solidarity that blurred the bounds of what we might call identitarian aggregation stemming from political, social, and cultural belonging or, more broadly, notions and feelings of community grounded in common history, ideology, experience, or empathy. This solidarity was an expression of attention and co-commitment. The primary risk one faced in expressing this kind of solidarity was not posed by the threat of some opposing force, but rather by the possibility that one's words and actions might be misunderstood, unvalued, or rejected.

It seemed to me that Niko was not just talking about social solidarity as supportive social interdependence and cohesion. There was something concerning the activation of this kind of solidarity that seemed to set apart what was happening at the shelter. There was something about the way people came to act—about anticipation—that changed his thinking. I asked him to clarify. Niko said he had recently taken a path he never expected. He had done something that he had not told me about. This piqued my interest.

Niko began, "Do you remember the chick I came with when we last met?" Niko paused, looking at me. Of course I remembered. "Anitsa?" I began. Niko continued, "Right. Well, we're together, you know. No secret there. What you don't know is that she works for a big NGO. She's like a social worker."

He explained that he met Anitsa after someone from the medical NGO she worked for came to the shelter to offer them help. This happened soon after Niko had spent that night outside with Hassan looking out for Golden Dawn. Niko thought regular visits by an outreach team from this organization might somehow suggest the shelter was affiliated or at least under the protection of a large, well-connected organization. What followed was not what Niko expected. After a visit from a health care team, a number of people from the organization arrived to get the shelter organized. Anitsa was on this second team. She came in with one other person and made a list of problems with the site: there was a lack of supplies for new mothers, insufficient food storage, a lack of safe play space for young children, unsteady electricity supply, no connection with services (state, NGO, or other) to help individuals secure important paperwork or income, either from some form of employment or through social benefits, and so on.

Niko took a breath, "Basically, Anitsa told us we had no idea what we were doing, that we were fucking around. Babies need nappies! Occupying and holding the building was fine, and the residents were trying to make some kind of normal life from the base we provided, but we needed to do more."

"So, nappies?" I ventured.

"Yes!" He replied. "And other things. I'll never forget it. Anitsa told me that a shelter should help people be alive. A shelter should make things possible or even likely. I told her that we refused to tell the residents what to do and that their lives were definitely improved by being there. I think I took her criticism personally! Anyway, she said this wasn't enough. I think she rolled her eyes. . . . She knew I wasn't on her level yet!" Niko laughed. "She told me that people always try to make something normal again as soon as they find stability, and that the shelter must be a statement in support of that. She said our statement was not as strong as it could be. Then she told me to shake off the idea that we're all saints! She said shelters like ours exclude lots of people. I hadn't thought about this, because the shelter was full; but she was right, we have ideas about where migrants should come from and how they should look and act. . . ."

"You mean solidarians have these ideas?" I asked.

"Mostly . . . fuck, I still hate that word . . . yes, although migrants have a say too. She told me that we are no better than the state! Can you believe that? Then she called me an asshole! I fell in love with her immediately."

I thought Niko's talk of Anitsa's observation regarding the exclusion of some people from the social solidarity projects of this crisis was very worthy of further consideration: people perceived to be without the right needs, without the right histories, whose appearances and narratives did not communicate the right story (cf. Cabot 2013), were indeed being turned away. How these lines were being drawn, the implications of this forming of groups and segmenting others, who was benefiting and in what ways, were fascinating open questions. For Niko, however, Anitsa's criticism opened his eyes to the biopolitics playing out at the shelter—and, indeed, to the biopolitics playing out at humanitarian spaces more broadly.[2] Niko rejected what he described as Anitsa's "crude" accusation that the shelter was replicating neoliberal abandonment or some other state violence, as he understood it; however, he began to wonder, insofar as the shelter did not directly contest the ambiguous social existence of its residents, if the shelter was perhaps replicating or complicit with a violence of the humanitarian system specifically—a violence that not only preserved, but also perpetuated diminished lives, as she had implied.[3] "Anitsa made me think that we had to rewrite some things to make our statement stronger," he explained.

Life at the shelter began to improve again as soon as Anitsa and her coworkers became involved. Tensions eased, and although there was no great flourishing of close relationships between residents and solidarians, there was co-cooperation, communication, and a return of positive feelings. Niko conceded that Anitsa and her team managed to do what the solidarians could not. I nodded and suggested that perhaps this was their business, that they knew how to "do shelters." At this, Niko bristled. He explained that Anitsa and the others had not been sent "by some manager," as he put it. They had exceeded the NGO's mandate by reaching out to the shelter. They spent resources—both material resources and expertise—to help a group of people who were not supposed to be there, doing something they were not prepared to do. This far exceeded her organization's normal operations. Again, I sensed a politics of indirect activism at play. Perhaps helping the shelter to get it right produced some sort of positive effect for Anitsa's group. Perhaps the mode of solidarity Niko observed was a reflection of this—a kind of social solidarity that benefits all parties by encouraging others to act.

Unlike Durkheimian notions of solidarity grounded in ideas of support, cohesion, and unity (which were more in line with Niko's old understandings of solidarity), and even more contingent and open-ended formulations such as solidarity as work and commitment of diverse individuals (Ahmed 2004, 189), a solidarity of indirect activism can be understood as grounded in, and expressive of, social critique—in this case critique informed by and formed within a position of desubjugation. Anitsa's group came, and a spirited, although respectful, dialogue ensued, ultimately resulting in changes and a sustained relationship. Indeed, the solidarity Niko described reverberated from agonism; that is, it ensued from affirmative and generative engagement and contestation with others. This was a disruptive solidarity. As Niko later put it, "this was solidarity with teeth." In this, the solidarity Niko was struggling to understand had as much to do with pushing against manifold injuries as it did with a kind of self-growth encouraged by new ideas and different perspectives cultivated, again in this case, beyond normativities.

So why did solidarity not matter to Niko? Faced with this question again, my interlocutor explained that the shelter had not asked Anitsa and her group for help. They came unexpectedly, not as representatives of their organization, but as individuals with particular expertise who had informally decided to support disobedient humanitarian initiatives like the shelter, because these initiatives were doing necessary work the humanitarian system was not, and in a different way: supporting them was the right thing to do. Similar to the apparatus Amalia participated in and relied on in health care settings in chapter 3, Anitsa's group came together horizontally, through activations of logics, norms, and moral narratives. However, unlike the apparatus at work in the health care setting, Anitsa's group exceeded the structure of the institution, both in terms of its operations and in terms of the regulations, funding agreements, and other frameworks that delimited its operations. What's more, all those involved understood their participation in terms of a critique of various normative limits; they drew in various others, and the expanding initiative grew adaptive, responsive, and regular, if not normal. The shelter remained an awkward site and a site of becoming awkward. Now, however, it resonated more strongly with and through the broader social space, communicating and locating the possibility of hope through stronger inessential, anti-foundationalist sentiment and expanded practice.

Niko explained that Anitsa and her group were *philótimi*: literally, "honorable friends"—ones who will help because it is the right thing to do, regardless of the cost. This word derives from ancient Greek *philótimia*: a combination of social service, sense of responsibility, and ambition for recognition. We might think of this combination as sympathetic participation in the fate of others, for the promises bound up with human connection. I was surprised to hear Niko evoke a concept that many Greeks were lamenting as dead in the era of crisis-driven self-interest and survival. Niko went on to say that there was an implicit connection, which he described as a form of mutual recognition between small groups who were working and struggling toward *something different*. They came together, he explained, not because they called on each other to do so, but because they saw themselves in each other—that is, as being positioned outside of things as they were expected to be, and moving in the same direction. The impulse to interact, to support and help one another in big and little ways, was the right thing to do, and doing so strengthened a new shared domain of finding ways. Niko explained that solidarity doesn't matter because "there is a different, more natural kind of energy pulling people together in Athens. This is much stronger and more reliable than the solidarity of the past, and it brings people you would have never thought to ask for support . . . and these interactions leave something with you. You know? They leave a good feeling, and you become more open."

"So, this is the new solidarity? Is street action dead?" I challenged.

"Of course not," Niko laughed, then added, "but I think people coming together like these NGO workers did for us, and like we do for each other, can be much more consequential."

"How so?" I asked.

Niko thought for a moment. "People will always fight for what they believe in when it's threatened. They'll also fight for the people they love. This is true, but this is also destructive. Things get burned down. People get burned. But acting in a way that builds something unexpected and unfettered in people, that might come out in different ways . . . that's something else."

This understanding of solidarity as a trace of some sustained and sustaining impulse to engage with others, to undertake acts that inscribe and affirm one's sense of self within a co-emerged domain of action in a shared world that exceeded but did not confront the normative cultures of intelligibility, would not have been possible for the pre-2015 Niko. My interlocutor had to see things differently, understand them differently, have a different sense of self and be willing to act accordingly with others within a world of chaos (Berardi 2012) for this idea of solidarity to take root. For me, this exchange summed up the transformation Niko had undergone. Niko was not his past, the places or the people he knew, the fights he had taken up, the labels he once placed on himself, although he carried these with him. He and his politics could not be summed up or located in a particular text or symbol. Niko's new politics was an echo of his big, crisis-driven mistake. It was seeded by the one response that changed everything for him, the lesson from where he began to see things differently and began to see again the possibility of finding a way for himself. It was within this space of new relations, where he found solace in harmony, that he began to see a future once more in the world.

The shelter allowed this same story to play out for all those individuals who came through its doors. People found ways that were revealing paths. Sometimes these paths were shared with others, sometimes not; but they were becoming visible, nonetheless, as features of a consolidating social topography emerged by critical relationality. Some found paths that led to their eventual departure from the shelter. Niko's path led him to stay, for the time. Although things were becoming clearer for him, he could not talk about the past without bad feelings taking him over. Maybe this would never go away. Maybe this is something he had to learn to live with. He was haunted, the city was haunted, by his failed efforts, their traces on the streets and in his archives, by abandonment, isolation, and grief. He was still finding a way to deal with the injuries he sustained when he became unfixed, confused, and alone. Yet, in the small, awkward space of the shelter, he was building something out of the need to bring order to his personal tragedy. As were others. In this, the shelter was a site that nurtured resilience in Niko, and those others who engaged with it. It also rendered visible a broader topography of similar undertakings, a spectral field of resonant milieus growing heavy. The materials, tensions, and expressions that defined the space held, enabled, and encouraged working and reworking, fingering at the stuck pages in one's mind, looking up and planning—alone and with others, toward something different.

FIGURE 6. Graffiti declares that the government's perceived betrayal of the winning "no" vote in the controversial 2015 referendum would not be forgotten. Athens, 2018. Photo by the author.

Epilogue

Vasilo still lives at the Roma compound. I lost contact with George shortly after our conversation at the end of chapter 2, although Thanos talks to him occasionally. Amalia quit HMA to work more hours at the hospital. Nefeli's father continues to visit his daughter's room and cleans the hallway. Samba and Taj still collect and sell metal and a variety of other things; and Samba is now in touch with Jigo, who found his way to Italy. Niko and Anitsa are still together. They planted jasmine in a large rusty can that once held olive oil. They keep the plant on his dusty balcony. She prunes it occasionally, to help it grow stronger.

These stories sketch coming to resilience. They also evoke a complex image of love—awkward love—as counterpower, awkward love and its various forms, intensities, and expressions such as care and attention, between people of disparate backgrounds, situations and trajectories, languages, habits, and understandings of the world, possibility, and trust, made unruly inscriptions on the social topography of Athens. These inscriptions marked figuring and finding, becomings and other transitions near and beyond the limits of lives in crisis-driven chaos, across the city. When resonant with and within the bounds of trying despite everything, they charged coming durative forms with radical possibility. The imprints of coming to resilience grow the wherewithal of change, no matter how uncertainly.

Acknowledgments

I want to express my sincere gratitude to all the people in Athens who allowed me to spend time with them, who talked with me, and who let me into their lives for this project. I know this was very difficult at times. I thank them for their extraordinary generosity. Thanks also to the members of my family in Greece who were often my thinking partners and my most productive critics. Thanks especially to my grandparents Eleni and Othon Alexandrakis.

I have been fortunate in my teachers, friends, colleagues, and students. Thanks to James Faubion for his comments on dissertation chapters, article drafts, and other writings that eventually became chapters in this book, and for his continuous support and encouragement. I could not have found a better adviser. Nia Georges was also gracious with her support throughout my graduate training and beyond. Thank you for the many big and little lessons that have shaped my career. The Department of Anthropology at Rice University really is a special place. I am grateful to have studied there.

I was also fortunate to spend a year as a postdoctoral fellow at the Seeger Center for Hellenic Studies at Princeton University in 2010, where parts of the book were drafted and critiqued. For this I thank Dimitri Gondicas for his insights and advice, Elizabeth Davis and Carol Greenhouse for critical comments and inspiring conversations, and my fellow postdocs who were supportive writing partners during my time at Princeton. Thanks especially to my friend Heath Cabot for her thoughtful feedback and encouragement. I am also grateful for invitations to participate in seminars and symposia at other universities over the course of my postdoctoral year. I took these opportunities to try many of the ideas in this ethnography. Thanks in particular to George Syrimis at the Hellenic Studies Program at Yale University and to Yannis Ioannides and Michael Herzfeld, who organized the Greek Study Group at Harvard's Center for European Studies.

I would also like to thank a host of friends and colleagues for their camaraderie, and for the numerous opportunities to share my work at conferences and retreats: Daniel Knight, Charles Stewart, Elisabeth Kirtsoglou, Katerina Rozakou, Dimitrios Theodossopoulos, Tina Palivos, Aimee Placas, Tracey Rozen, Dimitris Dalakoglou, Konstantinos Kalantzis, and especially Neni Panrougiá. Thank you Neni for your generous comments on different aspects of my work, for your support and attention, your passion and your willingness to share your insights and critiques. I have profited greatly from our discussions over the years.

I am deeply indebted to my colleagues in the Department of Anthropology at York University who read chapters and parts of chapters as I prepared the manuscript for this book. I am particularly indebted to Ken Little, whose generous comments helped me discover what this book is actually about. My thanks to Daphne Winland and Zulfikar Hirji for their critical comments and insights, and to all those who participated in the Working Paper Series where I shared drafts of chapters, and especially David Murray and Wangui Kimari for their close reading and critical comments on chapter 2. My mentor at the department, Albert Schrauwers, has been a source of inspiration and steadfast support. Thanks Albert, for everything.

Financial support for the research that led to this book was provided by the Social Sciences and Humanities Research Council of Canada. I am also very grateful to College Year in Athens (CYA), for providing me with a space to write and access to their library collection while I completed the manuscript on my sabbatical year in Athens, 2018–19. Thanks to Alexis Phylactopoulos, Vasso Matrakouka, and especially Georgia Katsarou for her generosity and for providing resources and assistance that made the final stages of this project possible.

Thanks to Kathe Gray, who prepared the final manuscript for submission to Cornell University Press. Thanks also to Clare Jones, who received the manuscript and saw it through to production, to senior production editor Karen Laun, who saw this book through final stages of publication, and to Cameron Duder, who prepared the index. Finally, I owe many thanks to my editor, Jim Lance, for his generous comments, support, patience, and encouragement. Jim, thank you for believing in this project.

Notes

INTRODUCTION

1. I use the term "interlocutor" throughout the book to refer to research participants, acquaintances, contacts, collaborators, consultants, and other individuals who have in one way or another been a part of, contributed to, and otherwise shaped the project of researching and writing this book. In using this term, I do not intend to distance or otherwise diminish or abstract those people whose lives, thoughts, and actions informed and shaped the book before you. To the contrary, and with Edward Said's critique of "interlocutor" in mind (1989), I use this term reflexively and with respect. First, I hope it will evoke the complex, manifold, multifaceted legacies, gaps, and limits that texture ethnographic projects—including this one. Second, I use this term in recognition of those individuals who understood their participation in this project strictly in terms of an interaction with me and were skeptical of the idea that this interaction might be understood to entail some form of coauthorship or that it may lead to meaningful connections between their worlds and those of the book's audiences. Although I do not share this sentiment—my thoughts on connections and ethnography's potentials are more aligned with Taussig's writing on the matter (2011)—I feel it is important, nonetheless, that this doubting be registered and incorporated.

1. EVERYDAY, ILLEGIBLE

1. At this point forward in the book, I use pseudonyms and take various other measures to protect the identities of all my interlocutors.

2. In Milton's *Paradise Lost* (book 2) Sin, born of Satan, is raped by Death (her son with Satan) and gives birth to hellhounds (dogs), which return hourly to her womb, feed on her bowels, and are reborn. I later asked Niko if he was referencing Milton specifically. He was.

3. Andrea Muehlebach explores a similar line of thinking in her work on the rise of voluntarism in the wake of neoliberal welfare reform in the Lombardy region of Italy (2012).

4. By "less valuable" Niko was referring to the potential of individuals and groups to, through labor, generate economic wealth for elites. Most of Niko's thoughts on labor, class relations, and the workings of the economy were unambiguously Marxist.

5. In season two, episode one of the television show *Monty Python's Flying Circus* (first aired in 1970), John Cleese plays a civil servant in a fictitious British government ministry responsible for developing silly walks.

6. *Light* was launched on September 3, 1861.

7. The assassination made the front page of the *New York Times* on March 19, 1913. Of note, Alexandros Schinas worked in the pantry of the Fifth Avenue Hotel in New York City before moving to Greece to start an anarchist school.

8. Nea Smyrni is an inner suburb of south-central Athens.

9. Murray Bookchin was a Trotskyist communist rather than a Stalinist. His appeal to many modern anarchists is his stand against urbanization and for ecological awareness, thus providing a nice supplement to classical anarchist theory, which does not address these issues adequately (see Bookchin 1992, 1995, 1999, 2007).

10. Ano Liosion is a poor working-class suburb in the west end of Athens.

11. This was an editorial group that produced several books and translations of anarchist political theory.

12. Neni Panourgiá (2009) used the term "political DNA" to refer to one's inherited political affiliation—or the taking up of the same political identity as one's family. Passing on political affiliations had social and economic benefits in pre-crisis Greece.

13. The celebration of "name days" is common across Greece. Individuals celebrate on the day (or days) of the year dedicated to the memory of a saint or martyr whose name they share. People without Christian names often choose to celebrate on All Saints' Day.

14. The details of what happened that night are documented in the proceedings of the murder trial of the two policemen involved in Grigoropoulos's death. Briefly, the two policemen had been involved in an exchange with another group of young people several blocks away from the intersection where Grigoropoulos was shot. The two policemen claim that the group threw bottles at their passing police car, but eyewitnesses suggest the group in question was only shouting insults. Regardless, when the police officers radioed the central command to report the incident, they claimed that they had been fired at. Central command ordered the police officers back to the base. The officers ignored the order, stopped their car just down the road, and got out. At this point a different group of people started yelling at them while running away toward the spot where Grigoropoulos and his friends were. This is the sound that drew Grigoropoulos to the street, where he was shot.

15. Of note, experts and observers would make the same complaint of the Occupy movement some years later.

16. Here Niko was referencing Gil Scott-Heron's famous poem and song "The Revolution Will Not Be Televised" (1971).

17. At the time, the best known example of the persecution and intimidation of an independent journalist was that of Kostas Vaxevanis, who published a copy of the infamous "Lagarde List"—a document containing the names of roughly two thousand Greek tax evaders with undeclared accounts at Swiss HSBC bank's Geneva branch, including various high-profile Greeks, some with political ties. For more, see Andrew Rosenthal's editorial titled "Greece Arrests the Messenger" in the October 29, 2012, edition of the *New York Times*. Greece sank to eighty-fourth place in the Reporters without Borders Annual Press Freedom Index for 2013, the lowest in Europe alongside Bulgaria.

18. The ambiguity of the referendum question caused much debate among legal scholars and politicians, even if citizens seemed broadly unconcerned. Voters were asked to consider a bailout proposal that was subsequently withdrawn by the troika. So, voters were then asked to consider two previous documents titled "Reforms for the Completion of the Current Program and Beyond" and "Preliminary Debt Sustainability Analysis." They could vote "Not approved / No" or "Approved / Yes."

2. BECOMING LOST

1. Thalassemia is an inherited blood disorder in which the body makes an abnormal form of hemoglobin. Symptoms of thalassemia include jaundice, enlarged organs, frequent infection, and severe (sometimes life-threatening) anemia. Thalassemia sufferers, like Vasilo's sons, often require regular blood transfusions.

2. All the ages in this chapter are estimates. None of my Romani consultants were sure how old they were, and most doubted that their birth certificates and driver's licenses were correct.

3. In *Gender Trouble* (1990), Judith Butler refers to the production of normative frameworks that circumscribe who can be conceived of as a subject in terms of "cultural intelligibility."

4. Working age for the Halandri Roma was about fifteen. While individuals younger than this often did work in the form of panhandling or aiding family members in their work, fifteen was the age when youths were expected to begin looking for employment on their own. This was also the age when most Greek students were legally allowed to drop out of school (although Romani youth from the Halandri compound rarely finished school).

5. In her introduction to *Cultural Anthropology*'s Hot Spots, "Beyond the 'Greek Crisis': Histories, Rhetorics, Politics," Penelope Papailias (2011) notes the blatant use of Orientalist tropes in international and domestic reporting on the crisis. Several contributors to the collection, including Aimee Placas and Stathis Stasinos, explore this issue in further detail.

6. Loutsa is a seaside resort town in East Attica. It was renamed Artemida in 2011.

7. This was a show popular with adolescent youths at the compound in which an American rap artist repaired and "enhanced" the vehicle of an underprivileged fan in each episode. Enhancements included adding unexpected touches like waterfalls and chandeliers to the vehicle interiors.

8. Which, incidentally, the boy's father was forced to abandon shortly thereafter when competition from Bangladeshi collectors and Greek collectors heated up.

9. Talk about this episode was the first time I heard my Romani interlocutors mention "cultural guards." In follow-up conversations, they explained that these guards were more dangerous than police, that they were better trained and given extra powers to protect "Greek" objects. My interlocutors talked about "cultural guards" as though they were special military commandos. The closest thing to "cultural guards" I ever saw in Greece, however, was for-hire private security.

10. The Roma living at the Halandri camp where I conducted my research were mostly from the Halkidiki clan, or had married in. Roma from other clans often visited or came to stay for short periods but never built their own homes.

3. ORDINARY GHOSTING

1. The abbreviation HMA is a pseudonym.

2. This is not unprecedented in Greece. During the military junta, doctors changed medical records to protect student protesters from persecution.

4. COMMON MATTERS

1. Of note, Amit and Rapport use the term "consocial" to describe a connection between people based on what is shared rather than in oppositional categories between insiders and outsiders (2002, 59). Consocial relationships are contextual rather than based on ascribed identities or boundaries such as race, religion, ethnicity, or gender. In the case here, however, we will see how shared matters come to bleed out and into identity, rendering increasingly visible, expanding, and texturing a situated sense of self with others in social place.

2. "Gypsies," or Roma, have a long history of collecting, scrapping, and recycling in Athens. In fact, the compound I described in chapter 2 was home to two door-to-door collectors who specialized in reusable and repairable materials. They capitalized on the surplus value of these items, discarded by better-off communities, either by keeping the items for themselves, trading them, or selling them. They prided themselves on having good reputations in the neighborhoods where they worked (Gmelch 1986). Other traditional door-to-door services provided by Roma include day laboring, fortune telling, and various kinds of specialized repair work.

5. RADICAL POSSIBILITY

1. Of note, Papataxiarchis discusses the coming together of activists (including anarchists) with diverse, if compatible, ideological commitments in the establishment of a rural squat, Platanos, in Lesbos (2018, 240–43). In this work he describes the tensions and anxieties solidarians negotiated with volunteers, NGOs, and other humanitarians, and the eventual transformations of Platanos and those who established it. Similar transformative intensities ran through the site I describe here, although the primary source of tension and intensity was internal to the site itself.

2. Anthropologists have well documented the biopolitics of humanitarian spaces (see for example Ticktin 2006 and Redfield 2005), with Katerina Rozakou exploring the case of Greek humanitarian spaces specifically (2012).

3. Rozakou describes the ambiguity produced in humanitarian settings as being between full social existence and biological life (2012). In our conversation, Niko put it more bluntly in terms of "life and death."

References

Adib, Parinaz. 2018. "What Are We Doing? Grasping at Solidarity in Athens, Greece." MA thesis, York University.

Agamben, Giorgio. 1998. *Homo Sacer: Sovereign Power and Bare Life*. Translated by Daniel Heller-Roazen. Meridian: Crossing Aesthetics. Stanford, CA: Stanford University Press.

Agamben, Giorgio. 1999. *Potentialities: Collected Essays in Philosophy*. Edited and translated by Daniel Heller-Roazen. Meridian: Crossing Aesthetics. Stanford, CA: Stanford University Press.

Ahmed, Sara. 2004. *The Cultural Politics of Emotion*. New York: Routledge.

Alexandrakis, Othon. 2003. "Between Life and Death: Violence and Greek Roma Health and Identity." MA thesis, University of Western Ontario.

Alexandrakis, Othon. 2010. "The Struggle for Modern Athens: Unconventional Citizens, Shifting Topographies, and the Shaping of a New Political Reality." PhD diss., Rice University.

Alexandrakis, Othon. 2015. "Transformative Connections: Trauma, Cooperative Horizons, and Emerging Political Topographies in Athens, Greece." *History and Anthropology* 27 (1): 32–44.

Alexandrakis, Othon. 2016a. "Incidental Activism: Graffiti and Political Possibility in Athens, Greece." *Cultural Anthropology* 31 (2): 272–96. https://doi.org/10.14506/ca31.2.06.

Alexandrakis, Othon. 2016b. "Introduction: Resistance Reconsidered." In *Impulse to Act: A New Anthropology of Resistance and Social Justice*, edited by Othon Alexandrakis, 1–18. Bloomington: Indiana University Press.

Almedom, A. M., Evelyn A. Brensinger, and Gordon M. Adam. 2010. "Identifying the Resilience Factor: An Emerging Counter Narrative to the Traditional Discourse of 'Vulnerability' on 'Social Suffering.'" In *Global Perspectives on War, Gender and Health: The Sociology and Anthropology of Suffering*, edited by R. H. Bradley and G. Hundt, 127–46. Farnham, UK: Ashgate.

Amit, Vered, and Nigel Rapport. 2002. *The Trouble with Community: Anthropological Reflections on Movement, Identity and Collectivity*. London: Pluto.

Anthopoulou, Theodosia, Nikolaos Kaberis, and Michael Petrou. 2017. "Aspects and Experiences of Crisis in Rural Greece: Narratives of Rural Resilience." *Journal of Rural Studies* 52:1–11. https://doi.org/10.1016/j.jrurstud.2017.03.006.

Argenti, Nicolas. 2019. *Remembering Absence: The Sense of Life in Island Greece*. Bloomington: Indiana University Press.

Argenti, Nicolas, and Katharina Schramm. 2012. "Remembering Violence: Anthropological Perspectives on Intergenerational Transmission." In *Remembering Violence: Anthropological Perspectives on Intergenerational Transmission*, edited by Nicolas Argenti and Katharina Schramm, 1–40. Oxford: Berghahn.

Athanasiou, Athena. 2011. "Becoming Precarious through Regimes of Gender, Capital, and Nation." Hot Spots, Fieldsights, October 28. https://culanth.org/fieldsights/becoming-precarious-through-regimes-of-gender-capital-and-nation.

Athanasiou, Athena, and Othon Alexandrakis. 2016. "Conclusion: On an Emergent Politics and Ethics of Resistance." In *Impulse to Act: A New Anthropology of Resistance and Social Justice*, edited by Othon Alexandrakis, 246–62. Bloomington: Indiana University Press.

Bal, Mieke. 1997. *Narratology: Introduction to the Theory of Narrative*. 2nd ed. Toronto: University of Toronto Press.

Barrios, Roberto E. 2016. "Resilience: A Commentary from the Vantage Point of Anthropology." *Annals of Anthropological Practice* 40 (1): 28–38. https://doi.org/10.1111/napa.12085.

Berardi, Franco. 2012. *The Uprising: On Poetry and Finance*. Los Angeles: Semiotext(e).

Berlant, Lauren Gail. 2011. *Cruel Optimism*. Durham, NC: Duke University Press.

Biehl, Joao, and Peter Locke. 2010. "Deleuze and the Anthropology of Becoming." *Current Anthropology* 51 (3): 317–37.

Bookchin, Murray. 1992. *Urbanization without Cities: The Rise and Decline of Citizenship*. Montréal: Black Rose Books.

Bookchin, Murray. 1995. *From Urbanization to Cities: Toward a New Politics of Citizenship*. Rev. ed. London: Cassell.

Bookchin, Murray. 1999. *Anarchism, Marxism, and the Future of the Left: Interviews and Essays, 1993–1998*. Edinburgh: AK.

Bookchin, Murray. 2007. *Social Ecology and Communalism*. Edinburgh: AK.

Butler, Judith. 1990. *Gender Trouble: Feminism and the Subversion of Identity*. New York: Routledge.

Butler, Judith. 2002. "What Is Critique? An Essay on Foucault's Virtue." In *The Political: Readings in Continental Philosophy*, edited by David Ingram, 212–26. London: Basil Blackwell.

Butler, Judith. 2004. *Precarious Life: The Powers of Mourning and Violence*. London: Verso.

Butler, Judith, and Athena Athanasiou. 2013. *Dispossession: The Performative in the Political*. Cambridge: Polity.

Cabot, Heath. 2012. "The Governance of Things: Documenting Limbo in the Greek Asylum Procedure." *Polar: Political and Legal Anthropology Review* 35 (1): 11–29.

Cabot, Heath. 2013. "The Social Aesthetics of Eligibility: NGO Aid and Indeterminacy in the Greek Asylum Process." *American Ethnologist* 40 (3): 452–66.

Cabot, Heath. 2014. *On the Doorstep of Europe: Asylum and Citizenship in Greece; The Ethnography of Political Violence*. Philadelphia: University of Pennsylvania Press.

Cabot, Heath. 2016. "'Contagious' Solidarity: Reconfiguring Care and Citizenship in Greece's Social Clinics." *Social Anthropology* 24 (2): 152–66. https://doi.org/10.1111/1469-8676.12297.

Campbell, John Kennedy. 1964. *Honour, Family, and Patronage: A Study of Institutions and Moral Values in a Greek Mountain Community*. Oxford: Clarendon.

Chiotaki-Poulou, Irini, and Alexandros Sakellariou. 2014. "Ē Koinōnikē Kataskeuē Tēs 'Genias Tōn 700 Eurō' Kai Ē Anadusē Tēs Ston Ēmerēsio Tupo: Mia Koinōniologikē Prosengisē" [The social construction of the "700 euro generation" and its emergence in the daily press: A sociological approach]. *Greek Review of Social Research* 131 (131). https://doi.org/10.12681/grsr.80.

Comaroff, Jean. 1985. *Body of Power, Spirit of Resistance: The Culture and History of a South African People*. Chicago: University of Chicago Press.

Comaroff, Jean, and John L. Comaroff. 1991. *Of Revelation and Revolution: Christianity, Colonialism, and Consciousness in South Africa*. 2 vols. Chicago: University of Chicago Press.

Cons, Jason. 2018. "Staging Climate Security: Resilience and Heterodystopia in the Bangladesh Borderlands." *Cultural Anthropology* 33 (2): 266–94. https://doi.org/10.14506/ca33.2.08.

Corsín Jiménez, Alberto. 2011. "Trust in Anthropology." *Anthropological Theory* 11 (2): 177–96. https://doi.org/10.1177/1463499611407392.

Cossette, Julien. 2016. "Critical Encounters on the Road: Walking Migrants on an 'Island Full of Busses.'" MA thesis, York University.

Coutinho, Jenna Leigh. 2016. "Navigating Health in 'Crisis': The Minimal Biopolitics of Humanitarian Aid in Greece." Master's thesis, York University.

Dalakoglou, Dimitris, and Giorgos Poulimenakos. 2018. "Hetero-Utopias: Squatting and Spatial Materialities of Resistance in Athens at Times of Crisis." In *Critical Times in Greece: Anthropological Engagements with the Crisis*, edited by Dimitris Dalakoglou and Georgios Agelopoulos, 173–87. New York: Routledge.

Dalakoglou, Dimitris, and Antonis Vradis. 2011. "Spatial Legacies of December and the Right to the City." In *Revolt and Crisis in Greece: Between a Present Yet to Pass and a Future Still to Come*, edited by Antonis Vradis and Dimitris Dalakoglou, 77–88. London: AK Press & Occupied London.

Das, Veena. 2000. "The Act of Witnessing: Violence, Poisonous Knowledge, and Subjectivity." In *Violence and Subjectivity*, edited by Veena Das, Arthur Kleinman, Mamphela Ramphele, and Pamela Reynolds, 205–25. Berkeley: University of California Press.

Davis, Elizabeth. 2015. "'We've Toiled without End': Publicity, Crisis, and the Suicide 'Epidemic' in Greece." *Comparative Studies in Society and History* 57 (4): 1007–36. https://doi.org/10.1017/s0010417515000420.

De Genova, Nicholas, and Nathalie Mae Peutz. 2010. *The Deportation Regime: Sovereignty, Space, and the Freedom of Movement*. Durham, NC: Duke University Press.

Deleuze, Gilles. 1990. *The Logic of Sense: European Perspectives*. New York: Columbia University Press.

Deleuze, Gilles. 1995. *Negotiations, 1972–1990*. New York: Columbia University Press.

Deleuze, Gilles. 1997. *Essays Critical and Clinical*. Minneapolis: University of Minnesota Press.

Deleuze, Gilles. 2009. *Difference and Repetition*. London: Continuum.

Deleuze, Gilles, and Félix Guattari. 1986. *Kafka: Toward a Minor Literature*. Minneapolis: University of Minnesota Press.

Derrida, Jacques. 1994. *Spectres de Marx*. Translated by P. Kamuf. New York: Routledge.

Dimakos, I., and K. Tasiopoulou. 2003. "Attitudes towards Migrants: What Do Greek Students Think about Their Immigrant Classmates?" *Intercultural Education* 14 (3): 307–16.

Douzina-Bakalaki, Phaedra. 2017. "Volunteering Mothers: Engaging the Crisis in a Soup Kitchen of Northern Greece." *Anthropology Matters* 17 (1): 1–24.

Dressler, William W., Mauro C. Balieiro, and José E. Dos Santos. 1997. "The Cultural Construction of Social Support in Brazil: Associations with Health Outcomes." *Culture Medicine and Psychiatry* 21 (3): 303–35.

Economides, Spyros, and Vassilis Monastiriotis, eds. 2009. *The Return of Street Politics? Essays on the December Riots in Greece*. London: Hellenic Observatory, LSE.

Economou, Marina, Michael Madianos, Lily Evangelia Peppou, Christos Theleritis, Athanasios Patelakis, and Costas Stefanis. 2013. "Suicidal Ideation and Reported Suicide Attempts in Greece during the Economic Crisis." *World Psychiatry* 12 (1): 53–59.

Economou, Marina, Michael Madianos, Christos Theleritis, Lily E. Peppou, and Costas Stefanis. 2011. "Increased Suicidality amid Economic Crisis in Greece." *Lancet* 378 (9801): 1459.

Fassin, Didier. 2016. "Hot Spots: What They Mean." Hot Spots, Fieldsights, June 28. https://culanth.org/fieldsights/hot-spots-what-they-mean.

Faubion, James D. 2011. *An Anthropology of Ethics.* Cambridge: Cambridge University Press.

Faubion, James, Eugenia Georges, and Gonda Van Steen. 2016. "Greece Is Burning." Hot Spots, Fieldsights, April 21. https://culanth.org/fieldsights/865-greece-is-burning.

Featherstone, Kevin. 2008. "'Varieties of Capitalism' and the Greek Case: Explaining the Constraints on Domestic Reform?" Hellenic Observatory Papers on Greece and Southeast Europe. London: London School of Economics.

Featherstone, Kevin. 2015. "External Conditions and the Debt Crisis: The 'Troika' and Public Administration Reform in Greece." *Journal of European Public Policy* 22 (3): 295–314.

Feldman, Allen. 1994. "On Cultural Anesthesia: From Desert Storm to Rodney King." *American Ethnologist* 21 (2): 404–18.

Feldman, Gregory. 2005. "Essential Crises: A Performative Appraoch to Migrants, Minorities, and the European Nation-State." *Anthropological Quarterly* 78 (1): 213–46.

Feldman, Gregory. 2011. "If Ethnography Is More Than Participant-Observation, Then Relations Are More Than Connections: The Case for Nonlocal Ethnography in a World of Apparatuses." *Anthropological Theory* 11 (4): 375–95. https://doi.org/10.1177/1463499611429904.

Feldman, Ruth, and Shafiq Masalha. 2007. "The Role of Culture in Moderating the Links between Early Ecological Risk and Young Children's Adaptation." *Development and Psychopathology* 19 (1): 1–21.

Foucault, Michel. 1997. "What Is Critique." In *The Politics of Truth*, edited by S. Lotringer, translated by Lysa Hochroth and Catherine Porter. 41–82. New York: Semiotext(e).

Giovanopoulos, Christos, and Dimitris Dalakoglou. 2011. "From Ruptures to Eruptions: A Genealogy of the December 2008 Revolt in Greece." In *Revolt and Crisis in Greece: Between a Present Yet to Pass and a Future Still to Come*, edited by Antonis Vradis and Dimitris Dalakoglou, 91–114. Oakland: AK Press & Occupied London.

Gmelch, Sharon Bohn. 1986. "Groups That Don't Want In: Gypsies and Other Artisan, Trader, and Entertainer Minorities." *Annual Review of Anthroplogy* 15:307–30.

Gourgouris, Stathis. 2012. "Greece at the Global Forefront: The Elections in Greece Are a Dramatic Articulation of the Essential Contradiction between Democracy and Captialism." *AlJazeera*, May 3, Opinion.

Green, Linda. 1999. *Fear as a Way of Life: Mayan Widows in Rural Guatemala.* New York: Columbia University Press.

Gropas, Ruby, and Anna Triandafyllidou. 2007. *Greek Education Policy and the Challenges of Migration: An Intercultural View of Assimilation.* Athens: ELIAMEP.

Guattari, Félix. 1996. *The Guattari Reader.* Edited by Gary Genosko. Blackwell Readers. Oxford: Blackwell.

Hage, Ghassan 2005. "A Not So Multi-sited Ethnography of a Not So Imagined Community." *Anthropological Theory* 5 (4): 463–75.

Herzfeld, Michael. 1985. *The Poetics of Manhood: Contest and Identity in a Cretan Mountain Village*. Princeton, NJ: Princeton University Press.

Herzfeld, Michael. 2005. *Cultural Intimacy: Social Poetics in the Nation-State*. 2nd ed. New York: Routledge.

Inda, Jonathan Xavier. 2006. *Targeting Immigrants: Government, Technology, and Ethics*. Malden, MA: Blackwell.

Ingold, Tim. 2000. *The Perception of the Environment: Essays on Livelihood, Dwelling and Skill*. New York: Routledge.

Ingold, Tim. 2007. *Lines: A Brief History*. London: Routledge.

Ingold, Tim. 2011. *Being Alive: Essays on Movement, Knowledge and Description*. New York: Routledge.

Jackson, Michael. 2013. *The Wherewithal of Life: Ethics, Migration, and the Question of Well-Being*. Berkeley: University of California Press.

Jarrett, Robin L. 1997. "Resilience among Low-Income African American Youth: An Ethnographic Perspective." *Ethos* 25 (2): 218–29. https://doi.org/10.1525/eth.1997.25.2.218.

Kalyvas, Andreas. 2010. "An Anomaly? Some Reflections on the Greek December 2008." *Constellations* 17 (2): 351–65.

Karanikolos, Marina, Philipa Mladovsky, Jonathan Cylus, Sarah Thomson, Sanjay Basu, David Stuckler, Johan P. Mackenbach, and Martin McKee. 2013. "Financial Crisis, Austerity, and Health in Europe." *Lancet* 381 (9874): 1323–31.

Karathanasi, Effie. 2000. *To Katoikeín tōn Tsingánon: O vio-khốros kai o koinōnio-khốros tōn Tsingánon* [The home of the Roma: The natural environment and the social environment of the Roma]. Athens: Gutenberg.

Katsimi, Margarita, and Thomas Moutos. 2010. "EMU and the Greek Crisis: The Political-Economy Perspective." *European Journal of Political Economy* 26 (4): 568–76.

Knight, Daniel M. 2015a. *History, Time, and Economic Crisis in Central Greece*. New York: Palgrave Macmillan.

Knight, Daniel M. 2015b. "Wit and Greece's Economic Crisis: Ironic Slogans, Food, and Antiausterity Sentiments." *American Ethnologist* 42 (2): 230–46.

Knight, Daniel M. 2017. "Fossilized Futures: Topologies and Topographies of Crisis Experience in Central Greece." *Social Analysis* 61 (1). https://doi.org/10.3167/sa.2017.610102.

Kokkevi, Anna, Marina Terzidou, Kyriaki Politikou, and Costas Stefanis. 2000. "Substance Use among High School Students in Greece: Outburst of Illicit Drug Use in a Society under Change." *Drug and Alcohol Dependence* 58 (1–2): 181–88.

Koonings, Kees, and Dirk Kruijt. 2015. *Violence and Resilience in Latin American Cities*. London: Zed Books.

Koselleck, Reinhart. 2004. *Futures Past: On the Semantics of Historical Time*. Translated by Keith Tribe. New York: Columbia University Press.

Laclau, Ernesto. 1990. *New Reflections on the Revolution of Our Time*. London: Verso.

Laclau, Ernesto, and Chantal Mouffe. 2001. *Hegemony and Socialist Strategy: Towards a Radical Democratic Politics*. 2nd ed. London: Verso.

Lewis, Sara E. 2013. "Trauma and the Making of Flexible Minds in the Tibetan Exile Community." *Ethos* 41 (3): 313–36. https://doi.org/10.1111/etho.12024.

Lorey, Isabell. 2015. *State of Insecurity: Government of the Precarious*. London: Verso.

Lovell, Anne M. 2007. "Hoarders and Scrappers: Madness and the Social Person in the Interstices of the City." In *Subjectivity: Ethnographic Investigations*, edited by

Byron Good, João Biehl, and Arthur Kleinman, 315–40. Berkeley: University of California Press.

Lydaki, Anna. 1997. *Balamé kai Romá: Oi Tsingánoi tōn Ánō Liosíōn* [Balamé and Roma: The Gypsies of Ano Liosion]. Athens: Ekdóseis Kastaniótis.

Lydaki, Anna. 1998. *Oi Tsingánoi Stēn Pólē: Megaló nontas Etēn Agía Varvára* [Roma in the city: Growing up in Agía Varvára]. Athens: Ekdóseis Kastaniótis.

Malkki, Liisa. 1992. "National Geographic: The Rooting of Peoples and the Territorialization of National Identity among Scholars and Refugees." *Cultural Anthropology* 7 (1): 24–44.

Massumi, Brian. 2002. *Parables for the Virtual: Movement, Affect, Sensation.* Durham, NC: Duke University Press.

Mikkonen, Kai. 2007. "The 'Narrative Is Travel' Metaphor: Between Spatial Sequences and Open Consequence." *Narrative* 15 (3): 286–305.

Mili, Hayder, and Benjamin Crabtree. 2014. *The Illicit Drug Trade through South-Eastern Europe.* United Nations Office on Drugs and Crime (UNODC).

Muehlebach, Andrea Karin. 2012. *The Moral Neoliberal: Welfare and Citizenship in Italy.* Chicago: University of Chicago Press.

Nahar, Papreen, and Sjaak van der Geest. 2014. "How Women in Bangladesh Confront the Stigma of Childlessness: Agency, Resilience, and Resistance." *Medical Anthropology Quarterly* 28 (3): 381–98. https://doi.org/10.1111/maq.12094.

Nail, Thomas. 2015. *The Figure of the Migrant.* Stanford, CA: Stanford University Press.

Napolitano, Valentina. 2015. "Anthropology and Traces." *Anthropological Theory* 15 (1): 47–67. https://doi.org/10.1177/1463499614554239.

Navaro-Yashin, Yael. 2012. *The Make-Believe Space: Affective Geography in a Postwar Polity.* Durham, NC: Duke University Press.

Nelson, Donald R., and Timothy J. Finan. 2009. "Praying for Drought: Persistent Vulnerability and the Politics of Patronage in Ceará, Northeast Brazil." *American Anthropologist* 111 (3): 302–16. https://doi.org/10.1111/j.1548-1433.2009.01134.x.

Ngai, Sianne. 2004. *Ugly Feelings.* Cambridge, MA: Harvard University Press.

Ong, Aihwa. 1987. *Spirits of Resistance and Capitalist Discipline: Factory Women in Malaysia.* SUNY Series in the Anthropology of Work. Albany: SUNY Press.

Paleologou, Nektaria. 2004. "Intercultural Education and Practice in Greece: Needs for Bilingual Intercultural Programmes." *Intercultural Education* 15 (3): 317–29.

Panourgiá, Neni. 1995. *Fragments of Death, Fables of Identity: An Athenian Anthropography.* Madison: University of Wisconsin Press.

Panourgiá, Neni. 2009. *Dangerous Citizens: The Greek Left and the Terror of the State.* New York: Fordham University Press.

Panourgiá, Neni. 2010. "Stones (Papers, Humans)." *Journal of Modern Greek Studies* 28 (2): 199–224. https://doi.org/10.1353/mgs.2010.0423.

Panourgiá, Neni. 2016. "Surreal Capitalism and the Dialectical Economies of Precarity." In *Impulse to Act: A New Anthropology of Resistance and Social Justice,* edited by Othon Alexandrakis, 112–31. Bloomington: Indiana University Press.

Panourgiá, Neni. 2018. "New-Poor: The Being, the Phenomenon, and the Becoming in 'Greek Crisis.'" In *Critical Times in Greece: Anthropological Engagements with the Crisis,* edited by Dimitris Dalakoglou and Georgios Agelopoulos, 132–47. New York: Routledge.

Panter-Brick, Catherine. 2014. "Health, Risk, and Resilience: Interdisciplinary Concepts and Applications." *Annual Review of Anthropology* 43 (1): 431–48. https://doi.org/10.1146/annurev-anthro-102313-025944.

Papadaki, Maria, and Stefania Kalogeraki. 2017. "Social Support Actions as Forms of Building Community Resilience at the Onset of the Crisis in Urban Greece." *Open Journal of Sociopolitical Studies* 10 (1). https://doi.org/10.1285/i20356609v10i1p193.

Papadopoulos, Dimitris, Niamh Stephenson, and Vassilis Tsianos. 2008. *Escape Routes: Control and Subversion in the Twenty-First Century*. London: Pluto.

Papailias, Penelope. 2011. "Beyond the 'Greek Crisis': Histories, Rhetorics, Politics." Hot Spots, Fieldsights, October 10. https://culanth.org/fieldsights/243-beyond-the-greek-crisis-histories-rhetorics-politics.

Papataxiarchis, Evthymios. 2016a. "Being 'There': At the Front Line of the 'European Refugee Crisis'—Part 1." *Anthropology Today* 32 (2).

Papataxiarchis, Evthymios. 2016b. "Being 'There': At the Front Line of the 'European Refugee Crisis'—Part 2." *Anthropology Today* 32 (3).

Papataxiarchis, Evthymios. 2018. Afterword in *Critical Times in Greece: Anthropological Engagements with the Crisis*, edited by Dimitris Dalakoglou and Georgios Agelopoulos, 227–47. New York: Routledge.

Pautz, Hartwig, and Margarita Kominou. 2013. "Reacting to 'Austerity Politics': The Tactic of Collective Expropriation in Greece." *Social Movement Studies* 12 (1): 103–10. https://doi.org/10.1080/14742837.2012.704180.

Peano, Irene. 2016. "Emergenc(i)es in the Fields: Affective Composition and Counter-camps against the Exploitation of Migrant Farm Labor in Italy." In *Impulse to Act: A New Anthropology of Resistance and Social Justice*, edited by Othon Alexandrakis, 63–88. Bloomington: Indiana University Press.

Pelagidis, Theodore. 2010. "The Greek Paradox of Falling Competativeness and Weak Institutions in a High GDP Growth Rate Context (1995–2008)." Hellenic Observatory Papers on Greece and Southeast Europe. London: London School of Economics.

Philogene Heron, Adom. 2018. "Surviving Maria from Dominica: Memory, Displacement and Bittersweet Beginnings." *Transforming Anthropology* 26 (2): 118–35. https://doi.org/10.1111/traa.12133.

Placas, Aimee. 2011. "Trickle-Down Debt." Hot Spots, Fieldsights, October 31. https://culanth.org/fieldsights/257-trickle-down-debt.

Placas, Aimee, and Evdoxios Doxiadis. 2018. "Introduction: Crisis and Austerity." In *Living under Austerity: Greek Society in Crisis*, edited by Evdoxios Doxiadis and Aimee Placas, 1–12. New York: Berghahn Books.

Potter, Jonathan. 1996. *Representing Reality: Discourse, Rhetoric and Social Construction*. London: Sage.

Povinelli, Elizabeth A. 2011. *Economies of Abandonment: Social Belonging and Endurance in Late Liberalism*. Durham, NC: Duke University Press.

Puar, Jasbir K. 2007. *Terrorist Assemblages: Homonationalism in Queer Times*. Durham, NC: Duke University Press.

Rafael, Vicente L. 2003. "The Cell Phone and the Crowd: Messianic Politics in the Contemporary Philippines." *Public Culture* 15 (3): 399–425.

Raffaetà, Roberta, and Cameron Duff. 2013. "Putting Belonging into Place: Place Experience and Sense of Belonging among Ecuadorian Migrants in an Italian Alpine Region." *City & Society* 25 (3): 328–47. https://doi.org/10.1111/ciso.12025.

Rakopoulos, Theodoros. 2014. "Resonance of Solidarity: Meanings of a Local Concept in Anti-austerity Greece." *Journal of Modern Greek Studies* 32 (2): 313–37.

Rakopoulos, Theodoros. 2015. "Responding to the Crisis: Food Co-operatives and the Solidarity Economy in Greece." *Anthropology Southern Africa* 36 (3–4): 102–7. https://doi.org/10.1080/23323256.2013.11500048.

Rakopoulos, Theodoros. 2016. "Solidarity: The Egalitarian Tensions of a Bridge-Concept." *Social Anthropology* 24 (2): 142–51. https://doi.org/10.1111/1469-8676.12298.

Ralph, Laurence. 2014. *Renegade Dreams: Living through Injury in Gangland Chicago.* Chicago: University of Chicago Press.

Rapp, Rayna. 1999. *Testing Women, Testing the Fetus: The Social Impact of Amniocentesis in America.* New York: Routledge.

Redfield, Peter. 2005. "Doctors, Borders, and Life in Crisis." *Cultural Anthropology* 20 (3): 328–61.

Reynolds, Pamela. 2000. "The Ground of All Making: State Violence, the Family, and Political Activists." In *Violence and Subjectivity*, edited by Arthur Kleinman, Veena Das, Mamphela Ramphele, and Pamela Reynolds, 141–70. Berkeley: University of California Press.

Roitman, Janet L. 2014. *Anti-Crisis.* Durham, NC: Duke University Press.

Rozakou, Katerina. 2012. "The Biopolitics of Hospitality in Greece: Humanitarianism and the Management of Refugees." *American Ethnologist* 39 (3): 562–77. https://doi.org/10.1111/j.1548-1425.2012.01381.x.

Rozakou, Katerina. 2016. "Socialities of Solidarity: Revisiting the Gift Taboo in Times of Crises." *Social Anthropology* 24 (2): 185–99. https://doi.org/10.1111/1469-8676.12305.

Rozakou, Katerina. 2018. "Solidarians in the Land of Xenios Zeus: Migrant Deportability and the Radicalisation of Solidarity." In *Critical Times in Greece: Anthropological Engagements with the Crisis*, edited by Dimitris Dalakoglou and Georgios Agelopoulos, 188–201. New York: Routledge.

Said, Edward W. 1989. "Representing the Colonized: Anthropology's Interlocutors." *Critical Inquiry* 15 (2): 205–25.

Scott, James C. 1985. *Weapons of the Weak: Everyday Forms of Peasant Resistance.* New Haven, CT: Yale University Press.

Silver, Lauren. 2008. "The Politics of Regulation: Adolescent Mothers and the Social Context of Resiliency." *Voices* 8 (1): 1–11. https://doi.org/10.1111/j.1548-7423.2008.tb00040.x.

Sotiris, Panagiotis. 2010. "Rebels with a Cause: The December 2008 Greek Youth Movement as the Condensation of Deeper Social and Political Contradictions." *International Journal of Urban and Regional Research* 34 (1): 203–9. https://doi.org/10.1111/j.1468-2427.2010.00949.x.

Spyridakis, Manos, and Fani Dima. 2017. "Reinventing Traditions: Socially Produced Goods in Eastern Crete during Economic Crisis." *Journal of Rural Studies* 53:269–77. https://doi.org/10.1016/j.jrurstud.2017.04.007.

Stasinos, Stathis. 2011. "Eat That!" Hot Spots, Fieldsights, October 31. https://culanth.org/fieldsights/eat-that.

Stavrides, Stavros. 2016. *Common Space: The City as Commons.* London: Zed Books.

Steinfort, Lavinia, Bas Hendrikx, and Roos Pijpers. 2017. "Communal Performativity—a Seed for Change? The Solidarity of Thessaloniki's Social Movements in the Diverse Fights against Neoliberalism." *Antipode* 49 (5): 1446–63. https://doi.org/10.1111/anti.12351.

Stewart, Kathleen. 2007. *Ordinary Affects.* Durham, NC: Duke University Press.

Stewart, Kathleen. 2010. "Afterword: Worlding Refrains." In *The Affect Theory Reader*, edited by Melissa Gregg and Gregory J. Seigworth. Durham, NC: Duke University Press.

Stewart, Kathleen. 2011. "Atmospheric Attunements." *Environment and Planning D: Society and Space* 29 (3): 445–53.

Stewart, Michael. 1989. "'True Speech': Song and the Moral Order of a Hungarian Vlach Gypsy Community." *Man* 24 (1): 79–102.

Stewart, Michael. 1997. *The Time of the Gypsies*. Boulder, CO: Westview.

Sutherland, Anne. 1975. *Gypsies: The Hidden Americans*. London: Tavistock.

Taussig, Michael T. 1980. *The Devil and Commodity Fetishism in South America*. Chapel Hill: University of North Carolina Press.

Taussig, Michael T. 1999. *Defacement: Public Secrecy and the Labor of the Negative*. Stanford, CA: Stanford University Press.

Taussig, Michael T. 2011. *I Swear I Saw This: Drawings in Fieldwork Notebooks, Namely My Own*. Chicago: University of Chicago Press.

Theodossopoulos, Dimitrios. 2013. "Infuriated with the Infuriated?" *Current Anthropology* 54 (2): 200–221.

Theodossopoulos, Dimitrios. 2014. "The Ambivalence of Anti-austerity Indignation in Greece: Resistance, Hegemony and Complicity." *History and Anthropology* 25 (4): 488–506. https://doi.org/10.1080/02757206.2014.917086.

Theodossopoulos, Dimitrios. 2016. "Philanthropy or Solidarity? Ethical Dilemmas about Humanitarianism in Crisis-Afflicted Greece." *Social Anthropology* 24 (2): 167–84. https://doi.org/10.1111/1469-8676.12304.

Thrift, Nigel. 2004. "Intensities of Feeling: Toward a Spatial Politics of Affect." *Geografiska Annaler. Series B: Human Geography* 86 (1): 57–78.

Ticktin, M. 2006. "Where Ethics and Politics Meet: The Violence of Humanitarianism in France." *American Ethnologist* 33 (1): 33–49.

Ticktin, M. 2011. *Casualties of Care: Immigration and the Politics of Humanitarianism in France*. Berkeley: University of California Press.

Ungar, Michael. 2008. "Resilience across Cultures." *British Journal of Social Work* 38 (2): 218–35.

Vradis, Antonis. 2009. "Greece's Winter of Discontent." *City* 13 (1): 146–49. https://doi.org/10.1080/13604810902770754.

Vradis, Antonis, and Dimitris Dalakoglou, eds. 2011. *Revolt and Crisis in Greece: Between a Present Yet to Pass and a Future Still to Come*. Oakland: AK Press & Occupied London.

Williams, Patrick. 2003. *Gypsy World: The Silence of the Living and the Voices of the Dead*. Chicago: University of Chicago Press.

Zraly, Maggie, Sarah E. Rubin, and Donatilla Mukamana. 2013. "Motherhood and Resilience among Rwandan Genocide-Rape Survivors." *Ethos* 41 (4): 411–39. https://doi.org/10.1111/etho.12031.

Index

Note: page numbers in italics refer to illustrations

Afghanistan, migrants from, 118
Agamben, Georgio, 16
Ahmed, Sara, 48, 168
Albanian Roma, 87, 89, 90, 136
Alex, 54–56, 60
Amalia, 94–95, 96–98, 101–3, 108–10; and
    Nefeli and her parents, 26, 98–100, 103,
    104–8, 111–14
Amit, Vered, and Nigel Rapport, 177n1
    (chap. 4)
anarchism: in Greece, 47–48; Niko's historical
    account of, 39–42, 44; and recruitment,
    42–43, 45
Anik, 54–56
Anitsa, 162–65, 166–69, 171
Ano Liosion (Athens suburb), 41,
    176n10
anti-austerity activism, 52
Arab Spring, 4
Argenti, Nicolas, 9
Athanasiou, Athena, 6, 22, 54
austerity program. *See* neoliberal austerity
    measures
auté den eínai zōế (this is not a life), 8, 15

bailout agreement. *See* troika and austerity
    measures
balamé (non-Romani): employment and,
    71–73, 75, 80; marginalization and
    segregation of Roma, 69–70, 78–79, 86;
    social contacts with Roma, 67–68, 81, 85,
    88–89, 90
Bangladesh, migrants from, 46–47, 49, 54, 90,
    144–45, 177n8
barely living, 8–9, 15–17, 22, 25
becoming-in-common, 27, 121–22, 132–33,
    161
Berardi, Franco, 27
Berlant, Lauren, 14, 27, 98, 101, 121
Bookchin, Murray, 41, 175n9
Butler, Judith, 14, 22, 26, 114, 139,
    177n3

censorship. *See* journalists, persecution of
Chiotaki-Poulou, Irini, and Alexandros
    Sakellariou, 3
Cleese, John, 38, 175n5
Communist Youth of Greece, 60
communists, 40–41, 60, 165, 175n9
community, political form of, 148, 155–56,
    166
construction sector, 66, 71, 84, 118
corruption, 4, 33, 34, 57, 92–94, 110, 112
cultural guards, 84, 177n9
cuts to services, 6, 14, 97, 102, 103, 109.
    See also pension cuts

Dadaoglou, Emanouil, 39
Daesh/ISIL (ISIS), 4
Davis, Elizabeth, 7–8
December events, the (2008), 51–52, 61,
    176n15
Deleuze, Gilles, 23, 26, 27, 28, 48, 59
Derrida, Jacques, 79
desubjugation, 22–23, 26, 37, 90, 121, 150,
    168
drug trafficking, 34, 67, 76–77, 78, 85–86, 88,
    89, 90
Durkheim, Émile, 8, 168

education: collective, 54, 57; and prejudice
    against Roma, 68–69; system, 33, 41, 50, 69.
    See also schools, occupation of
ERT (public broadcaster), closure of,
    52–53
European Central Bank (ECB). *See* troika and
    austerity measures
European Union (EU). *See* troika and austerity
    measures
Exarchia (Athens neighborhood), 4, 30, 31,
    50–51, 54–55, 56, 146

Feldman, Gregory, 102
field notes, 46, *115*
Foucault, Michel, 22, 26, 121, 139

George, 26, 80–86, 89, 90, 114, 171; and employment, 68, 70, 72, 73–78; relationship with mother Vasilo, 67, 68–69, 73–74, 77–78, 81, 82–87, 88

Germany: occupation of Greece during World War II, 2, 11, 12, 33; as part of the troika, 60, 108; as safe haven for migrants, 119, 130–32, 139

global financial crisis, 3–4, 5

Golden Dawn Party, 78, 90, 95, 107, 133, 135, 158, 161; attacks by, 27, 53–56, 88, 131, 141, 147–48, 155–56; resistance against, 55–56, 60, 62, 146, 152, 153, 166

Greek Civil War, 1, 11

Grigoropoulos, Alexis, murder of, 4, 31, 50–51, 176n14

Halandri. See Roma compound in Halandri

Hassan, 147, 155–56, 158, 160, 161, 162, 165, 166

health care and neoliberal austerity, 94, 95–96, 101–4. See also Amalia; Maria

Herzfeld, Michael, 103

HMA (aid agency, pseudonym). See Amalia; Maria

human trafficking, 5, 34, 77. See also sex trafficking; smugglers

identity documents, 134–35

Ingold, Tim, 132

International Monetary Fund. See troika and austerity measures

Jigo, 124–25, 128, 129–30, 171

journalists, persecution of, 53, 61, 176n17

Knight, Daniel, 8–9, 20

Koselleck, Reinhart, 98

Kypseli (Athens neighborhood), 49, 50–51, 99

labor: exploitation, 5, 96, 97, 175n4; laws, 3; migrant, 45, 130; unions, 40, 53; women's, 101. See also construction; Romani jobs; scrap metal collecting; street selling

Lesbos, Greece, 126, 128–29, 130, 178n1

Light (Phós), 39, 175n6

Loutsa (town in East Attica renamed Artemida), 74, 177n6

Lovell, Anne, 137

maps, 144–45, 145

Maria, 92–94, 97–98, 101, 112–13; on corruption in the hospital system, 92–93

Mauritania, migrants from, 118–19, 128–29

migrants, 33–34, 53–54, 70, 91, 94, 95, 97; and employment, 45–47, 49–50; and protest, 51, 52; and refugee crisis, 5; travel stories of, 118–19, 123–32. See also Amalia, and Nefeli and her parents; Golden Dawn Party; Samba; shelter for migrants; Taj

military junta (1967–1974), 32–33, 40, 53, 177n2 (chap. 3)

Milton, John, Paradise Lost, 34, 175n2

Molotov cocktails, 51, 63, 154

Muehlebach, Andrea, 175n3

Mustafa, 45, 46–47, 49

Nahar, Papreen, and Sjaak van der Geest, 20

name days, 50, 176n13

Nea Smyrni (Athens suburb), 41, 175n8

neo-Nazis. See Golden Dawn Party

neoliberal austerity measures. See troika and austerity measures

neoliberal governmentality, 6, 14, 28, 35–36, 45, 50, 61, 87, 97, 107, 110; and deployment of crisis, 146–47. See also troika and austerity measures

Nigeria, migrants from, 46, 49, 91, 129

Niko, 25–26, 27, 31–32, 114, 146, 171, 175n2, 175n4; anti-austerity activism, 52–53, 57–59, 60–62; anti-Golden Dawn activism, 53–56, 60, 155–56, 161; anti-police activism, 37–38, 51; historical account of anarchism in Greece, 39–42, 44; and migrant workers, 33–34, 45–50; questioning of solidarity, 35–37, 62–63, 147, 148–54, 156, 158, 160, 161–70; recruitment of anarchists, 42–43, 45

nonviolent collective action, 53, 54, 137

not knowing, state of, 25–26, 36–37

Occupy movement, 176n15

Pakistan, migrants from, 91

Panourgiá, Neni, 6, 33, 39, 53, 78, 103, 162, 176n12

Panter-Brick, Catherine, 17

Papailias, Penelope, 177n5

Papataxiarchis, Evthymios, 35, 178n1

Peano, Irene, 155

pension cuts, 6, 14, 26, 52, 62, 87. See also cuts to services

pensioners, 51, 64

personal debt, 35–36, 60, 133

Pimp My Ride (television show), 74, 177n7

police, 34, 53; activism against, 37–38, 41, 49, 61; and migrants, 70, 73, 99, 118, 133, 134–35; and Roma, 78, 84, 85–86, 88, 105, 107. *See also* cultural guards; Grigoropoulos, Alexis, murder of

potentializing solace, 27–28, 44, 119, 120–21, 143, 148

Povinelli, Elizabeth, 14, 16, 25–26, 50

precariatization, 19, 25, 59, 95–96, 156–57

privatization, 3, 52, 60–61, 70–71

prostitution. *See* sex trafficking

protests: against neoliberalism, austerity measures, and corruption, 4, 6, 41, 50–54, 61–62, 70–71, 107; students against the military junta (1967-1974), 40, 177n2 (chap. 3). *See also* Amalia; Niko; resistance

Puar, Jasbir, 22, 148

Red Thread (*Kókkino Níma*), 41, 176n11

referendum on bailout conditions (2015), 61–62, 150, 153, *170*, 176n18

refugee camps, 5

refugee crisis (2015), 5, 16–17, 24

resilience, concept of, 17–25, 28

resistance: collective, 18, 20, 24, 37, 52, 53, 58–59, 79, 157, 164; against Golden Dawn Party, 53–57, 60, 62, 146, 152, 153, 166; scholarly literature on, 6–7, 18–21. *See also* Amalia; Niko; protests

Reynolds, Pamela, 19

Roitman, Janet, 22, 90

Roma: marginalization and segregation of, 69–70, 78–79, 86; and Romani identity, 67–68; 79–80, 84; social contacts with balamé, 67–68, 81, 85, 88–89, 90. *See also* George; Roma compound in Halandri; Romani jobs; Spiro; Thanos; Vasilo

Roma compound in Halandri: architecture of, 83–84; child care in, 66; emptying of, 66–68; location and history of, 65–66, 78–79. *See also* Roma

Romani jobs, 66, 70–72, 73, 82, 177n4 (chap. 2), 177n2 (chap. 4). *See also* construction; scrap metal collecting; street selling

Romanians, 90

Rozakou, Katerina, 156, 178nn2–3

Said, Edward, 175n1 (intro.)

salary cuts, 14, 26, 52, 87

Samba, 27, 116–18, 171; collecting icons, 142–44; journey to Greece, 118–19, 123–30; and scrap collecting, 118, 119–20, 122–23, 128, 130, 133–41, 144–45

Schinas, Alexandros, 39, 175n7

schools, occupation of, 42, 53

Scott-Heron, Gil, "The Revolution Will Not Be Televised" (1971), 53, 176n16

Scott, James C., 18–19, 37

scrap metal collecting: Greeks and, 140, 144–45, 177n8; migrants and, 27, 46, 117–20, 122–23, 128, 130, 133–45, 177n8; Roma and, 80–81, 140, 177n2 (chap. 4)

Senegal, migrants from, 27, 91, 98–99, 124–26, 128–29

sense, shared, 9–10, 45, 48–49, 59, 98, 138, 157

sex trafficking, 5, 76

shelter for migrants: attacks on, 27, 147–48, 154, 155–56, 161; conflict between solidarians and residents at, 147, 155–63, 166–68, 170

smugglers, 126–27, 130, 131

social solidarity movements, 6, 151, 166, 167

social topography of resilience, 10, 25, 170

social wayfinding. *See* trust as an activation of social wayfinding

solidarians: and coining of term "solidarian," 27, 151; and Golden Dawn attacks, 154, 155–56, 161; relationship with Niko, 151–52, 155, 158, 160, 162–66; relationship with shelter residents, 147, 156–59, 167, 178n1. *See also* solidarity

solidarity: meaning of, 52, 113, 147, 148, 153, 165–66, 168–69; social, 6, 18–19, 151, 155–57, 160–61. *See also* Amalia; Anitsa; Niko

sovereign debt crisis, 4, 16, 24, 27, 36, 52–53, 76, 118, 133

Spiro, 82

squats, 37, 47, 53–54, 128, 151, 156, 158, 178n1; Romani youth and, 67, 77, 85–86, 87, 88–90

Stavrides, Stavros, 155

Stewart, Kathleen, 28, 132

street selling, 70

students, 40, 41, 42, 45, 50, 51–52, 54, 57, 68–69, 177n2 (chap. 3). *See also* Grigoropoulos, Alexis, murder of

suicide, 7–8, 111
Syrians, 4–5, 144
Syriza party, 60, 62

Taj, 27, 171; journey to Greece, 118–19, 128, 130–32; and scrap collecting, 117–18, 119–20, 122–23, 128, 133–45
Takis, 87–89, 145
Taussig, Michael, 175n1 (intro.)
tax increases, 52, 62
thalassemia, 64–65, 176n1
Thanos, 72, 79, 83, 84, 90, 171
Theodossopoulos, Dimitrios, 151
Ticktin, M., 97, 178n2
tourism, 4, 11
troika and austerity measures, 4, 6–7, 34–35, 52–53, 60–61, 62, 71, 95–96, 97, 108, 176n18

trust as an activation of social wayfinding, 27, 47, 48–49, 119–22, 128, 138–39, 143–45, 159, 171
Tsipras, Alexis, 60–61, 62

unemployment, 26, 35–36, 66, 71–72, 75, 118, 130, 163
unions, 40, 51, 53

Varoufakis, Yanis, 60
Vasilo, 64–67, 76, 88, 171, 176n1; concern about son George, 68–69, 73–74, 77–78, 81, 82–87
Victoria, 54–56, 129

wedding ring, *90*
work cooperatives, 7
World War II, 1, 11; German occupation of Greece during, 2, 11, 12, 32